A Century of Dance

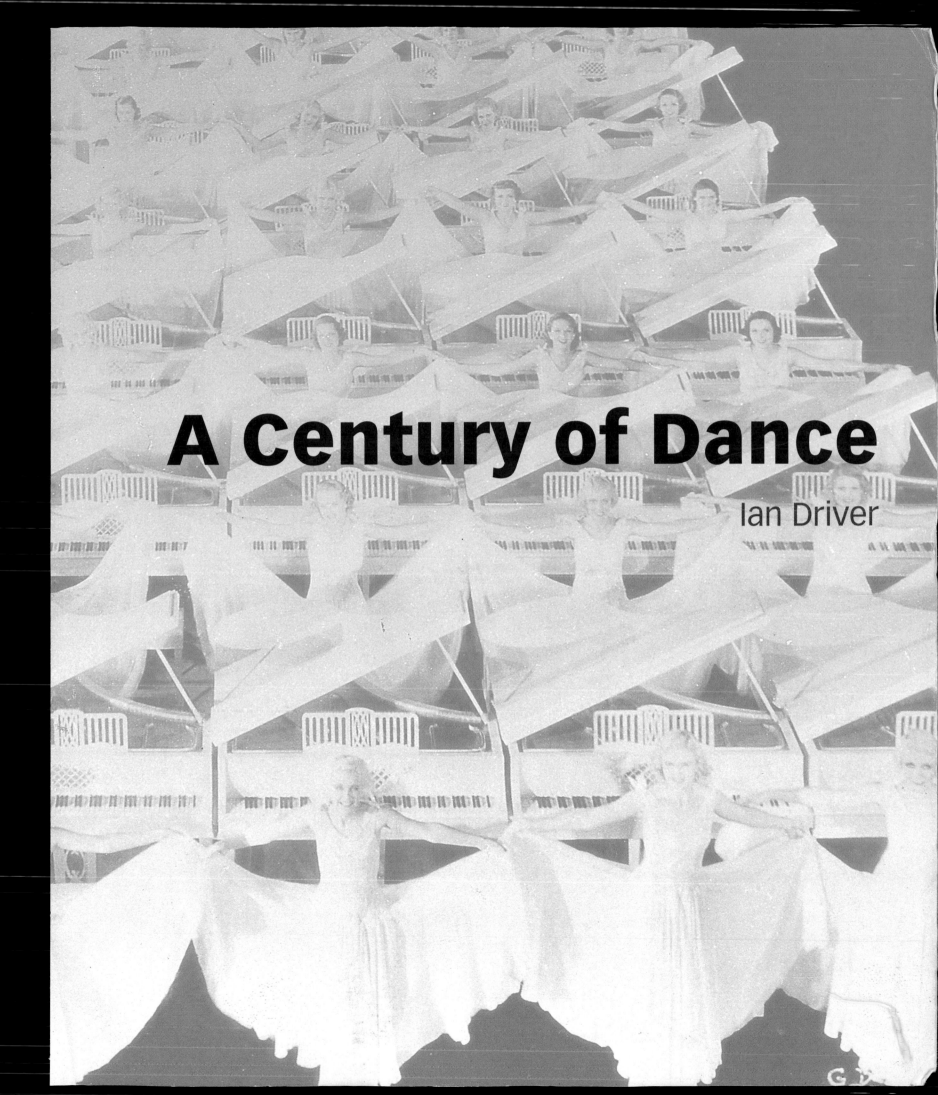

A Century of Dance

Ian Driver

Executive editor: Mike Evans
Senior editor: Trevor Davies
Creative director: Keith Martin
Design manager: Bryan Dunn
Executive art editor: Geoff Fennell
Design: Mark Stevens
Picture Research: Claire Gouldstone
Production Controller: Louise Hall

Additional ephemera supplied by Mike Evans
and Roy Carr

First published in Great Britain in 2000 by
Hamlyn, an imprint of Octopus Publishing
Group Limited, 2–4 Heron Quays,
London E14 2JP

First Cooper Square Press edition 2001

This Cooper Square Press paperback edition
of *A Century of Dance* is an unabridged
republication of the edition first published
in London in 2000. It is published by
arrangement with Hamlyn, an imprint of
Octopus Publishing Group Limited.

Copyright © 2000
Octopus Publishing Group Limited

Produced by Toppan
Printed in China

Contents

Right: A contemporary illustration showing a flapper and her beau Twenties style, in the era of the Charleston.

Below: A diagram of a dummy 'partner' figure, a device patented in 1921 for the self-tuition of ballroom dancing.

Non-classical dance has occupied a major place in the popular culture of the last hundred years, as social ritual, leisure activity and entertainment. Dance through the twentieth century and into the twenty-first has been as varied as the music, whether the ragtime style of the Charleston, Latin-tinged rhythms of the samba and salsa, the Hollywood classic of Fred Astaire and Ginger Rogers or dance crazes from the hokey cokey to hip-hop. Driven by records, radio, cinema and television, dance has occupied a bigger place in our lives than ever before.

Introduction

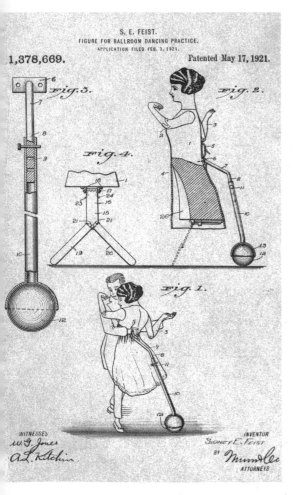

Historically dance has always been important in the lives of ordinary people. Folk dance goes back, like folk music, to earliest times. From the start it had connotations as social ritual in fertility rites, religious ceremony and most importantly mating rituals. And even more sophisticated, stylized forms of dance in the courts of kings and nobles, rich in etiquette and mannerism, functioned as a meeting point and courting ground for members of the opposite sex. When Jerome Robbins choreographed the dance in the gym in *West Side Story*, the boy-girl tension was not a million years away from the masked ball in *Romeo and Juliet* upon which it was based.

But while the function of dance has remained broadly the same, what has been notable over the past hundred years has been the promotion and accessibility of dance, driven as most things in the twentieth century by technological change.

The first of these innovations was on the domestic front in the form of the gramophone record. People could listen to all kinds of music in their own homes, and much of this happened to be dance music. Waltzes, foxtrots, fashionable dances like the tango and Charleston, were all available for private consumption, encouraging dancing as a social activity outside the home, in dancehalls and ballrooms, and more recently discos and clubs.

Likewise the rapid spread of radio during the 1920s further exposed people to dance music of all kinds. The huge popularity of the big bands, whose music was designed to be danced to, not simply listened to, just would not have happened were it

'When Jerome Robbins choreographed the dance in the gym in *West Side Story*, the boy-girl tension was not a million years away from the masked ball in *Romeo and Juliet*.'

Opposite: Detail of a female contestant getting ready for a ballroom dancing competition in Berlin, 1985.

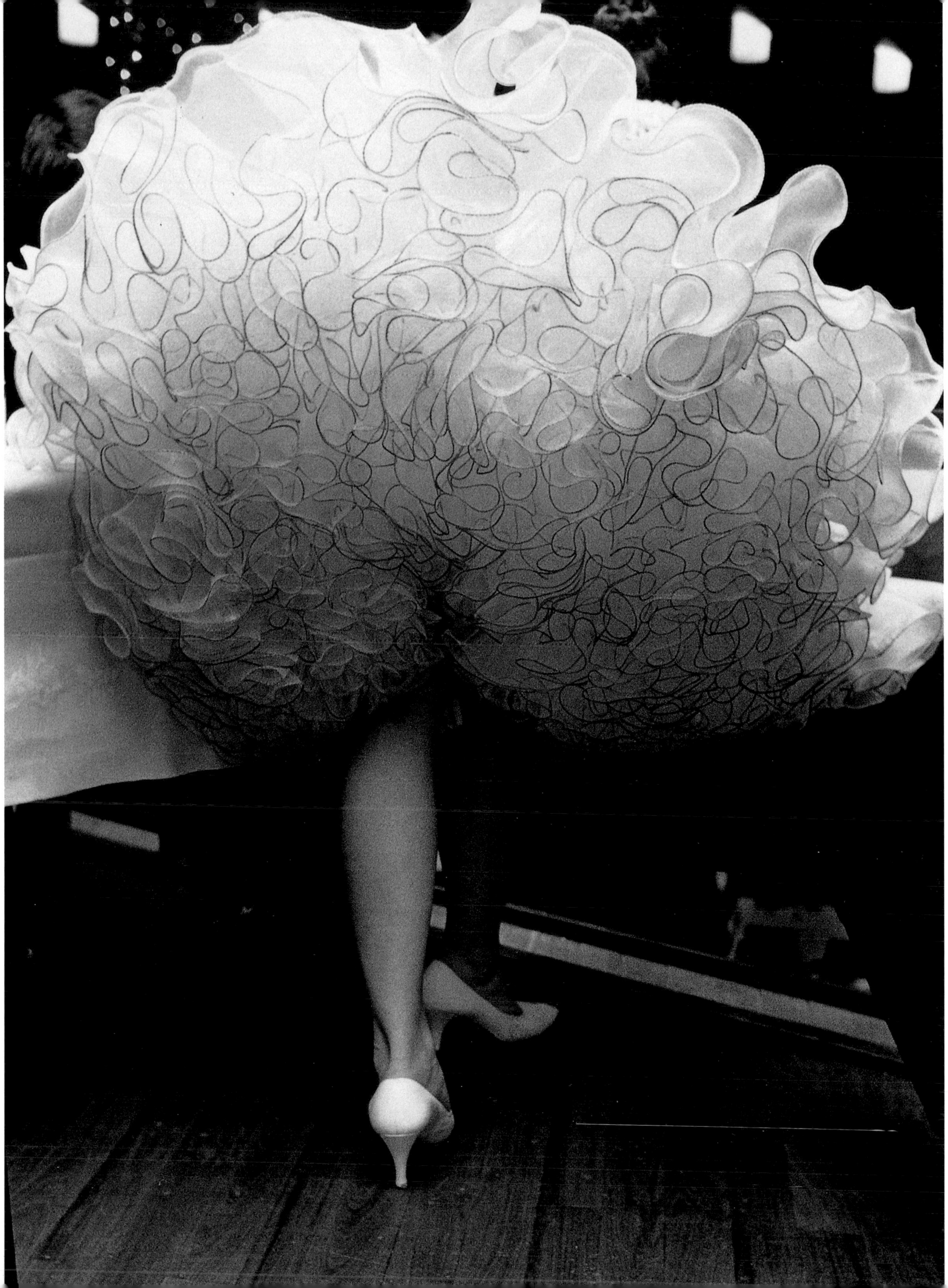

Introduction

not for records and radio. And the same could certainly be said for rock and roll and popular music since.

The other great medium of mass communication in the first half of the twentieth century was the cinema. When sound came to the silver screen in the late 20s, the film musical was born, and with it a whole new era of dance as spectator entertainment. Although many Hollywood musicals were based on hit Broadway shows, they now had audiences of literally millions worldwide and, loosened from the restrictions of stage choreography, a whole new dance genre evolved. By the mid 1930s Fred Astaire, Ruby Keeler, Ginger Rogers and Jack Buchanan were household names; Busby Berkeley revolutionized the cinematic dance set piece with extraordinary spectaculars; and in the 50s Gene Kelly took modern dance to new heights in films like *Anchors Aweigh*, *An American In Paris* and the seminal *Singin' In The Rain*.

While cinema widened the scope of dance, and offered an (albeit kitsch) view of more exotic forms from around the world

'Although many Hollywood musicals were based on hit Broadway shows, they now had audiences of literally millions worldwide.'

Above: Poster for *Chicago*, one of the hottest hit musicals of recent times, with the emphasis very much on the dancing.

Right: Dancers jiving at the legendary Savoy Ballroom in 1940s Harlem.

(the Carmen Miranda version of Latin American springs to mind) the other great influence – again, as with music – was that of African-American culture. From ragtime and tap dance (with its curious ancestry that includes African elements and Lancashire clog dancing) through jive to hip-hop, and the further flung dance forms of Cuba, Central and South America, all have made their mark on popular dance around the world over the last century.

Even in the twenty-first century of electronic information and digital technology, the role of dance has not diminished. Dance based hit musicals come and go – a recent sell-out everywhere was *Fosse*, the celebration of the work of Bob Fosse, the ever-burgeoning club scene is completely dance-based, pop acts thrive on dance routines, competition ballroom dancing is now a worldwide phenomenon, and the great Hollywood musicals are now set-in-aspic classics of modern popular culture.

Althrough Isadora Duncan and others have attempted to express themselves through unaccompanied movement, dance can usually be defined as movement to music, and in this has reflected the huge proliferation of all kinds of popular music over the past hundred years. Dance has enabled people to participate in music to an unprecedented degree, be it in the ballrooms of a bygone era or in the ubiquitous club culture of the present day.

Above: A shot from the Hollywood version of the stage musical *West Side Story*, in which Jerome Robbins' choreography set new standards in dance on the movie screen.

Left: Madonna, whose stage performances relied as much on her talents as a dancer, and those of the dancers around her, as they did on the actual musical elements.

May I have the pleasure?

Waltzing around the world

Social dance does not stand alone in the world of popular culture: it is born of a marriage between popular music and contemporary style. It is a manifestation of how individuals, groups or generations experience, interpret and emotionalize their social surroundings, and for this reason it is constantly subject to change. The rapidity of economic and social change throughout the twentieth century was mirrored by the increasingly frenetic pace of change in social dancing. Styles originated, developed and died away at an almost dizzying rate.

May I have the pleasure?

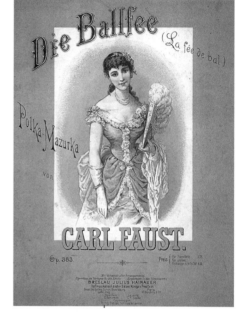

Another reason for the fast-changing nature of social dance styles was the recognition at the dawn of the century of the possibilities inherent in New World culture. For most of the preceding centuries Europe had been the sole source of original social dance styles. The staple dances of the nineteenth century, for example – such as the polka, the varsovienne (varsoviana), the mazurka, the polonaise and, of course, the waltz – originated in central or eastern Europe, while the trend for sentimentalizing rural life had led to the popularization of Scottish folk dancing.

Moreover, in the nineteenth century new styles and innovations percolated down through society. It was to the state ball or county dance that people turned for the latest in fashion. It may be true that, more often than not, new styles evolved from European rural or peasant dances, but unlike the twentieth century, these were taken up by high society with little appreciation of the cultural climate from which they sprang.

Across the Atlantic, too, Old World manners and European styles largely determined the social aesthetic of North America. All this was about to change, however. Although not particularly visible in 1900, both North and South America had within them the seeds of dance revolution. In the United States it was jazz; in

Above: Music for Carl Faust's 'The Fairy of the Ball' (c.1885), a polka-mazurka – both dances exploited the popularity of central and eastern Europe dance forms in the late-19th century ballroom.

Left: The German sheet music for 'The Washington Post', a polka-march by John Philip Sousa, best known for marching tunes.

'... social dancing is in a constant state of flux, shifting from one trend to another. Any attempt to pin down a style to a particular date or period is almost doomed to failure ...'

South America it was the tango and Latin music. Not only would these transform the way the world danced, but they would also mark the beginning of new styles coming, as it were, directly off the 'street'.

Change would also be hastened by the development of media technology. The rise of cinema, radio, television and recorded sound (not to mention the revolution in information technology at the century's close) furthered a cross-cultural fertilization already set in progress by mass human migration. The result would be an explosion of dance at the beginning of the twentieth century, which progressed throughout the decades that followed.

In fact, social dancing is in a constant state of flux, shifting from one trend to another. Any attempt to pin down a style to a particular date or period is almost doomed to failure because its roots can be found in generations past and its offspring discovered in dances to come. For this reason, anyone seeking to trace the path of dancing's development may be guilty of hunting a will-o'-the-wisp – but anyone who attempts it will be dazzled by the grace, exuberance and sheer ingenuity of mankind's celebration of the modern world.

Above: The stately polonaise, a Polish dance made popular by Chopin amongst other composers, as portrayed in a woodcut (c.1900) from a drawing by Stanislaw Rejchan.

May I have the pleasure?

Above: The waltz revolutionized ballroom dancing in the early nineteenth century, and by the dawn of the twentieth had reached new heights of popularity in Europe and North America.

Waltzing around the world

The fact that even today, after nearly a century of rebellion and progression, the waltz remains one of the best known of all social dances is testimony to its lasting appeal. The popular image of a man and woman, arm in arm, circling the dance floor, eyes only for each other, still represents the epitome of romance and sophistication. The grace and flavour of the waltz seem to remind us of happier times, when life was calm and love was sweet. The waltz is a dance of a world that is easier to understand.

At the dawn of the twentieth century the waltz ruled the dancehalls (or assemblies, as they were known then) of Europe and North America, its elegance and control perfectly symbolizing the taste and moral certainties of the Edwardian era: the man led, the woman followed: its and manners of behaviour as precisely structured as the society from which it sprang, and yet in many ways it represented a great leap forward for social dancing.

'Couples revolved around each other and around the dance floor in a manner that was considered by the moral harbingers of the day to be physically dangerous if not morally decadent.'

Before the waltz became popular, people danced, as often as not, turned out and away from their partners – if, indeed, they could be said to have a single partner at all. The evolution of the waltz changed all that. Here, for the first time, couples turned in and towards each other and away from their fellow dancers. The man took the intimate step of placing his right hand around the waist of his partner. Couples revolved around each other and around the dance floor in a manner that was considered by the moral harbingers of the day to be physically dangerous if not morally decadent, but the waltz was here to stay.

The importance of this moving together of the dancing couple cannot be overestimated. If in earlier days the minuet or the quadrille had allowed for the possibility or perhaps celebration of a couple's courtship, the waltz allowed them to practise it. The waltz became so phenomenally popular not simply because of the hypnotic nature of its 3/4 rhythm or the then shocking intimacy of its hold, but also because it allowed the individual to revel in his or her own pleasure. Personal pleasure and the individual search for expression were to become the over-whelmingly dominant themes in the evolution of dancing throughout the twentieth century.

In 1900 the social dance scene had remained almost wholly unchanged for nearly a century. Since its arrival in the early years of the nineteenth century, the waltz had experienced such expo-nential growth that by the beginning of the twentieth century it stood unrivalled as the social dance of choice. By 1910 most dance programmes were dominated by the waltz to an unprece-dented degree – it has been estimated that roughly three-quarters of all dances were waltzes. It would be fair to say that the popular dance venues of the time were saturated by the waltz's rhythm, and for many its ubiquity was making the dancing scene predictable and jaded.

Other dances were popular, and some, like the polka, survive today (although only in specialized environments). The galloping quality of the polka eventually found another outlet in the military two-step, which was popular immediately before 1900. The two-step – an energetic mix of marching and skips – had a simplicity that can be found in today's line dancing, and it was particularly popular in Europe. A large amount of its popularity can be attributed to the American composer and musician, John Philip Sousa (1854–1932), who wrote and performed military marches but went on to be one of the chief purveyors of cakewalks (see pages 25–26) when the craze hit Europe in the late 1880s.

Below: Sousa's marches were very popular in Europe as well as in his native country, and military two-step was one of the few challenges to the dominance of the waltz.

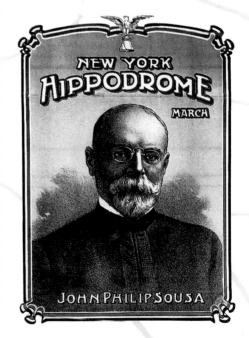

'The idea of the dashing Prussian officers and their ladies cavorting around the ballrooms at ever-increasing speeds to the music of Johann Strauss is still a powerful image today ...'

It was, however, the waltz that ruled. The waltz evolved from an Austro-German folk dance called the *Ländler*, its name deriving from the German word *walzen* (to revolve, to rotate). Its intimate hold and the speed of the dancers' revolutions around the dance floor had caused an outcry at its inception. Even the poet Byron objected:

Round the confines of the yielded waist
The strongest hand may wander undisplaced.

By the beginning of the new century, however, what had once been scandalous had long become tame and old fashioned. The waltz was still undeniably popular, but the speed and manner in which it was danced had become hotly contested. Of all the modifications and evolutions that the dance had gone through during the nineteenth century, it was the version thought of as the 'Viennese waltz' that had most strongly implanted itself in the popular imagination. The idea of the dashing Prussian officers and their ladies cavorting around the ballrooms at ever-

Above: Sousa, seen here with his musicians in 1893, was originally a band master, but his style of composition also lent itself to the more genteel atmosphere of the ballroom.

Right: Stanislaw Rejchan captured the romance, grace and sophistication of the late-nineteenth-century society ball in this painting *Dancing the Cotillion* (1893).

increasing speeds to the music of Johann Strauss is still a powerful image today, but by 1900 the old-style rotary waltz was beginning to lose its appeal. The reason lay in the rapid social changes taking place in the industrialized world.

By the beginning of the century Europe and North America had long since established themselves as industrialized societies with primarily urban populations. There were, of course, huge disparities between rich and poor, but it could be said that working people were gradually finding themselves with more time to pursue leisure activities and a little more cash to spend on them. Naturally, one of the major sources of entertainment was dancing, but in the years before the First World War there were few places where the average person could dance.

In Britain at this time, for example, access to dancing venues was as strictly defined as society itself. At the top of the social scale were state balls and the lavish entertainments of the landed gentry and those made rich through industrialization. Lower down the scale came county or hunt balls, which were held in local hotels or assembly rooms. Subscription dances offered dancing to all those who subscribed throughout a season, but for the majority of the population dancing could be enjoyed only occasionally at local 'assemblies' or through 'academies' run by dance teachers, both for a modest price. Otherwise, there were few outlets to meet the ever-increasing demand.

In the recently evolved entertainment centres of Britain's seaside towns, however, where the emerging leisure-seeking class

May I have the pleasure?

Above: Social change in the twentieth century would eventually signal the demise of lavish Viennese balls like this one in 1900 attended by Emperor Franz Josef.

took their holidays, a new idea was developing – the permanent dancehall. In one of the best known of England's seaside resorts, Blackpool, there were at least three permanent halls designed exclusively for dancing. Within their walls, under the expert guidance of teachers who acted as MCs, a new generation of dancers emerged, ready to challenge the old assumptions about waltz style. Frustrated by the rigid steps and the fast speed of the old-time waltz, they were seeking something fresher, newer and more relaxed. It came from North America, it was called the Boston, and it brought waltzing into the twentieth century.

The birth of the Boston is disputed. It appeared, as the name suggests, in the northeast United States sometime before 1905, and in the years before the First World War it crossed the Atlantic and was taken up by the more popular dancers of the day. Its popularity was short lived, but its legacy would be great: in so far as it replaced self-conscious style with relaxed movement, it did much to usher in what would become known as English Style.

While the old-time waltz continued to be danced in the ballrooms of the upper echelons of society, the Boston seeped into the dance programmes of the new popular venues. Although

'The old-style waltz was all about rhythm and beat, but the Boston was a dance that responded to the emotion of melody.'

technically a waltz, its only real similarity with the old rotary waltz was its 3/4 rhythm. Above all, the Boston was slower. A full turn in the Boston would take four bars of music, which is twice as long as it would take if one danced in the old style. This lack of concentration on the rotary pattern also meant that the old turned-out position of the feet was not as necessary. The new generation had found that position rigid and self-conscious, and it was abandoned, thus discarding the last vestiges of courtly style in popular dance (the five positions of the feet survive today only in ballet).

The naturalness of the feel, the holding of the partner hip to hip instead of directly in front and the concentration on lateral movement rather than on rotation marked out the Boston as something new and exciting. The old-style waltz was all about rhythm and beat, but the Boston was a dance that responded to the emotion of melody. The Boston began a trend towards insouciance in dancing that can be traced through Irene and Vernon Castle (see pages 34–35) and reached its pinnacle in Fred Astaire (see pages 128–133). It was a dance for a generation seeking to escape the rigid structures of the past.

Yet the Boston died away nearly as soon as it arrived. By the beginning of the First World War it had faded from the scene in Britain, and probably even earlier in the country of its birth. It has been suggested that it suffered the same fate as all 'travelling' dances as newly formed dance venues became ever more crowded and space became limited; more probably, however, it fell victim to the demand for new styles that it had created. Neither the Boston nor the old-time waltz could survive the coming of ragtime.

Above: Later known just as the Hammersmith Palais, the Palais de Danse in West London was arguably the most famous ballroom in Britain for half a century.

Ragtime crazy

DAGUERRE
chicago

'If I can't dance I don't want to be part of your revolution,' the American anarchist Emma Goldman once said. She was, perhaps, referring to the spirit of her own rebellion rather than to the new forces unleashed in the world of dance, but 'revolution' is, nevertheless, a good description of the spirit pervading dancehalls in the United States before the First World War. At first sight, the revolution appears to have sprung from the freshness and progressiveness of the New World itself, but a closer look reveals that its heart lies elsewhere – in the rhythms and culture of Africa.

Below: The minstrel show featuring parodies of African-American songs performed in black-face by white entertainers was pioneered by T.D. Rice, here seen performing as 'Jim Crow'.

Ragtime crazy

From its earliest days the black population of the United States used the sacred and emotional dance traditions they had brought with them from Africa as a means of reaffirming both private and public identity. Over time the African dance characteristics – such as exaggerated hip and pelvis movements or the vigorous use of foot stamping in relation to, or in place of, the rhythm of a drum – became mixed with the country jigs and clog-dances that white settlers carried with them from Europe. This intermingling of styles established a unique African-American aesthetic, and by midway through the nineteenth century it could be found throughout the great plantations of the southern United States. The popularity of this emerging black culture can be seen in the ambiguity with which it was greeted by the white establishment.

Outraged and threatened by visible displays of a new culture, white society sought to reduce and even, more often than not, completely curtail the outlets available for African-Americans to dance. Cut off from so many of the popular outlets for entertainment, the black community sought out the 'juke-joints' of the rural south.

Juke-joints were, like their urban counterpart the honky-tonk, self-contained premises, where the clientele could drink, gamble and dance, away from the prying eyes of an overbearing establishment. Shoddy in the extreme – most juke-joints were little more than run-down shacks – these establishments became the incubators for much of the new music and dance that would sweep across America a generation later. The word 'jukin' or 'jookin' came to describe the type of music that was played in these joints – a sort of embryonic blues – while alongside it many of the most important dances of the following 50 years took shape. The Charleston, the buzzard lope, the black bottom and the grind were all to emerge in the backrooms of juke-joints and honky-tonks.

Meanwhile, white America found itself in a quandary. On the one hand, African-American dancing was dangerous and threatening; on the other, it was undeniably attractive. How could white Americans enjoy it without celebrating the race from which it came? The answer came in the form of the minstrel show.

In the wake of the enormous success of T.D. Rice (1808–60), who was the first white man to rub burned cork on to his face and, as Jumping Jim Crow, perform a parody of black song-and-dance, came a myriad of other minstrel troops and shows. Ironically, some black performers started to black-up their own

Above and top: Performers in minstrel shows trod a fine line between respect for black American culture and mockery of it, as indicated by this advertisement.

'Outraged and threatened by visible displays of a new culture, white society sought to reduce and even, more often than not, completely curtail the outlets available for African-Americans to dance.'

PRIMROSE & WEST'S BIG MINSTRELS

OUR GREAT CHAMPION CAKE WALK OPEN TO ALL COMERS.

Above: An elegant cakewalk taking place in 1896, with the impressively ornate prize for the winners of the competition positioned on the table to the right.

faces, recognizing that the minstrel shows (and the countless carnivals and medicine shows that traversed the country) provided the only public platform on which they could display their skills. In the early days William Henry Lane, or Master Juba as he was known, was nearly as popular as Rice, and he brought the new hybrid of African-American dance to a wider audience. Nonetheless, the minstrel tradition did much to stereotype the new dances, and for generations to come the evolution of popular dance would be entwined with the African-American's search for respect and dignity.

It is worth noting, however, that it was a white minstrel, known as George Primrose, who left the greatest legacy to the development of dance in the beginning of the century. An Irish-Canadian, born in 1852, Primrose's real name was Delaney, and such was his reputation that many of the leading vaudeville dancers of the 1910s and 1920s held him up as their idol. Bill Robinson, Willie Covan and Jack Donahue, to name an illustrious few, acknowledged Primrose as a master. Towards the end of his career, long after the demise of minstrelsy, it was not unusual to find Primrose billed alongside black vaudeville acts. In many ways, he was the father of the soft shoe shuffle (see page 97), and many think of him as its greatest exponent.

'The end-of-act cakewalk would become the first indigenous African-American dance to attract mass public attention and infiltrate the dancehalls of the world.'

The cakewalk

By the turn of the century the minstrel tradition was dying out - vaudeville was evolving in its place – but one vital component of the minstrel show survived. The end-of-act cakewalk would become the first indigenous African-American dance to attract mass public attention and infiltrate the dancehalls of the world. Some writers have suggested that blacks from the southern states picked up the cakewalk from Seminole Native Americans, while others claim that it can be traced back to West African tribal rituals, but whatever its origins, by the second half of the nineteenth century it had established itself as a popular dance on the southern plantations. Not unnaturally, it became incorporated into minstrel shows, where its 'walkabout' nature was ideal for the end-of-act, or end-of-show, finale.

The dance itself had evolved effectively into a black parody of the intricate manners of white society. Smartly dressed dancers would process around the stage or dance floor, leaning back as they took precise and elaborate steps in time to heavily rhythmic music. Into this procession the dancers could insert leaps, impressions of other characters or even overtly elaborate acts of chivalry. As the dance developed, an element of competition was introduced, and prizes were awarded to the couples who best 'imitated' the social graces of 'their betters'. At first this prize consisted of ice cream or some other delicacy, but soon it became traditional for it to take the form of a grand cake, thus giving the dance its name (it also, interestingly, gave birth to the phrase 'take the cake').

By the turn of the century the cakewalk had become so popular that a black musical was produced, entitled *Clorindy* or *The*

Above: Although the cakewalk originated as a participatory dance in the southern USA, it was not long before a stylized form was seen on the vaudeville stage.

Right: Elements of the cakewalk satirized the manners of the white plantation owners, and its exponents took pride in their dress, emulating their bosses.

Origin of the Cakewalk (1898). This show established a precedent by which the stage became a springboard for a dance to enter the public domain, and the show's popularity made the cakewalk a craze throughout the dancehalls and ballrooms of Europe and North America. It is said that William K. Vanderbilt and his wife employed a black dance instructor to teach them the subtleties of the new craze in their Manhattan mansion.

Clorindy or *The Origin of the Cakewalk* starred Ernest Hogan (1865–1909), who was regarded by many, including Eubie Blake, the composer of *Shuffle Along*, as the greatest dancer and comedian of his day. Hogan's career was not a happy one. He was decried as an 'Uncle Tom' and died a frustrated man in 1909. Instead, the doyen of the black stage at the turn of the century was Bert Williams, who, with his partner George Walker, was one of the uncrowned but undisputed kings of the cakewalk.

Williams (1874–1922) and Walker (d.1911) had worked their way to the top via the familiar route of medicine and minstrel

'Walker would strut around the stage, and Williams would shuffle along behind him, unable to keep up and offering instead his own version of the mooche or grind.'

Top: Ernest Hogan helped popularize the cakewalk through his performances in the musical *Clorindy* or *The Origin of the Cakewalk* in 1898.

Left: Two other black performers of the turn of the twentieth century, Bert Williams and George Walker, delighted audiences in New York and London.

shows. Theirs was a traditional double act, adapted to the style and prejudices of the day. Walker was the flashy, street-smart man of the world, while Williams was the bumbling, naive, country bumpkin. Walker would strut around the stage, and Williams would shuffle along behind him, unable to keep up and offering instead his own version of the mooche or grind. In effect, Williams was what would become known as an 'eccentric' dancer (see page 40), and his use of traditional black dance took his audiences by storm.

Their greatest success was *In Dahomey*, which opened in 1902, the first black show to open in Times Square, New York. A year later it ran in London for seven months. As the title suggests, Williams and Walker were sensitive to the origins of many of their dances and would occasionally try to incorporate West African influences into their act, although their audiences were largely unaware of these inclusions. After Walker's death in 1911, Williams went on to become one of the leading lights of the vaudeville era, eventually becoming a headliner in the Ziegfeld Follies. Perhaps the years of working within the confines of racial stereotyping took its toll, however, because W.C. Fields once said of Williams: 'he was the funniest man I ever saw and the saddest man I ever knew.'

Ragtime

The cakewalk brought in its wake the new music that was coming out of the south and Midwest of the United States. The new dance required a new musical style. To be more precise, both the cakewalk and syncopation had their roots in a shared African past, and consequently where the cakewalk led, ragtime followed.

As Vernon Castle pointed out, ragtime music is made for dancing. Ragtime is born of European folk tunes mixed with West African drum rhythms. At its heart is the concept of syncopation – the unexpected displacement of a beat, or an accent, in a musical phrase. In the same way that the cakewalk grew out of the formal structures of 'marching' dances, so ragtime grew from the formal structures of marching music. The origin of the name is unknown, but it probably refers to the 'ragged' nature of the syncopation. Whatever its derivation, the name stuck.

The leading composer of the ragtime era was Scott Joplin (1868–1917). The son of a slave, Joplin was born in Texarkana, Texas, into a family of keen amateur musicians. Showing considerable musical promise, Joplin left home when he was 14 years

Above: Scott Joplin's popular composition 'The Entertainer' from 1902 gave him renewed fame in the 1970s when it was used in the soundtrack of the film *The Sting*.

Ragtime crazy

RAGTIME DANCE TUNES

'Alexander's Ragtime Band', Irving Berlin (1911). This world best-seller did much to secure Berlin's reputation and that of the musical genre within middle-class society. Scott Joplin always claimed that Berlin had taken the tune from his Ragtime opera *Treemonisha*.

'The Entertainer', Scott Joplin (1902). The best known ragtime tune today. Led the way in a revival of ragtime interest in the wake of its use in the film *The Sting* (1973).

'The Grand Old Rag', Billy Murray. This song, which was a take on George Cohen's 'You're A Grand Old Flag', provided the fledgling Victor record label with its biggest success of the decade.

'Maple Leaf Rag', Scott Joplin (1899). The so-called 'King of Ragtime', 'Maple Leaf Rag' made Joplin's name. Joplin wrote the song in 1897 but initially had difficulty finding a publisher for it. Eventually it sold more than one million copies.

'Mississippi Rag', William Krell (1897). The father of all ragtime tunes, Krell's tune was the first to carry the word 'rag'.

old against his father's wishes and pursued the typical career of the black itinerant musician. For the next 15 years he played either in St Louis, Missouri, or on the road, honing and developing his new musical ideas. By 1898 he found himself in Sedalia, Missouri, where he was studying harmony and composition at the George R. Smith College. It was here, in 1899, that he wrote 'Maple Leaf Rag', a work that made him world famous.

Between 1900 and 1916 Joplin's popular tunes led the way as the dance world went ragtime crazy. To paraphrase the words of the popular ragtime song, 'everybody was doin' it'. At the same time, popular music publishing was on the rise, and Joplin's 'Maple Leaf Rag' alone sold more than a million copies. Many of his better known compositions, such as 'The Entertainer' (1902), 'Gladiolus Rag' (1907) and 'Magnetic Rag' (1914), are still popular, but at the time they were just the leading compositions as syncopated tunes flowed out of an emerging Tin Pan Alley.

The turkey trot and animal dances

Music publishers and their composers soon realized that there was an easy way to supply the public's fast-growing taste for new dances and new tunes – to combine dance steps and instructions in the lyrics of popular songs. Now, through the visual medium of the stage, through the aural instructions of a song or even through a combination of the two, a dance could find its way on to the dance floor. Thus, ragtime opened up a passageway between the theatre, the composer and the dance-hall that for the next 30 years allowed dances to pass back and forth between stage, ballroom and studio. Only in the 1930s, as Broadway and Hollywood offered up dancers and routines far removed from the aspirations of the local dancehall, did this trend begin to fade.

Consequently, song-writers started trawling juke-joints and honky-tonks for new dances to sell to an eager public. Black vernacular dances were in vogue, and no venue was too small, no step too obscure, for the new craze. In the ballrooms and dance-halls of Europe and North America the formality of the waltz was cast aside for the frantic fun of animal dancing. It has been estimated that between 1912 and 1914 alone more than 100 new dances found their way in and out of fashionable ballrooms.

One of the most successful songwriters of the period was Perry Bradford (1893-1970). By his own admission, Bradford used steps that he had seen over the years as he travelled the variety

'Written in 1909, the 'Bullfrog Hop' came early in the craze for animal dances, and it has within it many of the seeds of popular dances of the next two decades.'

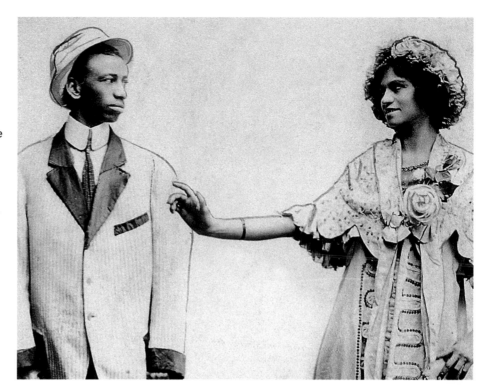

Right: Perry and Jeannette Bradford in 1918 on the vaudeville stage; Bradford was one of the most successful and influential of early twentieth century songwriters.

Below, right: Dances based on the movements of animals were considered ideal for ragtime, and the turkey trot was one of the most popular on both sides of the Atlantic.

circuits of the south performing in his own song-and-dance act. His songs were to do much to accelerate the hysteria for the Charleston and the black bottom in the 1920s (see pages 59–63), but before that he offered a demanding public a myriad of animal steps, too. One such lyric was called the 'Bullfrog Hop':

First you commence to wiggle from side to side
Get way back and do the Jazzbo' Glide
Then you do the Shimmy with plenty of pep
Stoop low, yeah bo', and watch your step
Do the Seven Years Itch and the Possum Trot
Scratch the gravel in the vacant lot
Then you drop like Johnny on the Spot
That's the Bullfrog Hop

Written in 1909, the 'Bullfrog Hop' came early in the craze for animal dances, and it has within it many of the seeds of popular dances of the next two decades. The 'Possum Trot' is an obvious example, while the 'Seven Years Itch' would surface again many years later in the mambo (see pages 86–88). Finally, the shimmy (see page 38) would go on to become one of the biggest

THE MOST TALKED OF DANCE IN THE WORLD TO-DAY
THE FAMOUS
TURKEY TROT

JOS. M. DALY
COMPOSER OF THE WORLD'S FAMOUS
CHICKEN REEL

Ragtime crazy

'He would finish sandwiched between his 'beauties', from where he would fire off a routine or a joke. This became known as "Fox's trot".'

sensations of the 1920s, with both Mae West and Gilda Gray claiming to have originated it. Bradford, of course, had seen it in the south years before either actress had taken it to the stage.

The bullfrog hop was just one of any number of animal dances that turned the dancehall into a rollicking zoo. The grizzly bear, the eagle rock, the snake hip, the chicken scratch and the bunny hug were just a few others that made their way to the dance floor. The nature of these dances is self-evident – they mimicked the characteristics of the animals after which they were named. Usually, they were accompanied by a matching ragtime tune. One dance, the turkey trot, became so popular in Britain that it was commonly known as the rag. The turkey trot was the best known of all the animal dances. Taking a single step to the beat, the man would 'trot' towards his partner, flapping his arms in the manner of an aroused fowl, while his partner did the same in retreat. Breathtakingly simple, the 'trotting' one-step was, by common consent, the animal dance best suited to ragtime music.

Like so many dances, the turkey trot came to New York from the provinces. It arrived from San Francisco in a show called *Over the River* – San Francisco was also, incidentally, the birthplace of the song 'Everybody's Doin' It' – but the most enduring 'trot' of them all came not from the rural south nor even from the west coast, but from the heart of Broadway itself. Uniquely, the 'foxtrot' was synonymous with one man – Harry Fox (1882–1959). Born in California, Arthur Carringford adopted the stage name Fox from his grandfather after settling on a career in variety when he was just 15 years old. By 1914 he was working the vaudeville theatres of New York. In that year he was asked to appear at the New York Theater, which was in the process of transforming itself into a cinema. Along with his company, American Beauties, Fox's job was to provide entertainment on the stage between films. It was not long before he had become the main attraction.

Realizing that the strict moral code of the day placed great restrictions on the movement of his alluring dressed 'beauties' – they could appear on stage only in frozen tableaux – Fox invented a dance that allowed him to move around them. Beginning with a slow walk that would take two beats of music, Fox would break into a series of short 'trots', each taking one beat. He would finish sandwiched between his 'beauties', from where he would fire off a routine or a joke. This became known as 'Fox's trot'.

Recognizing that there was a demand for this entertainment, the management of the New York Theater transformed the roof of the theatre into the Jardin de Danse, where Yansci Dolly and

Left: Harry Fox's Broadway act provided inspiration for another 'animal' dance, the foxtrot, which is still found in the ballroom dancing repertoire today.

Right: The Dolly Sisters presented the foxtrot when they appeared in revue in the USA, Britain, France and elsewhere, and it was imitated by amateur dancers everywhere.

the Dolly Sisters (who had teamed up with Fox elsewhere in vaudeville) performed the foxtrot in nightly revue. Customers took to the dance floor at the Jardin de Danse, imitated Harry and Dolly, and from there the craze seeped out into dancehalls around the world.

The root of the foxtrot's popularity was the easy-going and improvisational nature of the steps. People did not have to learn intricate steps and movements, as was necessary with the waltz or the tango, and it was consequently far more appealing to new

and inexperienced dancers. However, in an era of overcrowded dance floors, it could have gone the same way as the Boston or the cakewalk because, like those dances, it required a great deal of space. The fact that it survived is testament to its popularity and evidence of the foxtrot's ability to evolve and adapt to new styles.

Between 1916 and 1930 the speed of the foxtrot varied considerably, from anything between 32 to 50 bars per minute. An even slower, smoother version was introduced for a while,

Above: The animal dances were criticized for being too 'physical', but more refined versions soon emerged, like the 'Prince of Wales foxtrot', here danced by Mimi Palmer and Arthur Murray.

appropriately entitled the saunter. In the late 1920s the foxtrot combined with the Charleston (see pages 59–61) to create a dance known to dance teachers as the 'quick-time foxtrot and Charleston'. Everyone else knew this dance as the quickstep.

As ever, the arrival of a new and exciting dance style led to a corresponding frenzy by the moral defenders of the day. For the defenders of the status quo, animal dances were not only dances of African heritage but they positively encouraged physical contact – ironically, the same charge so vehemently hurled at the waltz a century before. Admittedly, not all the dances were particularly subtle. Both the bunny hug and the grizzly bear required dancers to embrace, and many girls took to the dance floor with protective padding to shield them from the physical

'... the bunny hug and the grizzly bear required dancers to embrace, and many girls took to the dance floor with protective padding to shield them ...'

excesses of their over-ardent partners. However, many of the more erotic moves of the original dances – the rotating hips of the Georgia grind, for example – failed to survive the journey on to the respectable dance floor.

Nevertheless, outrage ensued. In 1914 the Vatican officially denounced the turkey trot and also – for good measure – the tango. The Dancing Teachers Association of America refused to teach any form of syncopated dancing at all, while, unbelievably, in New Jersey a turkey trotter was sentenced to 50 days in jail. The dancehall was portrayed as one step away from Sodom and Gomorrah, and one popular anti-dance book of 1912 was entitled *From Dance Hall to White Slavery*. What was needed to ensure the survival of the ragtime dances was somebody to tame them and give them 'style'. Up stepped Vernon and Irene Castle.

Above: Demonstrations of the new dance craze were popular in the 1920s, as seen in the entertainment for customers at Lennards' shoe shop.

Right: The physical nature of the bunny hug led some women to protect themselves from over-amorous partners with a 'bumper' belt, comprising a number of padded sticks.

Ragtime crazy

Taking the lead:
Vernon and Irene Castle

The fact that today ballroom dancing is so widely associated with grace and sophistication, instead of with drugs and debauchery, is because Vernon and Irene Castle gave it that image. They tamed ragtime, gave it elegance, subtlety and style, and in the process became hugely famous. Vernon (1887–1918) was born in Norwich, England, and by 1907 he had given up his planned career in civil engineering to pursue a life on the stage. Irene Foote (1893–1969), who was six years his junior, came from New Rochelle, New York. They were married in 1911, and in Paris, one year later, they first made a name for themselves as a dancing team. Working the floor of the Café de Paris, they mesmerized their audiences with their ability to dance ragtime dances with grace and elegance.

By the time they returned to New York the Castles' reputation had been established. Opening Castle House, a school for the 'teaching of correct dancing', opposite the Ritz Hotel, they catered to high society's desire to learn ragtime dances. At night they performed in their own *Castles in the Air* cabaret. Irene became a vital figure in the evolution of women's fashion, devising a new style of dress that allowed her to dance more easily. Cutting her hair short and abandoning the heavy corset, she created the image that became associated with the bright young things of the 1920s.

Not only did the Castles standardize the improvisational steps of the turkey trot, the cakewalk and other animal dances, but they also created new dances of their own. They created the Castle walk – a series of steps, taken on the balls of the feet with the knees straight – which could be used for almost any animal dance, and for most people it was. They also developed the hesitation waltz and the one-step. Their technique was to refine and polish the rambunctious dances of the era. Thus, hips were not to be shaken, elbows were not to be flounced; hops were replaced with glides, while jumps were replaced with steps. In short, they gave syncopation sophistication.

In 1914 they published *Modern Dancing*, the definitive text of their ideas, and it quickly became a classic. They did not concen-

Right: Irene, the American wife of British dancer Vernon Castle, provided ragtime with an unexpected grace and style quite different from its origins.

Left: The Castles took Paris and New York by storm just before the First World War and they codified many of the era's new dances.

Right: Screen dance supremos Fred Astaire and Ginger Rogers acknowledged their debt to the Castles in the biographical film of 1939.

'..One can sit quietly and listen to them all; but when a good orchestra plays a "rag" one has simply got to move.'

trate only on ragtime but also led the way in developing the new waltz and that other great phenomenon of the era, the tango (see pages 69–70). It was their taming of the rag, however, that made their name, and it was ragtime that dominated their careers. As they said themselves: 'The waltz is beautiful, the tango is graceful, the Brazilian maxixe is unique. One can sit quietly and listen to them all; but when a good orchestra plays a "rag" one has simply got to move.'

A pilot of some renown during the First World War, Vernon Castle was killed while on a training mission in 1918, and the career of the world's leading arbiters of popular dance style was cut tragically short. The truth was, however, that the popularity of ragtime was beginning to wane. Its newer and wilder cousin – jazz – was starting to make its presence felt. Nevertheless, the breadth and influence of the Castles' work lingered on throughout the century, not least in the style, insouciance and charisma of Fred Astaire (see pages 128–133).

THE CASTLES FACTFILE

Vernon Castle
Born: Norwich, England 1887
Died: 1918 (Killed in action)
Real Name: Vernon Castle Blythe

Irene Castle
Born: New Rochelle, New York 1893
Died: 1969
Maiden name: Irene Foote

Married: 1911

Origins of success: After thrilling the audiences at the Cafe de Paris in 1912, the Castles returned to New York, where their mixture of teaching and performing became the talk of the town.

Key to success: An attractive husband-wife team, they pioneered a new way of dancing to the ragtime tunes of the day, replacing suggestiveness with sophistication, and improvization with standardization.

Dances: Originated the Hesitation Waltz, the Castle Walk and the One Step. Popularized the Turkey trot, the Maxixe and the Tango.

Legacy: The insouciant style of Fred Astaire and Jack Buchanan. The 'flapper' fashions of the Jazz Age.

Films: Fred Astaire and Ginger Rogers paid tribute to the Castles by making *The Story of Vernon and Irene Castle* their final film for RKO.

Running wild

The vaudeville era

Harlem hots up

The pleasure of the Charleston

Although new dance crazes, such as the cakewalk and the turkey trot, came directly from the African-American experience, there was still only one way that black performers could bring their new styles before the public – on stage. Williams and Walker (see pages 26–27) had proved that black performers could make the leap from minstrelsy to Broadway, but theirs was a rare journey. For the most part, black dancers were relegated to segregated theatres and circuits, while the dances they developed were poached by white artists who refused to recognize the origins of their acts. In this way, for instance, Mae West and Gilda Gray, two stars of 1920s Broadway revue, would fight to take the credit for originating the shimmy – a movement that involves vigorous shaking of the shoulders – when in truth it had been a staple of black dance routines for more than a century.

Running wild

Above: Dancers like Gilda Gray copied the style of black performers, sometimes unfairly claiming credit for 'new' forms that had actually been around for decades.

The vaudeville era

For young black dancers there was one way in which they could show off their dancing talents to the world and that was by becoming a 'pick' or 'piccaninny'. Picks – the word comes from the Portuguese *pequenino* (little one) – were black performers who were used by white artists as backing dancers for their shows. Often providing their own choreography, the picks would offer everything from soft-shoe to Russian dancing. Dancers as influential as Willie Covan, Bill Robinson and Eddie Rector all danced as picks at some time in their careers, and stars such as Sophie Tucker, Mayme Remington and Nora Bayes made use of them. The tradition of black picks was so ubiquitous that one performer, Canta Day, traded on the novelty of having white picks in her act.

In economic terms the tradition of employing picks was little short of child labour. Picks were cheap and effective, and the talent pool was huge, so many a headliner could get rich on the back of these boys, who were surviving on meagre payments. However, although the black dancers made little money, they did gain invaluable experience.

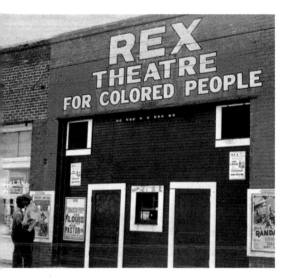

'... the picks would offer everything from soft-shoe to Russian dancing. Dancers as influential as Willie Covan, Bill Robinson and Eddie Rector all danced as picks at some time in their careers ...'

The career of the pick was short. When a young dancer became too old or too big he had no choice but to return to the fold of the 'Negro' show. In the main, black vaudeville developed separately from its white counterpart, and even though some performers, like Bill 'Bojangles' Robinson, graduated from black vaudeville to headlining revue, most did not. That a black circuit developed was largely thanks to Sherman Dudley, a retired comedian, who combined with various theatre owners to form the Theater Owner's Booking Association (TOBA), which by the 1920s had acquired theatres across much of the United States.

In spite of its unfortunate nickname, Tough on Black Artists, some black acts did very well on the TOBA circuit. A show called the *Smart Set* proved so successful that it ran for more than 20 years. The *Smart Set* combined a short play, *The Black Politician*, with dance and comic routines. The principal performers of the show were undoubtedly the comic dancers, and during its lifetime the *Smart Set* featured Dudley himself and Ernest Hogan. Hogan, who had changed his name from Reuben Crowder in order to sound more Irish, was considered by many to be a more accomplished eccentric dancer than the great Bert Williams himself. The quality of the *Smart Set*'s chorus earned it the title the Ebony Ziegfeld Follies.

The undoubted stars of black vaudeville, however, were the Whitman Sisters. The ebullient daughters of a Methodist bishop, Mabel, Essie and Alberta Whitman formed the Whitman Sisters' New Orleans Troubadours in 1904 (the title refers to the birthplace of the show). After the death of their mother in 1909, the girls were joined by their youngest sister, Alice, and the structure of their show was complete. Mabel was a fine singer, who toured with her own act, Mabel Whitman and the Dixie Boys, before joining with the others under the simple title of the Whitman Sisters. Mabel eventually retired from performing and managed the show instead. Essie was the comedienne of the troupe, creating a drunk act, which was rare for a woman, while Alberta (or Bert, as she was known) incorporated 'flash' dancing into a male impersonation routine, male impersonation being all the rage at that time. Finally, little Alice, who was billed as the Queen of the Taps, combined good looks with great flair to steal the show with her assortment of walkin' the dog, ballin' the jack and the shimmy.

Alongside this basic cocktail, the Whitman Sisters took a leaf out of white vaudeville and surrounded themselves with some of the best picks in the business, including Samuel Reed, Julius Fox-worth and Aaron Palmer. Palmer joined the show in 1910 when

Above, left: A blacks-only theatre in Leland, Mississippi; the black vaudeville circuit was separated from that of whites, and few black dancers crossed that divide.

Above: One dancer who did succeed in 'white' vaudeville was Bill 'Bojangles' Robinson, whom Fred Astaire paid tribute to in a sequence in the film *Swing Time*.

Running wild

he was 13 years old, and in 1919 he married Alice Whitman. They had a son, Albert, who by the age of four was appearing on stage and dancing the Charleston while dressed in a tuxedo. Little Albert, or 'Pops' as he was better known, grew up to be one of the great acrobatic dancers. His partnership with Louis Williams became as well known as – if not better known than – the show that had spawned them.

Although the centre of the show was always the family, the Whitman Sisters also acted as one of the best breeding grounds for young black talent. At the height of their fame, they employed a 14-strong chorus of girls, singers and dancing comedians – including a dancing midget, whom they billed as Princess Wee Wee – and made use of the best jazz bands around.

Mabel died in 1942, and although the show tried to continue, her death was a terminal blow. Tough in negotiation, severe in moral discipline and formidable in dance training, Sister May had been the engine that kept the show on the road. Between them, she and her sisters had taken black dancing one more step out of the mire of racial stereotyping and towards a greater appreciation of skill and artistry.

Below: The 'all singing, all dancing' caricature of black Americans that had its origins in the minstrel shows was perpetuated in many 20s and 30s stage and screen productions.

Above: Many vaudeville performers were to appear in some of the early film musicals, like *Broadway Melody of 1938*, starring Buddy Ebsen, who was later to find TV fame as Jed Clampett in *The Beverly Hillbillies*.

For the emerging dancers in black variety, however, Broadway was proving a tougher nut to crack. By the turn of the century popular variety had established itself as the premier form of entertainment in the cities of the world, with New York the centre of the art. A heady mix of headline vaudeville theatres, musical comedies and brash revues, Broadway's name would come to epitomize popular entertainment. Born from a mixture of European revue, immigrant nostalgia and minstrel tradition, it made some use of vernacular songs and dances of the New World, while barring performance by many of its greatest exponents.

The success of the cakewalk and the foxtrot shows how the popular stage was a filter through which contemporary dances could be put before the general public. Slowly the theatre began to do more than simply replicate social dances on stage; it began to celebrate the virtuosity of the dancers who danced them. A tradition of show dancing was born. The integrated musical, which seamlessly mixed dance, narrative and song was still a long way off, but its genesis was here, on the boards of the vaudeville stages and in the feet of the speciality dancers who trod them.

In a nutshell, vaudeville, like its British cousin music hall, consisted of from 10 to 15 individual variety acts all on one bill: comedians, jugglers, magicians, singers and dancers all performed in one show. Even when dance acts were not topping the bill, dance was often the glue holding the show together. Moreover the diversity of dance acts on display was immense – novelty dances, acrobatic dances, tap, toe, high-kicking chorus routines, ethnic folk dances – the list is almost endless. Like the country that bore it, vaudeville was a world in which if you could sell it, you could perform it.

In general, vaudevillian dance acts could be broken up into four distinct varieties: comic or eccentric routines; acrobatic routines; pseudo-classical or 'toe' routines; and tap. Of these, the last is the most famous and enduring of styles, and in Bill 'Bojangles' Robinson vaudeville had its biggest and most original dancing star.

Of the rest, novelty dancers were perhaps the performers who were totally rooted in the culture of the day. Novelty dancers or 'eccentric' dancers were, in effect, dancing comedians. Some, like Jack Donahue (1892–1930), who was more than 6 feet (2 metres) tall with comically long arms and legs, performed a 'shadow dance' routine. Others, like James Barton's drunk, and Buddy and Vilma Ebsen's brother-sister partnership, used com-

Top: 'Eccentric' dancers like Jack Donahue, here pictured with the songwriters Kalmar and Ruby in 1926, were essentially comedians but also talented dancers.

Above: James Barton, (here with William Harrigan and Addison Randall) made a career out of portraying a drunk through dance.

Running wild

edy dancing to highlight their comic creations. Both types reveal how much closer the disciplines of dance, comedy and acting were in the world of variety. Certainly, the skill of Charlie Chaplin, who began his career with his own version of the society drunk in the London music hall, was greatly influenced by the traditions of comic dance. Chaplin himself was a visible and outspoken celebrator of James Barton's talents.

The eccentric dancer was versatile. A performer like Harland Dixon, who had started as a regular hoofer with Primrose's Minstrels, developed into a leading comedic dancer by employing a mixture of dance parody, pantomime clowning and outright stereotype impersonation. (In vaudeville, dancing imitations of different nationalities was as widespread as racial impersonation.)

Ray Bolger (1904-87), who went on to find immortality as the Scarecrow in the film version of *The Wizard of Oz*, built his career on the appeal of the eccentric dancing technique. Bolger, perhaps more than anyone, epitomizes this breed of the new show dancer. Self-taught, improvisational and adept at giving the public what they wanted, he also passionately believed in the power of dance and putting before an audience the full breadth of its possibilities. Bolger's act was, in his own words, 'basically an

Right: Ray Bolger is well known today as the Scarecrow in the 1939 film *The Wizard of Oz* but he began his career on stage as an eccentric dancer.

'If the comic dances deliberately flouted the rules of classical ballet, toe dances embraced them and consciously used them in the development of their routines.'

Above: The semi-balletic styles of dancers like Adelaide and Hughes were an acknowledgement of the links between popular and more 'serious' dance forms.

actor playing the part of a little guy trying to dance', but in the same way that only a highly accomplished pianist can play the piano badly, it took a dancer of great skill to give the appearance of being a gangly klutz.

Like so many of his contemporaries, Bolger's was an instinctive talent. None of his routines were written down or notated, and much of his act was improvised and consequently never the same twice. Nevertheless, his admirers spread further than the back row of the vaudeville house, and it was just a matter of time before he made the move beyond the vaudeville world.

Bolger's career has been in some ways overshadowed by the enduring appeal of *The Wizard of Oz* (1939). His other films included *The Great Ziegfeld* (1936) and *Rosalie* (1937), alongside Eleanor Powell (see pages 104–107), and *Where's Charley?* (1948). He was so respected by George Balanchine that the choreographer hired him to create the part of the Sailor in his ground-breaking Broadway ballet, 'Slaughter on Tenth Avenue' (see pages 156–157). His stage act was so idiosyncratic that attempts to revive *Where's Charley?* – one of his greatest Broadway successes – floundered completely without the benefit of his unique personality.

At the other end of the spectrum of vaudeville dance acts were the pseudo-classical or 'toe' acts. If the comic dances deliberately flouted the rules of classical ballet, toe dances embraced them and consciously used them in the development of their routines. Here the undoubted stars were Adelaide and Hughes.

Adelaide Dickey and John Hughes came together in 1911, roughly the same year as that other celebrated dancing couple of the era, Vernon and Irene Castle (see pages 34–35). Of all the stars of vaudeville, Adelaide and Hughes were destined to hold

Running wild

'In its purest form acrobatic dance was exactly as it sounds: strong, muscular dancers executed daring and shocking acts of strength and flexibility.'

Right: The undoubted suppleness of Evelyn Law demonstrated here in her dressing room before she appeared on stage in revue.

the record for the longest engagement at the summit of the vaudeville stage, the Palace Theater in New York. A vociferous supporter of classical ballet, Adelaide Hickey was well trained in its technical disciplines, and she would bring many of its qualities into their acts whenever she could. (The descriptive name, toe dancing, refers to the tradition of point work in classical dance.) In spite of Adelaide's vocal support for ballet, her and her partner's routines were a mixture of styles, skilfully joined into a romantic whole, which carefully pandered to popular taste. Waltz and ragtime dances were combined with point work and ethnic dance, all bound up in routines that bore names like 'The Birth of Dance' or 'The Garden of the World'.

In truth, despite the often mutual respect of the practitioners, popular and classical dance have rarely mixed in the public's imagination. Despite the success of Adelaide and Hughes and others like them, it would take the particular skills of the great Broadway choreographers, such as Agnes de Mille, to bring it on to the Broadway stage (see pages 157–158).

Between these two poles of performance came what has loosely been described as acrobatic dance acts. In its purest form acrobatic dance was exactly as it sounds: strong, muscular dancers executed daring and shocking acts of strength and flexibility. Dancers would lift partners in every conceivable way and round off the routine with cartwheels, backflips and good, old-fashioned feats of contortion. The tradition was perhaps more akin to the circus than the dancehall, but in the great years of vaudeville it was hugely popular.

Some writers have also placed under the banner of acrobatic dancing that other craze of the vaudeville years: the high-kicking, or leg-splitting, dancing girl. Legomania, as the craze was known, was basically the desire to see female dancers with fine pairs of legs, who could perform the traditions of high-kicks or leg-splits in ever more ingenious ways (legomania has been defined more broadly and sometimes includes the tap and vernacular routines of eccentric dancers). Evelyn Law became famous with an act that consisted of simply advancing across the stage on one leg, while the other one was pointing straight up in the air towards the ceiling. In that age-old tradition of show-business, in vaudeville it paid to 'keep it simple'.

Of course, legomania was only the logical extension of the chorus work that lay, like a backdrop, behind all the acts on the popular stage, be it vaudeville, revue or the emerging musical comedy. It did not take long for either the impresarios or their

stars to realize that the success of an act depended on its being seen in the most flattering context, so dance directors were employed to give the shows the best presentation. The director's responsibilities lay in assembling the acts hired by producers into the most appealing and unifying package – always allowing for the vagaries of a star ego or billing. In essence, this consisted of hiring a chorus and choreographing the most inventive and eye-catching routine possible for it.

The origins of the chorus line can be traced back to the revue in Paris. At the Folies-Bergère lines of beautiful women would parade on stage in slight and extraordinary costumes, and by the end of the century lines of chorus girls dancing the can-can had become world renowned. Precision dancing, however, really evolved not within the decadent atmosphere of French revue but in the altogether more subdued world of the London stage – more specifically at the hands of John Tiller.

An English musical comedy, *A Gaiety Girl*, had stunned New York as early as 1893 with its novel line of chorus girls, but Tiller was the first to hit upon the idea of farming out precision troupes for the popular stage. A wealthy businessman with no previous professional experience, Tiller seized on the turn-of-the-century popularity of marches and parades and incorporated them into

Above: The Folies-Bergère in Paris – this poster is from the 1890s – provided a model for variety shows in Britain and the United States with its spectacular revues of the 1920s and 1930s.

Left: British businessman John Tiller's girls performed a precision, chorus-line style of dancing that was to achieve great success throughout the world, particularly in the USA.

Above: The Tiller Girls were graduates of John Tiller's own dance school, where they gained the understanding between them necessary for precise synchronized movements.

his amateur shows. So successful were these, that he began to be offered work within the professional circuit, culminating in the opening of his own dance school. Before long, Tiller was providing troupes of Tiller Girls for musical shows in London, New York and beyond.

An impresario buying one of Tiller's troupes would get for his money between 8 and 16 dancers, all with a variety of dancing skills and trained in the Tiller method, along with one or two pre-rehearsed routines that were ready to slot into the show. The success of the system was based on the fact that so many of the

'... the finale of a 1924 revue, *Vanities*, offered the spectator 184 'Vanity Girls' doing their thing ...'

dancers had grown up and trained together and were, consequently, imbued with that choral familiarity so necessary for precision dancing. In fact, Tiller would often take on dancers as young as eight years old and provide them with training, schooling and personal and professional support throughout their careers. The system not only made John Tiller very wealthy, but it also shielded many of his charges from the harsher realities of the professional dancer's life.

Where Tiller led, others followed. More and more chorus troupes were provided to meet an ever-increasing market. The Gertrude Hoffman troupe offered routines that mixed the precision style of John Tiller with the flowing modernism of Isadora Duncan, while the finale of a 1924 revue, *Vanities*, offered the spectator 184 'Vanity Girls' doing their thing on a giant revolving staircase. For the time being the Broadway choreographer offered not dancing virtuosity, but glorious spectacle.

Below: Although Gertrude Hoffman's 'nymphs' often performed in the freer style of Isadora Duncan, they also managed to incorporate some of the Tiller precision style.

The best known precision dance troupe of them all, though, is Radio City's Rockettes, a still living example of the stop-the-show choreography of the 1920s and 1930s. The Rockettes thrill audiences of more than 2 million annually with routines that have changed little since they were first devised. Founded in 1925 by Russell Market of St Louis, Missouri, they were originally called the Missouri Rockets, but by the time they reached New York, the founder of the Roxy Theater, 'Roxy' Rothafel, had taken them in hand. Rothafel doubled the size of the troupe before establishing them in the new Radio City Music Hall when it opened in 1932. Originally called the Roxyettes but then renamed the Rockettes, they have been hoofing ever since, with at least two routines – 'The Living Nativity' and the 'Parade of the Wooden Soldiers' – unchanged since their debut.

Whether a dance troupe was assembled for a show or brought in as a unit, the dance director had the ultimate responsibility for dance presentation. In an era when dance was often seen as light relief from the main act – 'personality' dance acts excepted – dance directors received little notice or appreciation, but this should not suggest that they were not highly skilled and influential. Choreographers such as Bobby Connelly and Le Roy Prinz were in the business of giving the audience what they wanted, which often meant the rehashing of familiar steps and kicks in the most imaginative manner possible instead of grappling with new forms of expression. That would come later.

The choreographer whose name is most associated with the great years of Broadway revue is Ned Wayburn (1874–1942).

Wayburn's career spanned the first 40 years of the century, a significant period, which saw stage dancing evolve from simple marches to the pioneering days of American ballet. He worked in London and New York and created numerous vaudeville shows and routines as well as directing musicals for Klaw and Erlanger, the Shubert Brothers and, most famously, Florenz Ziegfeld. In fact, it was Wayburn who created the famous Ziegfeld walk, a unique moement that allowed his dancers to traverse the steps

'... Bobby Connelly and Le Roy Prinz were in the business of giving the audience what they wanted, which often meant the rehashing of familiar steps and kicks in the most imaginative manner ...'

Above: Probably the greatest choreographer of Broadway revue, Ned Wayburn, who worked with the Shuberts and Ziegfeld, amongst others.

Above, left: Le Roy Prinz pictured at the Paramount studios with a group of chorus girls whose routines varied little, but of which audiences never seemed to tire.

Opposite: Radio City Music Hall and the Rockettes, who took over the precision dancing of the Tiller Girls and made it their own in this spectacular Art Deco theatre.

Above: The Ziegfeld Follies were portrayed in the 1936 MGM film *The Great Ziegfeld*, a tribute to the showman and his glamorous spectacles.

Right: Florenz 'Flo' Ziegfeld looking relaxed and confident, despite the stresses and strains that are the characteristics of an impresario's life.

of Joseph Urban's set without risk to life and limb. It has always remained one of the most potent images of the Ziegfeld era.

Wayburn recognized that show-dancing was a business and that most routines were based on similar techniques and disciplines. As a consequence, as well as being the best known choreographer of his day, he was also to become one of the most influential teachers. By recognizing, documenting and codifying contemporary dance practice, Wayburn not only managed to establish his own Institutes of Dancing but also to provide the historian of dance with a unique insight into the world of the 'hoofing' routines.

Reflecting the overriding taste of the day, Wayburn's choreography was built on precision dancing. With this as the bedrock of his routines, he could plunder every other dance style – from ballroom, tap, toe and ballet to musical comedy dancing – to realize his vision, and he coined the phrase 'fancy dancing' to describe a blend of balletic figures with tap and step, which, he maintained,

'The tallest, prettiest and most glamorous girls were called 'squabs', whose importance was not so much in dancing as looking wonderful in costume; 'peaches' and 'chickens' were speciality acts; while 'ponies' ... were, literally, work horses.'

was ideally suited to show routines. Kicks and moves were codified by Wayburn, and he drew up a means by which the stage could be broken up into 24 separate areas, with simple movement directions for crossing each one. This allowed him to notate and set down individual routines. Thus, the Ned Wayburn Institutes, along with his 19-volume *The Art of Stage Dancing* (1925), allowed countless students to make a living on the stage, either in his own shows or those of his contemporaries.

The training was quick, brusque and no-nonsense, matching the work of the mentor, and it provided a grounding in a world that was harsh and unerringly practical. Wayburn and his contemporaries were in the entertainment business, and there was no time to hide the practicalities of their profession. They needed dancers who could blend seamlessly into the chorus and understand the currency of the routines. Consequently, there was no room for the 'plain' face or the individual technique. Wayburn, Berkeley and Connelly all looked at the figure first and addressed dancing ability second. Typically, Wayburn even broke his dancers down into groups to which he gave idiosyncratic names relating to their skills. The tallest, prettiest and most glamorous girls were called 'squabs', whose importance was not so much in dancing as looking wonderful in costume; 'peaches' and 'chickens' were speciality acts; while 'ponies', who were, literally, work horses, made up in skill what they lacked in looks.

Left: The original 16 dancers of Ziegfeld's revue in typical 1920 outfits, although the staircase is not a long as it would later become.

HARLEM FACTFILE

Origin: The Dutch settlement of Nieuw Haarlem became an Irish residential area before becoming the epicentre of Black and Hispanic urban migration.

Location: Manhattan, New York. Traditionally 125th Street is the heart of Harlem.

Harlem renaissance: Between 1900 and 1930 Harlem became the centre of a flowering of African-American culture; writers like Langston Hughes and Claude Mackay celebrated the lives and achievements of African-Americans, and white audiences flocked to the neighbourhood to see new shows and song and dance acts.

Theatres: Lafayette, home of *Darktown Follies* and *Shuffle Along*, introduced Josephine Baker, Florence Mills and Blake and Sissle. The Lincoln, home of *Runnin' Wild*, the show that introduced the Charleston to the world.

Dancehalls: The Savoy Ballroom (the Home of Happy Feet); birthplace of the Lindy and centre of the evolution of the swing sound. Musicians included Dizzy Gillespie and Count Basie.

Cabaret: The Cotton Club, the heavily segregated home to many of the greatest dance acts of the era, backed regularly by the Duke Ellington Orchestra.

Harlem hots up

While Wayburn and his contemporaries were creating the American musical in midtown Manhattan, black musicals were beginning to make their presence felt uptown. In Harlem in 1913 an integrated theatre called the Lafayette had opened *Darktown Follies*, an all-black musical that pushed back the boundaries of jazz dancing on stage. *Darktown Follies* was the brainchild of the multi-talented John Leubrie Hill. Actor, producer, director and all-round inspiration, Hill fought to get *Darktown Follies* to Broadway with all the crusading zeal of a man with a mission. An actor who had worked for Williams and Walker and directed his own show, *My Friend from Dixie* in 1911, Hill had previous experience, but nevertheless, the fact that *Darktown Follies* proved so successful in an era that offered so many obstacles is testament to his character.

'... the Texas tommy was a vital signal of the way popular dance was headed, particularly in the way the dance allowed couples to break and improvise ...'

Darktown Follies was a simple story of a young wastrel who flees bad company and an overbearing wife (played by Leubrie Hill) and looks for a better life in the high social circles of Washington, D.C., before being dragged home by his spouse. It proved a milestone for two reasons. First, it broke the taboo of presenting a 'Negro' love scene on stage. Second, its dancing was of a breadth and originality never seen on the New York stage before. The show ended with the ubiquitous cakewalk, but before that it introduced the world to the Texas tommy and – the biggest sensation of the show – the circle dance.

The Texas tommy was one of many dances that had been brought north by the black migration. A dancer named Johnny Peters is said to have brought it from the south in 1911, dancing it at Lew Purcell's influential black cabaret in San Francisco. Peters wound up performing the Texas tommy for the Al Jolson troupe, partnered by a dancer called Mary Dewson. When Dewson fell ill, Ethel Williams took her place, and Peters and Williams made a reputation doing the dance in and around New York City. Spotted by Leubrie Hill, they were hired for *Darktown Follies*, and Ethel Williams went on to become the star of the show.

As Ethel Williams told the dance historians Marshall and Jean Stearns, the Texas tommy had, 'two basic steps – a kick and hop three times on each foot, and then add whatever you want, turning, pulling, sliding'. A precursor of the lindy hop and jitterbug of the next decade (see pages 140–141), the Texas tommy was a vital signal of the way popular dance was headed, particularly in the way the dance allowed couples to break and improvise steps on their own before rejoining hands. In this way the Texas tommy looked forwards to the defining characteristic of twentieth-century social dancing: the abandonment of couple dancing for individual expression.

Ethel Williams also featured in the other great sensation of *Darktown Follies*, the circle dance. The finale of the second act, the circle dance consisted of the whole company 'snaking' around the stage, singing 'At the Ball ... That's All', composed, of course, by Leubrie Hill. With their hands on the hips of the person in front, the dancers would move with a combination of a mooche and a slide, Ethel Williams bringing up the rear with her own clowning version of ballin' the jack. It caused such a sensation that Florenz Ziegfeld bought the entire routine for his own Follies, but even though Ethel Williams helped teach the routine downtown, neither she nor Leubrie Hill ever received any credit for its creation.

Opposite: The Lafayette theatre in New York's Harlem district, scene of the ground-breaking black musical *Darktown Follies*, which caused a sensation in 1913.

Above: Stepin Fetchit was an ex-vaudeville song and dance man who became a successful movie actor, playing what are now seen as racially stereotyped 'dumb' black parts.

SACK AMUSEMENT ENTERPRISES
PRESENTS
BILL ROBINSON
WORLD'S GREATEST TAP DANCER
IN
"HARLEM IS HEAVEN"
ALL-COLORED CAST
EUBIE BLAKE'S ORCHESTRA
And New York's Famous Cotton Club Entertainers

Left: A touring version of a night at the Cotton Club featuring Bill 'Bojangles' Robinson top of the bill.

COTTON CLUB FACTFILE

Location: 142nd Street and Lenox Ave

Nickname: Aristocrat of Harlem

Claim to fame: The most famous and most notorious cabaret venue in New York City. Provided a white audience with some of the greatest jazz and dance acts of the Prohibition era.

Origins: Opened in 1923 as a front for the illegal dealings of the bootlegging gangster, Owney Madden. Run by George 'Big Frenchy' Demange, it had a rigid whites-only policy. Many of the acts were African-American, but all the revues were written by white talent.

Talent: Musicians included Duke Ellington and Cab Calloway. Lena Horne began her career at the Cotton Club, and Ethel Waters was a frequent performer. Dance acts included the Nicholas Brothers, Coles and Atkins, Bill Robinson, the Four Step Brothers and 'Snake Hips' Tucker.

Film: The legend of the venue was revived in the 1984 film, *The Cotton Club*, directed by Francis Ford Coppola and starring Richard Gere and Gregory Hines.

'*Shuffle Along* opened on 21 May 1921 ... and finally put jazz dance on the map.'

Darktown Follies saw some of the first white audiences moving uptown, intrigued by what Harlem had to offer. Irene Castle was said to have learned the Texas tommy from Ethel Williams. However, it was 1921 before another show followed in the footsteps of *Darktown Follies*. *Shuffle Along* opened on 21 May 1921, at the 63rd Street Theater, and finally put jazz dance on the map.

With a plot written by Flournoy Miller and Aubrey Lyles (1883–1932), writers and performers of considerable reputation, and music composed by the established song-writing team of Noble Sissle (1889–1975) and Eubie Blake (1883–1983), *Shuffle Along* came with a good pedigree. Nevertheless, it too had great difficulty in making it to the stage, but once there it delighted audiences across the country for many years. It was revived twice more – in 1932 and 1952 – its longevity proof that much of the show's dancing was ahead of its time.

The plot was simple – a small town's election for mayor is complicated by the social pretensions of the candidates' wives – but *Shuffle Along* made stars of a largely unknown cast. Miller and Lyles took the leads, creating as a centrepiece for the show a 20-minute dance fight. (Dance fights were a regular part of the vaudeville circuit.) In Charlie Davis and Tommy Woods it possessed two great pioneers in the development of tap, and two glorious eccentric dancers in Bob Williams and Ulysses S. Thompson, but it was Thompson's wife, Florence Mills (1895–1927), who stole the show.

Shuffle Along made Florence Mills a star, and, during the Harlem renaissance, she burned brightly. Pretty, vivacious and with great comic skill, she left *Shuffle Along* to star in the *Plantation Revue* (1922), *Dixie to Broadway* (1924) and the 1926 season of *Blackbirds*. Despite her huge fame, she refused to recognize her own success, telling at least one reporter that: 'I have my own way of dancing – and singing – and it happens to be popular.'

Of all the unknown talent that *Shuffle Along* launched on an unsuspecting public, however, none was more sensational than

Above: The effervescent but modest Florence Mills achieved stardom through her appearances in *Shuffle Along* and later appeared in several other musicals.

Left: The successful black song-writing team of Eubie Blake (at the piano) and Noble Sissle, who wrote the jazz-dance musical *Shuffle Along*.

JOSEPHINE BAKER FACTFILE

Born: 3 June 1906

Died: 12 April 1975

Childhood: Born St Louis, Missouri. Survived a harsh childhood and two marriages before joining the chorus of *Shuffle Along* at the age of 15.

New York: Starred in Blake and Sissle's *Shuffle Along* and the *Chocolate Dandies*. Despite this early success she was never again as appreciated in the United States as she was elsewhere in the world.

Paris: Arrived in Paris with La Revue Negre in 1925. In 1926 she headlined at Folies-Bergère. Eventually opened her own venue, Chez Josephine.

Awards: Chevalier de la Légion d'honneur and Rosette de la Resistance for her work in wartime France.

Secret of success: Baker's mixture of dance, song, outrageous costume and ability to shock placed her at the heart of 'le jazz hot' Paris. She became an international icon and counted among her admirers the likes of Ernest Hemingway and Princess Grace of Monaco.

the young Josephine Baker (1906–75). Barely 16 – she had auditioned for the show a year before and been turned away when the producers discovered her age – she was the chorus line's end-girl, a position made famous by Ethel Williams a generation before. Either because she was unable to dance the steps expected, or because she recognized an opportunity to make a name for herself, Baker replaced the set choreography with her own inimitable mixture of clowning, mugging and cheeky improvisation. Whatever her reasons, it worked, and within a few years she was earning the astronomical sum of $125 a week in the chorus line of Blake and Sissle's the *Chocolate Dandies*.

Josephine Baker's ambition and self-confidence grew out of the harsh realities of a poverty-stricken childhood. One of four children, she was born in St Louis, Missouri, the illegitimate daughter of a black mother and a Spanish father. She was brought up by her mother and a black stepfather, but the lightness of her skin initially hindered her career within the heavily segregated world of American variety. This, and the horrifying experience of witnessing the destruction of her hometown by a white lynch mob, provided her with the crusading zeal to fight for civil rights in later life.

Above: The legendary Josephine Baker here appears on stage like a caged bird; her greatest success was at the Folies-Bergère in Paris in the 1920s.

Opposite, left: Baker's popularity in Europe was not restricted to the world of Paris cabaret, as proved by this Dutch poster for her 1935 movie *Princess Tam Tam*.

Opposite, right: A close encounter in 1927 with an elephant; despite her success in Paris and across Europe, Baker was little appreciated in her home country.

The real turning point in Baker's career was her arrival in Paris in *La Revue Nègre* in 1925. To a Paris engulfed in the *le jazz hot*, Baker came to embody the spirit of the land from which it came. With a mixture of eccentric dancing, idiosyncratic jazz singing and revealing and outrageous costumes, she took the city by storm. Paris in return wooed Baker, and despite the odd tour, she remained in Europe for the rest of her life.

In 1926 she headlined in the Folies-Bergère, famously taking to the stage dressed only in a girdle of bananas. Baker's success, however, was not solely due to the shock value of her performance or the undeniable force of her personality. She was bringing to a continent titillated and tantalized by the jazz dances and new sounds of America the raw experience, the genuine article. Indeed, she represents the missing link in the story of African-American dance as it swept across the world. Josephine Baker was the great dance exporter; when she danced the Charleston, Europe followed. When Europe got word of the black bottom, it was to Baker that it turned. She became a legend, and her stardom gave a girl from humble beginnings access to the greatest European figures of the day.

'Josephine Baker was the great dance exporter; when she danced the Charleston, Europe followed. When Europe got word of the black bottom, it was to Baker that it turned.'

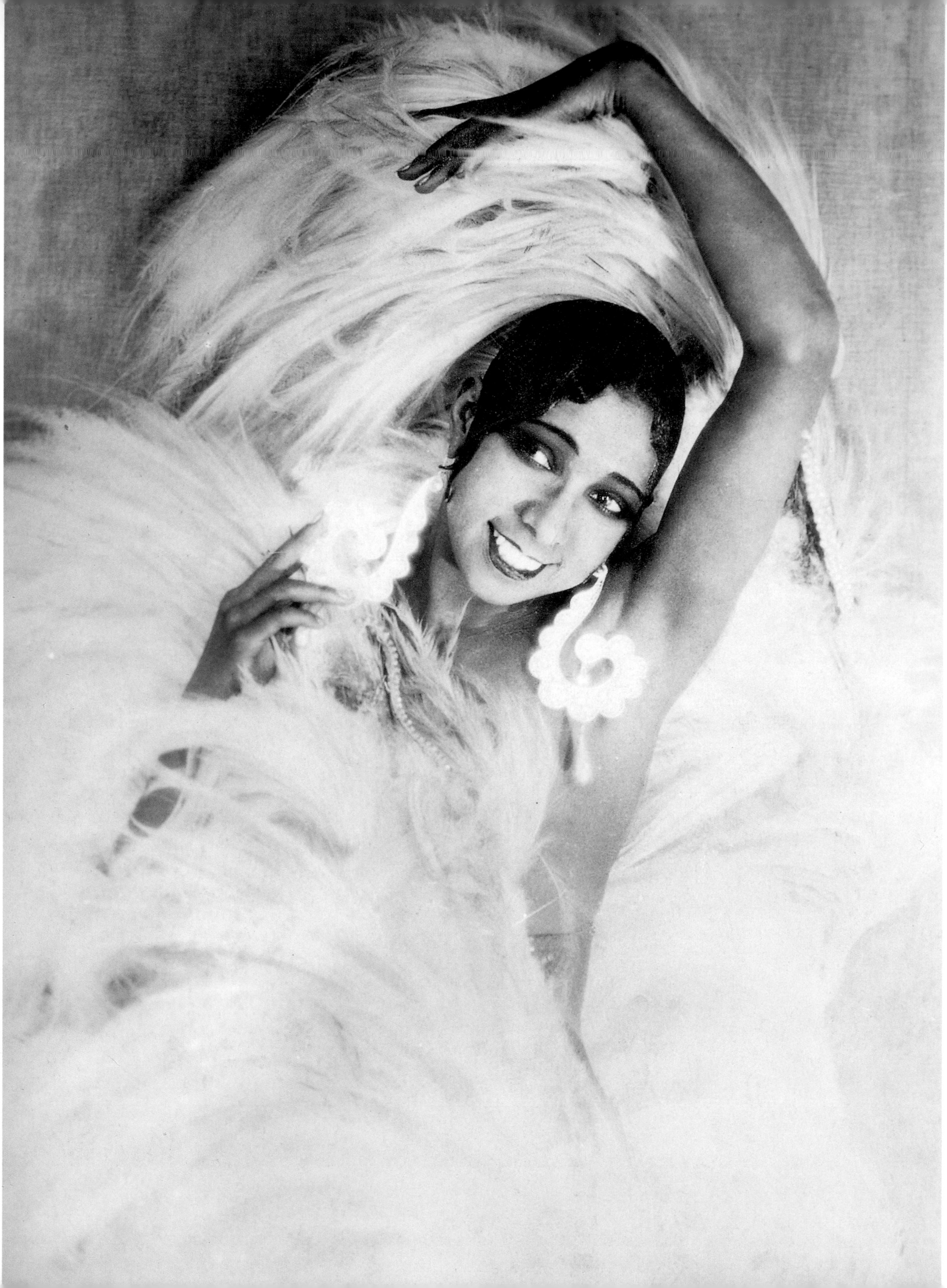

Despite her success, including becoming a Chevalier de la Légion d'honneur in her adopted France, in the United States her achievements were never really recognized. An appearance in *Ziegfeld's Follies of 1936* met with little acclaim, and her later visits became as notorious for her civil rights battles as the quality her performance. In truth, her unique style was perhaps better suited to the intimate cabarets of Europe, but it was only after her death that the Variety Club Foundation of New York recognized, with a celebratory tribute, one of its greatest exports.

The pleasure of the Charleston

For European audiences *La Revue Nègre*, which had launched Baker on to the international scene, was a real example of what was happening in New York in the aftermath of *Shuffle Along*. The black musical was in vogue, and Josephine Baker was only one, albeit the brightest, of the stars of the decade. *The Plantation Revue, Pat and Take* (with music by Perry Bradford), *Strut Miss Lizzie* and *Liza* were all shows that grew out of the fertile seeds sown by *Shuffle Along*. Show dancing, too, was to change in its aftermath, becoming more intricate and daring. It was almost as if a direct line had opened up between jazz musical development and show dancing evolution, and tap dancers and jazz drummers plundered each other's styles in turn for more dynamic and intricate rhythms.

The most successful show of the crop was *Runnin' Wild*. Devised by those two stars of *Shuffle Along*, Flournoy Miller and Aubrey Lyles, *Runnin' Wild* boasted an impressive cast list. Tommy Woods and George Stamper offered acrobatic tap and eccentric dancing respectively, while Adelaide Hall sang. The importance of the show, however, lay not in its personnel, but in its choreography, for *Runnin' Wild* was the production in which the Charleston came of age.

Such would be the impact of the Charleston that many people would later claim the credit for inventing it, although, like so many dances of the period, its birth lies in the history of African-American culture. An 1866 edition of *Harper's Weekly* contains a picture of a dance very like the Charleston, while dance historians have traced its roots back to the Ashanti dancers of Africa. Certainly, Noble Sissle claims that he was dancing it as early as 1905, and it was already part of a Whitman Sisters show by 1911. Certainly, its name suggests a history, if nothing more, in the southern state of South Carolina.

'Such would be the impact of the Charleston that many people would later claim the credit for inventing it, although, like so many dances of the period, its birth lies in the history of African-American culture.'

Left: A delightful publicity shot of Josephine Baker from the revue *Paris Qui Remue*, when she was at the height of her popularity.

Below: The Charleston was the dance of the 1920s; everyone was doing it, whether at private parties, in ballrooms or even on the top of a car.

Running wild

The Charleston's arrival on Broadway, too, is surrounded in myth. One story tells of Sissle and Blake introducing Ned Wayburn to a black boy, taken in off the street in 1923. The story goes that the boy danced an early version of the Charleston, and Wayburn evolved it into a Charleston routine for the *Ziegfeld Follies* in the same year. Over the years this story may have become mixed with another tale of the dance's creation that was told by Flournoy Miller. Miller said that he found three kids dancing for money on the pavement outside the Lincoln Theater during the rehearsals of *Runnin' Wild*. The trio was led by a dancer called Russell Brown, who later became one of the Three Browns, an acrobatic tap troupe, but at this time he went under the nickname of 'Charleston'. The kids improvised drums using garbage cans and kitchen tubs and took each other on in a form of challenge dancing, which survives today in the b-boy dancing of the Bronx (see page 236). Impressed, Miller took the lads into his rehearsals and developed the steps into a chorus routine. The boys themselves never made it on to the stage, but the routine, in which a male chorus, the Dancing Redcaps, danced the Charleston to James P. Johnson's song of the same name, brought down the house.

Runnin' Wild solidified a growing taste for the Charleston in the dancehalls of both Europe and America. By the middle years of the decade, the craze had swept all before it, and for a short period the public was dancing nothing else except the Charleston. A 1925 *Variety Magazine* reported that in 'Boston's Pickwick Club ... the vibrations of the Charleston were so strong that the dancers caused the place to collapse, killing fifty'. The success of the dance in Britain was immense, with even the Prince of Wales proving an accomplished exponent, in spite of

'The kids improvised drums with garbage cans and kitchen tubs and took each other on in a form of challenge dancing, which survives today in the b-boy dancing of the Bronx.'

Above, left: The Hollywood star Joan Crawford was known for her shapely legs in her early career, and the Charleston showed them off to great effect.

Right: A flapper from one of film director Mack Sennett's 'comedies', which often featured the eccentric dance that seemed to epitomize youthful exuberance.

Above: The Charleston even made the cover of *Life* magazine in 1926, although there might have been some implied criticism in the drawing.

Left: It may be a little dangerous, but it's fun! Flappers dancing the Charleston in 1926, apparently on top of Chicago's Sherman Hotel.

the *Daily Mail* newspaper denouncing it as 'reminiscent of Negro orgies' – a chilling and revealingly racist objection.

The craze was comparatively short lived – by 1927 the black bottom (see pages 62–63) had taken its place – but its importance and longevity in the popular imagination is due to a number of factors. First, the Charleston marked another step on the road away from intimate couple dancing towards individual expression. The dance was as popular with men as with women, and a culture of 'cutting-in' evolved, whereby a dancer could change partner in mid-routine. Second, the popularity of the Charleston contest meant that the line between stage performer and ball-room practitioner was blurred. Many of the greatest exponents of the Charleston never left the dance floor, although many notable dance careers began within its steps. Ginger Rogers (see pages 128–133) and Joan Crawford both began their careers as Charleston stars.

Finally, the lack of travel in the dance meant that the Charleston was relatively easy to film. Therefore, despite its briefly hysterical existence, there is a mass of social record confirming the Charleston's place as an icon of the jazz age. Its speed and cheek perfectly matched the spirit of a generation, eagerly fleeing from the memories of one world war and blind to the

Running wild

Right: The impresario George White was out to shock in his 1926 revue *Scandals*; here he teaches the stars how to dance the black bottom.

Below: George White supposedly auditioning some of the 75 girls who were to appear in a 1933 film based on his celebrated stage shows.

imposing shadow of the next. Although many Charleston steps would be integrated into the lindy hop (see page 140), and a Charleston quality can be found in the mashed potato (see page 193), the purest form of the dance will always be frozen in a time, linked forever with the bright young flappers who brushed their knees and kicked their feet in the heart of the 1920s.

The producer of *Runnin' Wild* was George White (1890–1968). In 1926 White produced another show, *Scandals*, which featured Ann Pennington dancing the black bottom. Again, a dance from the south – this time Nashville – caused a sensation, and again, the public went wild for it. Over the next few years, the black bottom rivalled the popularity of the Charleston itself. Although in

the ballrooms the dance consisted of little more than a few hops and a slap of the backside, the black bottom could be traced back to a considerably more intricate ancestor called the Jacksonville rounders dance. Perry Bradford was said to have reworked this into the black bottom in his 1919 'Original Black Bottom Dance'. Bradford knew, as well as anybody, that in the world of social dancing, there is nothing new under the sun.

White had probably seen the black bottom in a 1924 show in Harlem called *Dinah*, but he packaged it and resold it to a wider public. This meant that in the space of a few years George White had produced two shows that had launched the leading dance crazes of the decade.

But the Charleston and the black bottom probably represent the high-water mark for dances passing back and forth between stage and ballroom. Show dancers were becoming ever more accomplished and choreographers ever more daring. As the heady atmosphere of the 1920s collapsed into the harsh realities of the new decade, the public would be offered a lushness and virtuosity on stage and screen that they could not match in their local dancehall. For the time being at least, the two environments would follow their own paths, each aware of the other, but not inseparable.

'Although in the ballrooms the dance consisted of little more than a few hops and a slap of the backside, the black bottom could be traced back to a considerably more intricate ancestor.'

Above: The black bottom still had a place on the dance floor, as did the Charleston. Here Edith Wilson gives a rendition.

Latin American rhythms

The United States was not the only country forging new dance styles out of the clash between African slave dances and the dominant culture of their New World masters. In Central and South America the same reaction was taking place. However, in South America the dominant culture into which the African slaves were imported was not that of northern or central European but of the Iberian peninsula. The best illustration of this African-Latin fusion phenomenon was the habanera, a nineteenth-century folk dance born directly out of the Afro-Cuban clash. A Cuban adaptation of what was already a Spanish version of a French eighteenth-century dance known as the *contredanse*, the habanera came to dominate the fin-de-siècle South American dance scene and it survives today in the opera *Carmen* by Georges Bizet.

'In Argentina the habanera mingled with the more conspicuous European import, the polka, to produce a new dance unique to the region, the milonga.'

Below: Havana Central Park in the Cuban capital, where the dance the habanera originated and from which it takes its name.

Latin American rhythms

In fact, the *contredanse* itself was a French version of English pastoral dances, and, as such, it is a useful example of the old adage 'what goes around, comes around'. The habanera was born in Havana, Cuba, the city from which it takes its name. Supposedly brought to the island from Haiti and elsewhere in the West Indies by French planters, it spread throughout South America and back to Spain. In Cuba it helped to influence the extraordinary outpouring of styles that emerged from the island a hundred years later, but before that its biggest influence was in Argentina, particularly in the burgeoning metropolis of Buenos Aires. In Argentina the habanera mingled with the more conspicuous European import, the polka, to produce a new dance unique to the region, the milonga. Also known as the 'poor man's habanera', the milonga was a dance of the pampas, the extensive arable plains of northern and central Argentina, and the

Left: The tango was born in the seedier districts of Buenos Aires, the Argentinean capital, amongst adherents to a violent subculture found in the brothels.

Below: Before long the tango had shaken off some its underworld associations, and was beginning to be accepted in higher society, as this postcard implies.

gauchos, the bold cowboys who ranged the pampas during the eighteenth, nineteenth and twentieth centuries. However, unlike the culture it celebrated, the milonga survived. The reason is simple – it was the forerunner of the tango.

The birth of the tango

At the turn of the century the city of Buenos Aires was experiencing a period of enormous growth. Its economic prosperity and rapid industrial expansion and the large number of immigrants pouring into its streets every day made Buenos Aires compare favourably with New York City. The majority of immigrants were Spanish and Italian, and, as in New York City, they found accommodation in overpopulated *conventillos* (tenements) and *arraballes* (slums). Often sited on the outskirts of the city, the *arraballes* provided an environment where the old traditions of the pampas and the new culture of the immigrants could meet and mix, and it was in this environment that there developed the street culture of the *compadritos*, street-wise young men who aped the values of the *compadres* of the pampas with macho displays of pride. They also possessed a propensity for violence. Conspicuous in their trademark uniform of a white neckerchief tied around the neck, *fungi* (wide-rimmed hat) worn loosely over one eye, high-heeled boots and a knife hanging off the hip, the *compadritos'* domain was the seedier parts of the city.

In spite of its aspirations and burgeoning urbanization, Buenos Aires was still a port at heart and possessed more than its

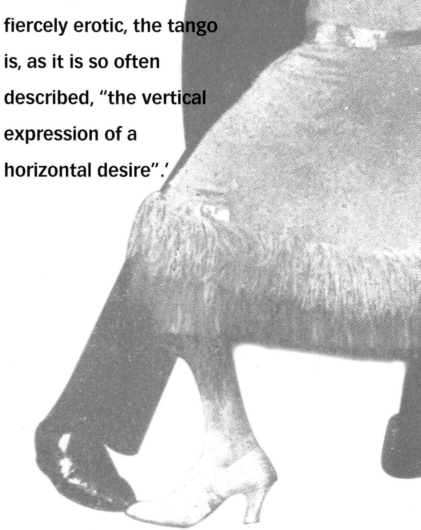

fair share of brothels. Here, and in bars of the *arraballes*, the *compadritos* came together to strut, brag and dance. At first, the *compadritos* danced the milonga, but in time they added to it dance styles they had seen elsewhere. Within the African community of Buenos Aires, which was small but tightly knit, they saw many dances of African descent, not least a new version of the *candomble*, which the African-Argentines called the tango. Although this dance did not allow for partners to touch and only loosely suggested the dance that was eventually to bear its name, the *compadritos* fell for it and incorporated parodies of it into the milonga.

The origins of the word 'tango' are open to conjecture. It may have come from African-Argentine dances – the word tango originally referred to any place where Africans congregated to dance

Below, left: The heady South American rhythms of the tango were surprisingly eagerly adopted by composers in the Germanic countries of central Europe.

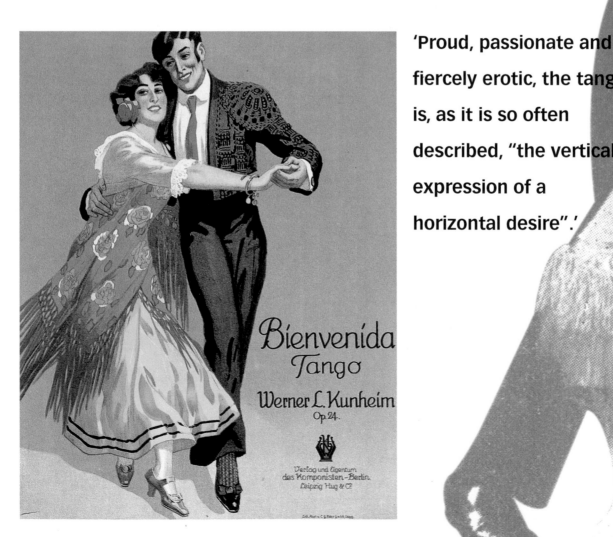

'Proud, passionate and fiercely erotic, the tango is, as it is so often described, "the vertical expression of a horizontal desire".'

– but it was possibly in use well before the turn of the century to describe the indigenous music evolving in the *arraballes*. (In 1886 the bandoneon, an accordion with buttons rather than keys, had been imported to Argentina and had become the essential accompaniment for the tango.) There is also a theory that the name comes from the Latin verb *tangere* (to touch), but this seems unlikely, and any suggestion that it came from the French verb *tanguer* (to sway, to reel) speaks more of the French craze for the dance a few years later than any serious contemplation of the provenance of the name.

In any event, the dance that became known as the tango possesses many of the hallmarks of the environment from which it sprang. Proud, passionate and fiercely erotic, the tango is, as it is so often described, 'the vertical expression of a horizontal desire'. With the dancers' bodies pressed together, their eye contact intense and the upper body still, the tango has none of the innocent romance of the waltz or the frivolity of ragtime. Instead, it has hidden within its choreography the lust of the lonely immigrant and the dispassionate sensuality of the prostitute. Lust, violence, sex – it is not surprising that the tango has been so often associated with melancholy and death.

Tangomania

It is remarkable that a dance that was conceived in a brothel and shunned by the upstanding citizens of its own country should have survived at all, but not only did the tango prosper, it conquered the world. The dominant dancing craze of its generation, its seedy reputation and suggestion of scandal did much to secure its fame. There is a popular saying in Argentina that the citizens of Buenos Aires are Italians who speak Spanish, think they are English and wish they were French. Certainly, it was the upper classes' desire to travel to Europe, France in particular, that was responsible for the spread of the tango abroad. Young, aristocratic Argentine men, who considered visiting brothels as important a part of their education as touring Europe, began to teach their European hosts the scandalous dance they had seen on their trips to the *enramadas* at home. From these clandestine demonstrations, the tango spread like wild fire across the ballrooms of Paris.

As the dance swept across Europe it brought with it sensation and outrage in equal measure. In London the tango performed by George Grossmith and Phyllis Dare in the West End musical, *The*

Above: Although its erotic associations would suggest that the tango was a dance of the night, it seems to have been accepted even at tea dances.

Latin American rhythms

Sunshine Girl (1912), spawned a host of imitators in the best tradition of the theatre/dancehall crossover. The Savoy hosted tango dinners, while *The Times* of London published letters from irate parents. In 1914 a tango was officially performed for Queen Mary at a ball given in honour of Grand Duke Michael of Russia. The queen's subsequent enthusiasm for the dance did much to dampen the hostility to the craze in her own country, although it had been a part of Russian society ever since the Tsar had asked his young nephews to give him a demonstration of the dance in 1911. In Germany a ban on officers in uniform performing the tango all but banished the dance from high society, while in Italy, Pope Pius X officially condemned its 'barbaric contortions'.

The centre of tangomania was, inevitably, Paris. Here the new craze affected everything from couture to cuisine. Ladies' fashions evolved to accentuate the visual effects of the dance and allowed for more freedom of movement – tango blouses with billowing sleeves, for example, and dresses with provocative slits. The demands for fast and frequent turns led in turn to smaller, more compact headgear. Men's evening dress became sleeker and more dramatic. The best known innovation of the period were the *thés tango* (tango teas), which were held wherever the fashionable congregated to see and be seen, from Paris to New York. The tradition of dancing between the courses of a meal in fashionable restaurants had begun in Vienna, but now – perhaps because the sedate surroundings countered the provocative nature of the dance - the idea took off. From Paris the *thé dansant* (tea dance) travelled to the chic seaside towns of the Channel coast, such as Le Touquet and Deauville, where it caught the attention of many of the vacationing revellers from abroad.

Respectability

The tango craze was brought to an abrupt end in 1914. The outbreak of the First World War left little time for a frivolous cult in recreational dancing, and the fad died down. However, the tango did not disappear completely, and after the war it returned to the cafés and ballrooms of Paris, even though, like the society in which it thrived, it had changed forever. The post-war tango was a less rebellious, more standardized version of the original. The steps may have been more provocative, but the music itself had lost something of the driving beat. Ironically, as the tango became increasingly detached from its South American origins – it was brought to heel by the Imperial Society of Teachers of

'The post-war tango was a less rebellious, more standardized version of the original. The steps may have been more provocative, but the music itself had lost something of the driving beat.'

Left: Carlos Gardel, the star of numerous inter-war South American films, encouraged a revival of interest in the tango in the country of its birth.

Dancing in their meetings in the 1920s – the myth surrounding its origins became more celebrated. Dancers and bandstands were flooded with dancers dressed in mythologized versions of Argentine national dress, and it was into this environment that the most iconic tango image of them all – Rudolph Valentino in the 1921 film *The Four Horseman of the Apocalypse* – seeped into public consciousness.

Ironically, as the passion for the tango was dying down in Europe, it finally became an accepted part of Argentine life. The middle classes of Buenos Aires, so sniffy towards the tango when it emerged out of the *arraballes* 30 years before, changed their tune when they saw the success of the dance in Europe. As the rest of the world's gaze turned towards new trends in dancing, Argentina finally took the tango to its heart and set about transforming it into high art (and, often, an effective tool of political expression). The centre of this movement was Carlos Gardel

(1887–1935), a South American variety and movie star, whose life mirrored the journey of the tango from *arraballes* to high society. He died tragically in an aeroplane crash, although his films, music and charisma survive to this day throughout Latin America.

Gardel's films are the most obvious example of the tango's commemoration on celluloid, but the dance has been a repeatedly popular motif in the movies. Aspects of the tango fed into Fred Astaire and Ginger Rogers's first film together in 1933, *Flying Down to Rio* (see page 130). Ken Russell's 1977 celebration of Rudolph Valentino, *Valentino*, included a tango danced by two of the greatest ballet dancers of the day, Anthony Dowell and Rudolf Nureyev, while the *Last Tango in Paris* (1972) by Bernardo Bertolucci made much of the metaphorical connection between sex and death in the dance. In fact, the constant use of the tango in novels, films and plays has kept the form present in world culture, culminating at the end of the twentieth century in stage

Above: The tango was ideal for the charismatic film star Rudolph Valentino, here performing with Alice Terry in *The Four Horsemen of the Apocalypse* of 1921.

extravaganzas like *Tango Argentino* and *Forever Tango*, whose commercial success has confirmed the popular taste for the tango even into the twenty-first century.

The immense popularity of the tango before the First World War meant that any dance style that could also be described as 'exotic', and possessed a South American beat had a good chance of arriving on the dance floors of Europe. One such dance was the Brazilian maxixe, an energetic and physical dance, which was characterized by swooping body movements. As always, the original exuberance in execution became tamed and modified as it made its way into polite society, but it nevertheless proved especially popular with the young in the years immediately preceding the First World War.

Unfortunately, the popularity of the maxixe was short lived. It rode, as it were, on the coat tails of the tango, and when tango-mania subsided so did interest in its derivatives. However, the maxixe was merely a ballroom flirtation with a fully fledged dance culture emanating from Brazil. The maxixe was a calling card for the arrival of the samba.

'Each *orixa* has its own identifiable drum rhythm and dance style that personifies the god – undulating shoulders for a sea god, for example, or stamping feet for the god of war. One of these gods, the *caboclo*, has a style known as the samba.'

Above. Dancers from Brazil's Mangueria Samba School performing their country's national dance in colourful costumes on the streets during the carnival festivities.

Left: The tango remains a staple in the ballroom dancing repertoire, although it has metamorphosed into something quite different from the pre-1914 dance.

The samba

Slavery played as important a part in Brazilian history as anywhere else in the New World. Brazil became, in 1888, the last country in South America to abolish the practice, and by that date between 3 and 4 million slaves had been imported into the country. However, the massive numbers of Africans working the great plantations of the country, particularly in the northeast, meant that there was a constant fear of uprisings among the colonists. The Portuguese answer to this threat was significantly different from the response to the same worry in the United States: in the USA African culture was suppressed and stifled, but in Brazil the West African culture of the slaves was allowed limited expression and consequently became relatively easily assimilated into the dominant Catholic culture. In effect, this meant that West African rituals were supplanted by Catholic festivals, and Yoruban deities swapped for Christian saints. In most other respects, however, African traditions survived.

In the northeastern region of Bahia one such dance ritual, the *candomble*, survives to this day. The *candomble* is an African ritual in which dancers seek 'possession' by divine spirits while they dance. Known as *orixas*, these deities possess individual characteristics and personalities, and the local women who perform the *candomble* believe that they are actually 'taken over' by the spirits during the ceremony. Each *orixa* has its own identifiable drum rhythm and dance style that personifies the god – undulating shoulders for a sea god, for example, or stamping feet for the god of war. One of these gods, the *caboclo*, has a style known as the samba.

The samba became the secular face of the *candomble* ritual. In the aftermath of the abolition of slavery at the end of the nineteenth century, the *candomble* and the samba spread across the country. Over time the samba's earthy and exhilarating style became a physical expression of Brazilian identity and an endless source of national pride.

One of the reasons for this was the role it came to play in carnival, and especially in the carnival of Rio de Janeiro. The samba is not the only dance to feature in carnival festivities – in the city of Recife the *capoeira* plays a central part – but it is the carnival in

Below: Sheet music for the 'true samba' apparently written by genuine Brazilian composers, but published in France; Latin American dances were enjoyed throughout Europe, and still are.

Rio and the *sambistas* who perform it who are internationally recognized. (The *capoeira* has recently emigrated to the United States, where it features in house and hip-hop dancing.) Brazilian carnival is itself a product of a hybrid culture. Partly a modern manifestation of medieval Christian festivals that marked the coming of Lent with subversive and anti-authoritarian festivities and partly a descendant of the African coronation traditions, carnival is today a means of articulating national pride and improving racial and religious relations.

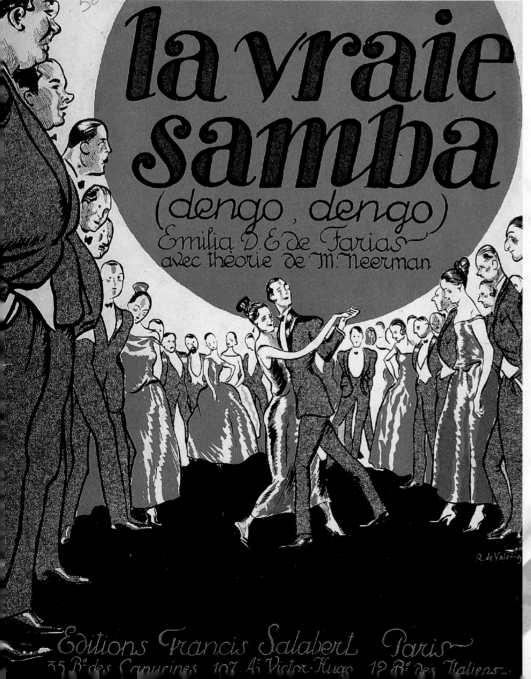

la vraie samba
(dengo, dengo)
Emilia D. & de Farias
avec théorie de M. Neerman

Éditions Francis Salabert Paris
35 B^d des Capucines 107 A^e Victor-Hugo 12 B^d des Italiens

'The samba school processions are a living expression of Brazilian culture and history, combining allegory and pastiche in a colourful mosaic of national hopes and aspirations.'

The samba made its way into the carnival at the beginning of the twentieth century as it travelled south from its roots, first appearing on the streets about 1917. Initially, the authorities frowned on the *escolas de samba* (samba schools), feeling threatened by their racial origins and perceived link to public disorder. In 1935, however, the authorities relented and the samba schools became a vital and central part of the festival. The aim of every samba school is to come first in the samba contest that is the centre of the carnival. The competing schools, which can be made up of several thousand people, spend the best part of a year building exotic floats and rehearsing samba songs and routines to present in the four-day extravaganza. The heart of the samba contest is the sambadrome – a long stretch of paving flanked by huge terraces able to accommodate more than 70,000 spectators. The sambadrome is where the judges sit and pontificate, and it is, consequently, the site of the *sambistas*' most energetic and complete performances. The samba school processions are a living expression of Brazilian culture and history, combining allegory and pastiche in a colourful mosaic of national hopes and aspirations. Dancers dressed as figures from Brazilian history rub shoulders with imitations of screen legends, and parodies of local politicians step out with carnival kings and queens. In the gay community in particular, one figure stands out as worthy of imitation – the Brazilian Bombshell, Carmen Miranda.

Left: A dancing competition in Mexico, where the liveliness of the performance often disguised the essential poverty endured by the contestants in their everyday lives.

Carmen Miranda

A singer, dancer and actress, Carmen Miranda (1909–55) is largely responsible for the surge in popularity in the samba in the 1940s. The Portuguese-born Brazilian singer became the embodiment of the new craze as it left its native shores and travelled to Europe and America as the latest dancehall craze.

As early as 1928, Carmen Miranda had secured a recording contract with RCA and was well on her way to becoming a major musical star in Brazil. Over the next 10 years she supplemented her variety work with appearances in Latin films, including *Alo, Alo Brasil* and *Estudantes*. In 1939 she travelled to the United States. The samba had been introduced to the United States at the 1939 World's Fair, and the dance was just beginning to become popular, so Carmen Miranda arrived at just the right moment to exploit its growing appeal. Her appearance in the Broadway revue, *The Streets of Paris*, in which she sang 'South American Way', caused a sensation, and she was subsequently signed by Twentieth Century Fox.

Throughout the Second World War Carmen Miranda starred in a series of colourful musicals that sold to the wartime public an image of fun and frivolous Latin life. With films like *Down Argentine Way* (1940), *Weekend in Havana* (1941), *The Gang's All Here* (1943) and *Copacabana* (1947) and songs as well known as 'I, Yi, Yi, Yi, Yi (Like You Very Much)', 'Chica Chica Boom Chic' and 'The Lady With the Tutti Frutti Hat', she was, by 1945, the highest-paid female performer in America. Her costumes in these films – always very extravagant dresses and fruit-laden hats – were a popularized version of the dress styles of the Baiana women of

> **'Throughout the Second World War Carmen Miranda starred in a series of colourful musicals that sold to the wartime public an image of fun and frivolous Latin life.'**

Brazil. Miranda's banana-bedecked headgear is a somewhat unlikely symbol of the origins of the samba.

Carmen Miranda's appeal proved to be short lived, however, and by the late 1940s she was returning to the cabaret and recording circuit, attempting to break out of the mould of the colourful stereotype. She never really achieved this, and when she died of a heart attack, live onstage in 1955, she was still identified in the popular imagination as the 'lady with the tutti frutti hat'.

Brazil's relationship with its greatest Hollywood export has always been ambiguous. She was recognized at the time of her death as an international star who had placed Brazilian culture on the map, and her death was followed by a period of national mourning. Her colourful personification of samba culture has

Opposite: The irrepressible Carmen Miranda in a publicity photograph taken for her film career, which began in 1930s Brazil, and continued in the 1940s in the USA.

Left: She may have been famous for her extravagant hats, but Carmen Miranda clearly had an almost as impressive shoe collection.

also led to accusations of stereotyping and 'selling-out' – as early as 1939 she had chosen not to return to Brazil after accusations of 'Americanization'. In fact, not unlike Bill Robinson (see page s 99–101), who endured similar attacks in the aftermath of his success, Carmen Miranda's popular persona had more to do with the prejudices of the mid-twentieth-century entertainment industry than the wilful perversion of reality by the artist.

Carmen Miranda's success led to a wave of popularity for the samba in the USA and Europe during the 1940s and early 1950s. The dancehall version of the samba was a watered-down couple dance, which had its roots in the maxixe (see page 72) of 30 years earlier. This was the dance that even Princess Margaret of the British royal family was dancing by the early 1950s. By the end of the decade, however, a new version of the samba was emerging.

Below: Carmen Miranda could be criticized, and was, for distorting the truth about Brazilian culture, but she nevertheless gave the national dance an international appeal.

CARMEN MIRANDA FACTFILE

Born: 9 February 1909

Died: 5 August 1955

Real name: Mario do Carmo Miranda da Cunha

Nickname: The Brazilian Bombshell

Early career: Born in Portugal but moved to Rio de Janeiro at an early age. Built up a successful career as singer and actress in Brazil before moving to the USA in 1939.

Hollywood: During the 1940s she was one of the most successful film stars in the world. Films included *Down Argentine Way*, *Weekend in Havana*, *Springtime in the Rockies* and *Nancy Goes to Rio*.

Songs: 'South American Way', 'The Lady with the Tutti Frutti Hat', 'I Yi Yi Yi Yi Yi (I Like You Very Much)', 'Chica Chica Boom Chic'.

Key to success: Trademark 'fruity' costumes and extravagant persona, based on the dress of the working-class fruit sellers of Bahia, offered sensuality and frivolity to an American and European audiences.

Above: Tenor saxophone star Stan Getz joined forces with guitarist Charlie Byrd on a 1962 album that was pivotal in the spread of the bossa nova, 'Jazz Samba'.

Right: Brazilian guitarist Laurindo Almeida made two influential Latin-jazz albums with his Quintet in 1954, featuring the American musician Bud Shank on flute.

'... the bossa nova required the same two-step movements as the samba and the same body movements. Again, its popularity was widespread but brief.'

Bossa nova

In America the samba rhythm had come within the orbit of the new cool jazz sounds of the 1950s. The pioneering work done by Dizzy Gillespie (1917–93), Machito (1912–84), Mario Bauza and others fed back into the samba culture of Rio and its environs. The result was the bossa nova.

In Portuguese, *bossa nova* literally means 'new trend' and this adequately describes the new sound. The music was in syncopated 2/4 time, as opposed to the 4/4 time of the original, and the instrumentation was simple. The vocal range was greater, and an increased importance was placed on improvisation. Perhaps the best known bossa nova song is the 1963 Stan Getz hit, 'The Girl from Ipanema'. In dance terms the difference was not so great, and the bossa nova required the same two-step movements as the samba and the same body movements. Again, its popularity was widespread but brief. The jazz sounds that had brought it to prominence it were evolving at a frenetic pace, and the musicians soon moved on to something new. The bossa nova was simply one of the myriad of sounds coming out of the bebop/Latin crossover, and it was by no means the longest lasting. Eventually, the sound, dance and culture of cu-bop would evolve into contemporary salsa, and to understand salsa we must return to Cuba and the origins of the rumba.

The rumba

The origins of the rumba are closely related to the origins of the samba. Both were born of an African tradition transplanted to the New World, and both claim antecedents in the Congolese and Bantu dances of the Kongo-Angolan complex in west central Africa (today this consists of Angola, the Democratic Republic of Congo and the Congo). Rumba – a Spanish word describing a collective festival event – originally referred to the celebratory gatherings of the slaves and free Africans of Cuba in the middle of the nineteenth century. As these gatherings evolved and, in the wake of abolition, filtered across the country, the dance styles of the gatherings came to acquire the same title. Rumba is today a generic term. It refers to the many folk dances that exist across Cuba and the West Indies, as well as the popular dance-hall versions that spread across the world. In Cuba there came to be as many forms of the rumba as there are provinces and com-

'... the rumba developed into a pantomime imitation of the sexual act. The man moves like a sexual predator ... while the woman counters with defensive and coquettish moves.'

Left: The sheet music for a rumba tune published in New York in 1936, entitled 'Pobre Pedro' ('Poor Pedro'), featuring some appropriate art work.

munities. In the rural parts of the island a solo version of the dance developed, while in Havana and other urban centres it became a vibrant couple dance. All the indigenous folk rumbas, however, share the same sensuality, vigorous hip movement and insistent rhythmic accompaniment. Like the tango, the rumba developed into a pantomime imitation of the sexual act. The man moves like a sexual predator, as it were, while the woman counters with defensive and coquettish moves. For this reason, in the rigid social structure that obtained in Cuba before the Second World War different forms of the rumba were danced by different levels of society, and the dance became increasingly less explicit as the dancers rose up the social scale. The middle classes danced a version known as the *son*, which was slower and less suggestive, while the upper classes danced the *danzón*, which was slower still and the hip movement was reduced to a minimum. It was the more restrained *son* that was introduced to the

Below: Xavier Cugat, here performing with his band and the singer Abbe Lane, was responsible for popularizing the rumba and other Latin American dances in the USA.

United States and Europe between the wars, and it is this style that became known internationally as the rumba.

In contemporary Cuba the rumba plays an important part in post-revolutionary identity. However, many of these native folk dances bear only the slightest resemblance to the internationally recognized 'Cuban rumba'.

As in the story of the samba, it was the United States that the rumba conquered first. It was officially introduced to the United States at the 1936 Chicago World's Fair, but it had been making its presence known long before that. As early as 1923 rumba musicians and dancers had been introduced by the bandleader Emil Coleman to New York City, and in 1925 a Latin club called El Chico opened its doors in Greenwich Village. In 1935 George Raft and Carole Lombard starred in the film *Rumba*, which showcased the style while working within the confines of the traditional love-through-dance plot. This narrative device, which allows actors to dance while holding on to the bare bones of a plot, has dominated the film dance genre since its inception. There is little difference in concept between *Rumba* and *Dirty Dancing*, although they were made 50 years apart.

One of the Cuban dance orchestras that led the rumba craze in the early 1930s was the Don Modesto Azpiazu Orchestra, which featured among its attractions a young Cuban dancer called Alicia Parla. The sensuous rumba demonstrations by the young Parla – she was not yet 20 – caused a sensation. As a well as becoming a conduit for the new craze, the young lady became a star of New York City society, numbering among her friends Ernest Hemingway and gossip columnist Walter Winchell, who referred to her as 'that lovely Havana torso flipper'. In Monte Carlo during a tour of Europe, she so entranced the Prince of

'There is little difference in concept between *Rumba* and *Dirty Dancing*, although they were made 50 years apart.'

Wales (the future Edward VIII) that he requested private lessons from her. His approval did much to secure the popularity of the style in Europe, although the rumba did not really catch on in Britain until after the Second World War. (In fact, the success of the rumba in Britain had more to do with the demonstrations of the style by the popular teachers Pierre and Lavelle, whose standardization of the dance led to the recognition of the 'Cuban rumba' in 1955.) Parla's reign as Queen of the Rumba was short lived, and by the time she was 20 she had retired to Cuba, where she stayed until the revolution, before moving to Miami. Her dancing career was never revived.

Xavier Cugat

The greatest popularizer of the rumba and, indeed, of the whole Latin sound, was Xavier Cugat (1900–90), a Spanish-born musician whose family had emigrated to Cuba when he was five years old. A classically trained musician, he realized at an early age that his interest was in popular music rather than in the classical sphere. Typically he would later say: 'I would rather play Chiquita Banana and have my swimming pool, than play Bach and starve.'

By the time tangomania hit New York in the mid-1910s Cugat was in New York performing with a tango band known as the

Above: Cugat, here again pictured with Abbe Lane, enjoyed popularity that lasted 40 years and spanned the time of the rumba to that of the twist.

Left: Dancers practising of the latest Latin American dance craze at the Copacabana, whose existence owes something to the influence of Xavier Cugat.

'... Cugat's band took to the stage in trademark bright red jackets, and he entranced his audience with a witty commentary on the show, while his dancers demonstrated the rumba and other Latin American dance styles ...'

Left: Latin American dances had a sexual energy that got under the skin of the more restrained North Americans, like these performers at the Tropicana in the 1930s.

Opposite: Husband-and-wife (for a time) Abbe Lane and Xavier Cugat, leading a spirited conga line from one of the many musicals they made for MGM in the 1940s.

Gigolos. The band dissolved in the wake of the tango's demise, but Cugat had realized the commercial appeal of Latin music in the United States, and he moved to Los Angeles where he reassembled his band and had some limited success in the emerging musical film business, most notably appearing in *In Gay Madrid* (1930). Xavier Cugat's real success coincided with the arrival of the rumba at the end of the 1920s. By 1930 Cugat and his Latin American Orchestra were performing at the Coconut Grove club in Los Angeles. His act proved so successful that before long he was invited to New York, where his orchestra became the resident band at the newly completed Waldorf Astoria Hotel. From this base, he spread the Latin American sound through the city, the country and the world.

Cugat's mixture of Latin dance sound, novelty tunes and extroverted showmanship – his band took to the stage in trademark bright red jackets, and he entranced his audience with a witty commentary on the show, while his dancers demonstrated the rumba and other Latin American dance styles – helped to keep the man and his orchestra in the public eye for the next 40 years. Although his initial success came on the back of the rumba, he was adept at recognizing the constant shifts in public taste, and his band provided the soundtracks for many of the Latin dance styles that followed in the rumba's wake, such as the conga, cha-cha-cha and mambo. Later, he even provided music for the twist (see pages 189–199), but it is the rumba with which he will be forever associated.

Cugat was a flamboyant character on and off stage, playing as fast and loose in his personal life as with his band. A husband to a fistful of wives and a keen collector of attractive female performers to his act – he offered the young Rita Hayworth (see page 169) one of her first breaks – the force of his personality led some to undervalue his musical achievements. However, he is probably the single biggest influence on the development of Latin music in America in the middle of the twentieth century, and without his work it is possible that bandleaders like Perez Prado would never have flourished.

Latin American rhythms

ican swing. However, this is to underestimate the ability of musical styles to cross international borders, and the origins of the mambo are more traditionally credited to the Cuban musician who felt the influence of North American jazz long before he set foot in the country, Perez Prado

Perez Prado (1916–89) may not be the undisputed father of the mambo – Arsenio Rodriguez and Orestes Lopez share some of the credit for its genesis – but he was undoubtedly the 'king' of the genre by the time of his death. Born in Cuba, he began his musical education in the classical tradition, not unlike Xavier Cugat. However, his training as a classical pianist did not prevent him from pursuing a career in popular music, and by 1947 he had acted as both a pianist and arranger to any number of bands in and around Havana. In 1947, however, he left Cuba and settled in Mexico, which at the time had a large expatriate Cuban population. One of the reasons given for his emigration was the increasing racial tension in Cuba immediately after the war – Prado was of African descent – although it is also suggested that his innovative combination of North American jazz with traditional Cuban music was not well received by the Cuban musical establishment. Whatever the reason, Cuba's loss was Mexico's gain, and over the next three years Prado developed the musical style that made his name. Alongside the singer and fellow Cuban Beny More, Prado released a number of mambo records that secured his reputation, and he began to make an impact in the United States, most notably with the 1949 recording 'Mambo No. 5'. By 1951 the American magazine *Newsweek* was reporting on the dance craze that was sweeping Mexico and South America, and Prado ventured north to pursue his career.

Perez Prado

Xavier Cugat showed how compatible the United States and Latin music had become, particularly in New York. Throughout the 1930s and 1940s a considerable Latin population had begun to live in the area that became known as Spanish Harlem, and many of these new residents were émigrés from Batista's Cuba. Here, Cuban musicians came into direct contact with other Latin expatriates, particularly from Puerto Rico, as well as with the already dominant African-American community, with its rich and influential musical legacy. Indeed, this is one theory for the evolution of the mambo, with its trademark mix of Cuban rhythms with Amer-

The mambo

The term mambo probably comes from the Nanigo dialect of Cuba, and although it has no specific meaning, the word may have made its way on to the dance floor through the Cuban phrase *abrecuto y guiri mambo* (open your eyes and listen), which was used in Cuban song contests. Certainly Orestes Lopez would shout out to his band members as they launched into a solo, *Mil veves mambo!* (A thousand times mambo).

If the sound itself was born from the fusion of Afro-Cuban rhythms and North American swing – Prado said that he used many of the natural rhythms of the Cuban countryside, such as work rhythms and birdcalls – the dance itself was a jazzier

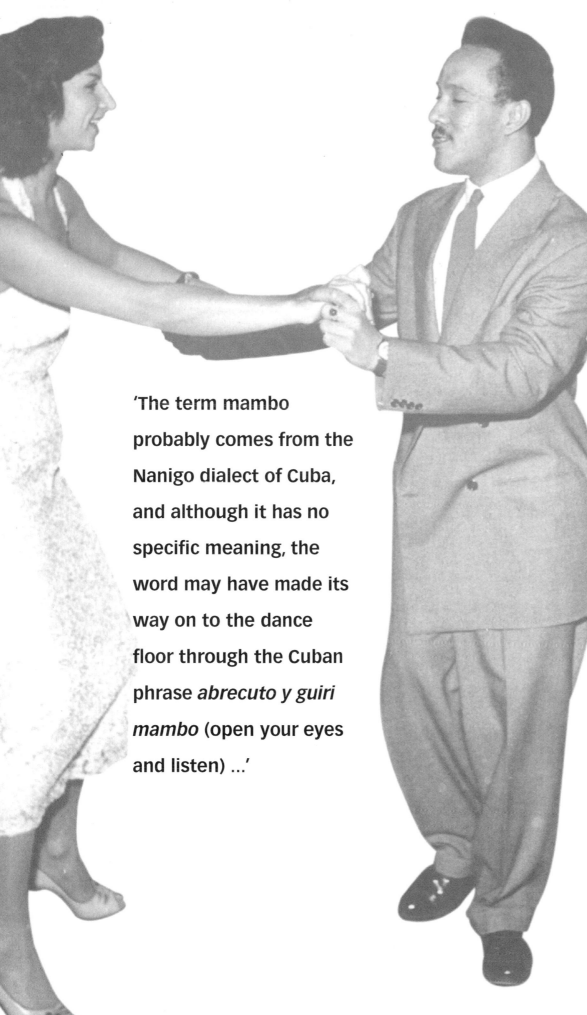

'The term mambo probably comes from the Nanigo dialect of Cuba, and although it has no specific meaning, the word may have made its way on to the dance floor through the Cuban phrase *abrecuto y guiri mambo* (open your eyes and listen) ...'

MAMBO HITS

'Abaniquito', Tito Puente Orchestra (1949). The first American mambo record. Helped to launch the craze on the US public and cemented Puente's career. Appeared on the album *Mamborama*.

'Cherry Pink and Apple Blossom White', Perez Prado (1955). Prado's biggest success. Went to the top of the US charts and stayed there for 10 weeks. Danced to by Jane Russell in the film *Underwater*.

'Mambo No 5', Perez Prado (1949). One of the first and biggest hits for the proclaimed 'King of Mambo'. Helped move Mambo records off Hispanic radio stations and into the mainstream. Reworked to great acclaim by Lou Bega in 1999.

'Papa Loves Mambo', Perry Como (1954). Recordings like this and 'Mambo Italiano' by Rosemary Clooney showed that even the most American of crooners were bitten by the Mambo bug.

'Rock an' Roll', Celia Cruz (1956). Recorded by the modern 'Queen of Salsa', reveals the close links between the two emerging styles of the 1950s.

Left: From the mambo, came the cha-cha-cha, here performed by Prado himself, which required less physical contact and so allowed greater individual freedom of movement.

version of the *son* and *danzón* styles that had spawned the rumba. The mambo's ragged rhythm and relatively simple steps made it an ideal dance for a North American public eager for some fun at the height of the Cold War. Prado's music led the way as America, particularly New York City, went mambo wild. By 1954 even such all-American acts as Perry Como ('Papa loves Mambo') and Rosemary Clooney ('Mambo Italiano') were celebrating the new dance craze in song.

Harlem may have been the incubator from which the mambo spread across New York, but the self-proclaimed 'Temple of Mambo' was the Palladium Ballroom on Broadway. The Park Plaza Ballroom in Harlem may have been more authentic, but the Palladium stood as testament to the mambo's cross-cultural appeal. Here, at the Wednesday night mambo dance contests, some of the best Latin dancers of the day came to demonstrate their skills. Dancers including Killer Joe Piro, Louie Maquina and the Mambo Aces showed how expressive and individualistic the new dance style could be. One dancer, 'Cuban' Pete, became

known as the 'Prince of the Palladium', and he is still in demand today as a teacher and performer of salsa. Superstars like Marlon Brando, Bob Hope and Lena Horne came to celebrate the dance and the music, often played by the best Latin orchestras of the day. Tito Puente, Tito Rodriguez and Jose Curbelo were among those who regularly appeared at the Palladium.

The mambo lost some of its lustre as it spread across the dance floors of the world, and consequently it brought in its wake a number of derivative dance styles. The best known is the alliterative cha-cha-cha, which is said to have acquired its name through the sound of Cuban slippers as they scratched along the dance floor. With its distinctive name – the number of 'chas' is variable – the cha-cha-cha became the biggest Latin craze to follow in the mambo's footsteps. With a faster rhythm than the mambo, the cha-cha-cha's mix of steps, shuffle and rolling hips left little room for physical contact, and it fed into the public demand for solo dancing that was evolving in the rock and roll scene (see pages 183–188).

Right: The sometimes stiff formality of ballroom dancing took on Latin dance styles like the mambo with varying degrees of success.

'With a faster rhythm than the mambo, the cha-cha-cha's mix of steps, shuffle and rolling hips left little room for physical contact, and it fed into the public demand for solo dancing that was evolving.'

Above: Like many Latin dances, the merengue has enjoyed repeated popularity over many years, most recently in versions that have adopted other influences like the Nicaraguan *punta* and Brazilian *lambada*.

The merengue

Also thrown into the Latin American pot was the merengue. The national dance of the Dominican Republic, the merengue's trademark 'limp' step is a thing of legend in its native country, where the dance had been known since the beginnings of the nineteenth century. It is said that a valiant general, returning to his village after a revolutionary war, could only drag his wounded right leg in the dances thrown for his return. Out of respect, the inhabitants of the village did the same, and the dance was born. Another story has it that the step evolved from the enslaved sugar-cane cutters as they worked the island chained from foot to foot. Whatever the truth, both stories show how closely linked the island and its dance have become. However, none of this was particularly relevant to the dance-starved Americans, who pounced on the merengue in the mid-1950s, eager to appropriate any Latin style that could satisfy their taste for 'exotic' dances.

Latin American rhythms

The salsa revival

Along with the bossa nova, the Latin dance trends receded from view as the British beat invasion swept the world before it in the mid-1960s. Rock music swept all before it, and by the end of the decade the Latin music business was in serious decline. Latin dance undoubtedly played a vital part in the development of disco, not least in the evolution of the hustle (see pages 206–208), but for the style itself what was really needed was a full-scale repackaging that could relaunch it on the international market. This is, in effect, what salsa is: the complete rebranding of Latin American dance music.

The rise of Latin dance music in the United States was inevitably linked to the growth of Hispanic communities within the nation's major cities. Cubans, Puerto Ricans and Dominicans were just some of the Hispanic immigrants moving into the Spanish sections of New York City alone, and this cultural mix clearly had an impact on the musical styles emanating from these communities. Indeed, to refer to Latin dance music of the 1960s as

'... In its bid to reposition itself in the market, salsa left behind its traditional 1970s style of driving rhythms and searing brass sections and adopted a softer, mellower style ...'

Right: From the 1970s, artists like Celia Cruz, here pictured in 1984, have helped the growth in popularity of the salsa sound, and the dancing that goes with it.

Cuban-derived would have been inaccurate. Working alongside the Cuban innovations of, for example, Perez Prado and Machito were Puerto Ricans, like Tito Rodriguez and Tito Puente, and it was a Dominican, Johnny Pacheco, a successful bandleader in his own right, who in 1964 recognized the need to promote new Latin dance acts in the light of the musical climate of the time. He began an independent record label, Fania Records, which in time both regenerated Latin dance and became a vital component in establishing Latin pride and identity. Under the umbrella title of 'salsa', Cuban-derived dance music had a catchy new name, free of the constraints of a historical connection to a single nation.

In the early days Pacheco's outfit was small – he distributed the records himself from the back of his car – but in 1967, with the help of an Italian-American lawyer, Jerry Masucci, the company became much more aggressive, and 'salsa' was created as a new marketing strategy, and Latin music sales soured.

Throughout the 1970s Fania Records promoted the work of many of the leading lights of the salsa movement. Stars such as Hector Lavoe, Ismael Miranda, Willie Colon, Celia Cruz and Ruben Blades recorded for Fania and helped to establish a vibrant salsa sound. Moreover, salsa had spread further afield than New York City and the countries from which it sprang; Venezuela and Colombia had also established vigorous salsa traditions, every bit as influential as the one that had sprung up in New York.

Above: Salsa is phenomenally successful today, and spans the divides between cultures and nations, and between the various individual Latin American dances themselves.

Above: A live album simply entitled 'Salsa!', from the Fania All Stars, the superstar group drawn from house musicians of the New York Fania label.

Right: One of today's salsa kings, Ricky Martin, an international star who has built his career on the wave of popularity of Latin American music.

By the end of the 1970s the first phase of salsa popularity was beginning to fade. The re-emergence of the merengue, and the appeal within, particularly, the New York Puerto Rican community of hip-hop, meant that salsa was in decline. In its bid to reposition itself in the market, salsa left behind its traditional 1970s style of driving rhythms and searing brass sections and adopted a softer, mellower style, known as salsa romantica. With its emphasis on love and romance, as opposed to community identity and political action, the new style was seen as a watering down of the genre by the purists, but salsa romantica did much to keep salsa alive, and the introduction of performers such as Eddie Santiago and Luis Enrique did much to lay the groundwork for the great salsa craze of the 1990s, which has made acts like Ricky Martin and Rickey Inglesia into international stars.

By the end of the twentieth century, salsa has brought Latin dance to a peak of popularity not seen anywhere else in the cen-

'Salsa dance today is an amalgamation of all the major Cuban-derived dance styles of the century. Rumba, mambo, cha-cha-cha and guaracha all feature within its moves ...'

tury, not even the 1950s. Major salsa venues, like the Copacabana in New York, the Salsa Palladium in Miami and Bar Tiempo in London, are symbols of the phenomenon that has spread Latin dance far away from its Hispanic roots and across the world. Today salsa is as vital a part of the dance scene in Holland, Sweden or Japan as it is in Spain or the United States. The enormous success of films like *Dirty Dancing* (1987), *La Luna* and *Dance with Me* confirms this breadth of appeal.

Salsa dance today is an amalgamation of all the major Cuban-derived dance styles of the century. Rumba, mambo, cha-cha-cha and guaracha all feature within its moves, and the clarity of its style and variability of its performance are, perhaps, the main appeals in a culture dominated by the self-expression of the clubland dance scene. In fact, it is the only area of social dancing, outside the arena of dance sport, where couple dancing remains. For this reason it is a popular way of bringing people together, and this may be one of the central reasons for its continuing appeal. However, the root of salsa's success may eventually lie in the ability of Latin music to constantly re-invent itself without compromising the timeless attraction of the Latin beat.

Above: Couple dancing still survives in South America, as evidenced by this scene in a dancehall on a Saturday night in northeastern Brazil.

Sight and sound: tap dancing

For the first 30 years of the century no dance style was more popular than tap. Those great originators and stylists who took on this amalgamation of Old World jigs and African tribal dances and turned it into a celebration of individual artistry and rhythm seemed to embody the dynamism of a burgeoning nation. Mass popularity can often cloud high artistry, however, and it is only comparatively recently, in the light of the tap renaissance, that the skill and story of those tap pioneers has come to be appreciated. Like jazz itself, tap dancing is a product of the New World's adaptation of Old World styles. At sometime in the distant past of American colonization, European step dances, such as the Irish jig and the Lancashire clog-dance, became mixed with the juba and ring dances that the slaves brought with them from Africa. No matter how long it took and whatever the process, by the middle of the nineteenth century the resulting hybrid form had found its way on to the stages of the minstrel tents that toured the nation.

Sight and sound: tap dancing

Over the years the Irish jig largely disappeared from mainstream view in the United States, although did it survive in Irish communities both there and in Britain and, of course, in Ireland itself, from where it eventually burst upon an unsuspecting world as the *Riverdance* phenomenon; see pages 117–119). Instead, the jig became an all-encompassing word, usually describing African-American dance steps. Both Jim Crow and Henry 'Juba' Lane were said to dance jigs. The clog-dance also survived on the minstrel stage, with many clog-dancers still performing at the beginning of the century. The most original style, however, and the one that marked out the birth of something new, was the soft shoe.

'The soft shoe placed its emphasis on grace and elegance, allowing for a more relaxed upper body posture.'

Above: Minstrel shows presented clog dancing of a kind that would have barely been recognized by the Lancashire folk amongst whom the form originated.

From clogs to soft shoes

The most obvious difference between clog-dancing and soft shoe was that the former was danced on wooden soles (clog) and the latter on leather (soft shoe), but there was more to it than that. The soft shoe placed its emphasis on grace and elegance, allowing for a more relaxed upper body posture, in turn allowing for light and cleaner taps. (One need only think of the body position of the modern *Riverdance* dancers to see how stiff and controlled the upper body can be in the old-style step dances.) In other words, soft-shoe allowed for the individual expression of personality.

The soft shoe evolved from one of the most popular dances of the minstrel era, the Virginia essence, which consisted of moving the body forwards across the stage by manipulating the toes and the feet and keeping the legs straight. According to at least one contemporary, it looked as if the performer was being pulled across the stage on 'ice skates' (in fact, the moonwalk made famous by Michael Jackson in the 1980s bears an uncanny resemblance to the Virginia essence).

The greatest exponent of the soft-shoe was George Primrose, who numbered among his admirers the likes of Harland Dixon, Eddie Rector and Bill Robinson (see pages 99–101). There were other practitioners of the soft shoe but none could match the precision, ease and panache of Primrose. With his lightness of touch, his insouciance and his ability to hold on to his steps (it was said that he rehearsed in private so that no one could steal his ideas), Primrose can be seen as the father of modern tap.

Great as his influence was, however, Primrose's dancing could still not really be called tap. For a start, his steps lacked that most vital of twentieth-century innovations – syncopation. Syncopation finally rose to the surface with the arrival of the buck and wing, the American stage's amalgamation of clog-dancing and soft shoe. The buck and wing was, in effect, the precursor of what would become modern rhythm tap, and even Ruby Keeler, who by the 1930s was the biggest tap sensation in the business, always referred to herself as a 'buck dancer'.

The buck and wing was really a mixture of all the old step dance styles mixed into one homogeneous whole. Dancers usu-

Above: One of the greatest film tap dancers, Ruby Keeler, in a still from *42nd Street* with Warner Baxter and, on the right, Ginger Rogers.

Above: A poster for *Born Happy*, **one of the many Broadway shows that starred Bill Robinson.**

was already traversing the country as a piccaninny (see pages 38–39) – just as Eddie Rector and Bill Robinson did – learning his trade in a vaudeville act known as Cosie Smith and Her Six Piccaninnies. The career-span of a pick was short, and by the time he was 12 years old Covan was already looking for ways to survive and develop a career on his own. His route to success lay within the circuit of buck and wing dance contests that were so popular at the time.

Tap dancing, like so much in American vernacular dance, evolved from competition. 'Cuttin'' contests on street corners, in which various dancers would try to outdo the steps already performed, were a breeding ground for dancers, and it was not long before organized competition came to the stage, too. In 1928 a buck contest held exclusively for Broadway performers produced a winning rostrum of amazing talent: Fred Astaire, Jack Donahue and Bill Robinson. Dance contests were a serious matter.

Willie Covan won the best known buck contest of them all: the contest incorporated in the minstrel show, *Old Kentucky*. This was his springboard to success, and as a recognized performer he devised new and exciting variations on the buck and wing, such as the rhythm waltz clog step. One of many admirers of George Primrose, Covan experimented with the concept of elegant soft shoe dancing (one of his later acts was subtitled, 'every move a picture'), and at the same time he anticipated the rise of the acrobatic tap, most famously with his invention of the 'around the world step without any hands'.

Willie Covan's skill and innovation received the recognition they deserved through his series of dance acts, which became world famous. In 1917 he formed the Four Covans, a group that within a few years was touring the globe, and his partnership with Leonard Ruffin was an integral part of the phenomenal success of *Shuffle Along* (see page 55). In an era of race segregation, few acts graduated from the black TOBA vaudeville circuit to the white halls, and only three 'black' acts ever headlined at the Palace Theater in New York. One was Bert Williams; one was Bill Robinson himself; and the other was Covan and Ruffin – proof of an enduring talent.

Later in his life, at the insistence of Eleanor Powell (see pages 104–107), Willie Covan became the head dancing instructor at MGM Studios, during the heyday of movie musicals. Here, he passed on his skill, grace and innovation to some of Hollywood's greatest musical stars, including Mickey Rooney and Ann Miller (see pages 107–109).

ally wore large, clog-like shoes with wooden soles, and it was performed almost entirely on the balls of the feet. A wing is as it sounds: one foot swishes outward and the ankle rolls, allowing for a varying number of taps. Again Ruby Keeler offers a good example of this. Think of the chorus routines in *42nd Street*: hundreds of girls banging out wings at a frantic pace, dancing mostly in one place, arms swirling like windmills.

The man who really took on the buck and wing and pushed back the barriers of its limited form was Willie Covan. Born in 1897, Covan had a long career that is a virtual map laid across the landscape of early tap history. By the time he was six years old he

Bojangles: the great improviser

With the evolution of the soft shoe, wings and that ubiquitous tool of the tap dancer's art, the time step, all the pieces were in place ready for the tap scene to explode. Between 1900 and 1930 tap dancing was the world's most popular form of stage dancing, and the language, technique and possibilities of the form changed and evolved at a truly blistering rate. Every act was different, seeking that certain something that would mark it out for fame, but perhaps all the skill, charm and bluster of the era really came together in the personality of one man – Bill 'Bojangles' Robinson (1878–1949).

By the end of his career, Robinson's fame had reached heights previously unimaginable for a black performer. More than just a dancer, Bojangles became an icon for his age, and 1.5 million people thronged the streets of Harlem and Brooklyn when he died in 1949. It remains to this day the largest funeral ever held in New York City. Writing after Robinson's death, Ed Sullivan, the television variety host, said: 'Despite the softness of his taps, no performer and very few Americans ever touched the heart of this city, this nation, with greater impact than "Bojangles".' Yet Robinson was well into middle age before he entered into the national consciousness – but he had perseverance to go along with his other talents.

Below: Bill 'Bojangles' Robinson performing in 1943 in Twentieth Century Fox's *Stormy Weather*, a critically acclaimed film featuring all black talent.

'... all the skill, charm and bluster of the era came together in the personality of one man – Bill 'Bojangles' Robinson (1878–1949) ...'

Above: 'Never appear with children or animals', but Bill Robinson got away with it – here with Shirley Temple in *The Little Colonel*.

He was born in Richmond, Virginia, in the heart of the segregated south. (Years later he attempted to return to Richmond, bringing his celebrated *Bill Robinson Revue* to his home town, but such was the strength of feeling within the cast that all the other performers threatened to resign rather than go with him.) His parents died when he was still an infant, and young 'Bo' was brought up by his grandmother, Bedila Robinson. She did not want him to pursue a career on the stage – she thought it lacked dignity – but the boy was determined, and he ran away to follow his dream. Like so many of his contemporaries, his first professional experience was as a pick, in his case supporting Mayme Remington. He, too, won the buck-dancing contest in *Old Kentucky* and appeared for a while in the minstrel show *The South Before the War*.

He had begun to rise to prominence when he joined forces with George Cooper, and the two men toured at home and abroad for a while, with Cooper teaching his younger partner much about the business of show-business, and Cooper and his first wife, Fannie Clay, had a considerable influence on Bojangles's personal development.

It was as a solo performer, however, that he gradually secured his reputation, becoming one of the few black performers to appear on the white vaudeville circuit. It was not until 1928, when he was hired for the Broadway show *Blackbirds*, that the New York critics finally took notice of his unique ability. It was in *Blackbirds* that he first introduced to New York his trademark 'stair dance', a 15-minute routine consisting of light and airy taps

BILL 'BOJANGLES' ROBINSON FACTFILE

Born: 25 May 1878

Died: 25 Nov 1949

Real name: Luther Robinson

Nickname: Bojangles; The Mayor of Harlem.

Theatre: Worked widely in vaudeville before eventually becoming a Broadway star in his 40s. His best known appearances included *Blackbirds of 1928*, *Brown Buddies* (1930), *Blackbirds of 1933*, and the *Hot Mikado* (1939).

Films: Appeared in 14 films from 1930. Best known for his partnership with Shirley Temple, with whom he appeared four times: *The Little Colonel* (1935), *Littlest Rebel* (1935), *Rebecca of Sunnybrook Farm* (1938) and *Just Around the Corner* (1938).

Key to success: Mixture of charm, skill and gift for publicity made him a huge dance star. Best known for his 'Stair Dance', his precision and lightness of touch made his tap legendary. He was largely responsible for bringing tap up on to the toes.

Favourite phrase: 'Everything is copasetic'.

Fact: Bill Robinson held the world record for running the 100 yards (91.4m) backwards.

rapped out with breathtaking precision over a flight of stairs. Along with his theme song, 'Doin' the New Low Down', the stair dance wowed New York and set the seal on his reputation. He never looked back.

A number of key factors came together in the Robinson phenomenon. He was not innovative, but he honed and perfected established steps to a previously unimaginable degree, and he brought to the execution of his tap a precision and lightness that had not previously been seen. It was not only his steps, but his entire body that seemed more airbound. Added to all this was the sheer force of his personality. A mixture of song, anecdote, dance and cheek, his whole act was 'copasetic' (his own word, meaning 'better than okay'), and it was backed by an instinct for self-promotion that served him well throughout his career. After his death, in fact, a 'copasetic' club was formed in which leading tap dancers would regularly get together to dance in honour of his memory.

Robinson's reputation rests primarily on the quality of his live performance. A workaholic, he danced long after many of his contemporaries had been forced to stop, and his name will forever be associated with shows like *Blackbirds of 1928*, *Brown Buddies* (1930) and *The Hot Mikado* (1939). His film work was far more limited, and he was often reduced to presenting racial stereotypes, most notably in his partnership with Shirley Temple (see pages 127–128), but accusations by the black community that he was an 'Uncle Tom' stung him deeply, and he denied them vociferously.

For many years Robinson was much admired within the world of tap dance without being considered a unique talent. However, like many other African-American figures of his time, his legend has been reassessed. In 1995 Savion Glover's *Bring in Da Noise, Bring in Da Funk* (see page 115) included a controversial portrayal of Robinson. That same year, when the US Congress was planning to establish a National Tap Dance Day with which to cement the tap renaissance, it chose 25 May, Robinson's birthday.

The Hoofer's Club

The tap dancing community was a tight-knit world that fed on gossip and speculation. Tap came directly off the street, and new steps and innovations were honed from what one could see and steal from other practitioners. The hub of this continual process of exchange and evolution was a room in Harlem, New York City.

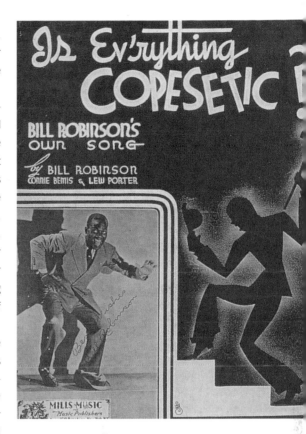

Above: Sheet music for Bill Robinson's featured song 'Is Everything Copesetic?', including a graphic reference to his famous stairs routine.

'Tap came directly off the street, and new steps and innovations were honed from what one could see and steal from other practitioners.'

Ostensibly, the room was just a backroom of the Comedy Club, a gambling joint adjacent to the Lafayette Theater on 131st Street, but throughout the tap dancing world it was known by another name – the Hoofer's Club.

The club was run by Lonnie Hicks, who liked and admired dancers enough to donate his backroom to their development. He made his money from gambling, and so the backroom, which was furnished with little more than a battered piano and some benches, was a free space. Open 24 hours a day, it also provided some much needed warmth and shelter throughout the dark days of the Depression. Within the confines of the Hoofer's Club, steps could be created, analysed and acquired; stories could be told and information exchanged. Here, Bojangles was not king, although he was much admired, and other names, many of whom would never break into the mainstream, were held up as the great innovators and stylists.

Chief among these was King 'Rastus' Brown. Almost unknown within the regular vaudeville circuit, where his lack of comic technique was a hindrance to a black performer, he was nevertheless considered by those who saw him as the master of tap. As with all legends, the line between truth and elaboration is murky, but one thing is uncontested: Brown brought to tap many of the innovations credited to Bill Robinson, but he lacked Robinson's force of personality with which to promote them. (He always claimed that he created Robinson's stair dance, although the origins of the routine probably predate both of them.) Brown's reputation within the confines of the tap world was huge, and he regularly appeared at the Hoofer's Club, where he would 'lay down some iron' and pass on to the younger generation some of his effects. Willie Covan, Eubie Blake, Prince Spencer and John Barton were just a few of the dancers who acknowledged the genius and influence of King 'Rastus' Brown. But then, during the 30 years of its heyday, nearly all the leading figures in the tap world passed through the doors of the Hoofer's Club. Some, like Eddie Rector and Toots Davis, were already acknowledged masters. Others, like John Bubbles, used it as a finishing school and sprang from its doors into stardom.

Eddie Rector and Toots Davis had made their names in the Harlem show, *Darktown Follies* (see pages 53–55). Rector did much to develop the smooth and easy style of tap that would become known as a 'class' act, while Davis was a more acrobatic dancer, representing the other great development in tap style, acrobatic or flash dancing. Together they unveiled in *Darktown*

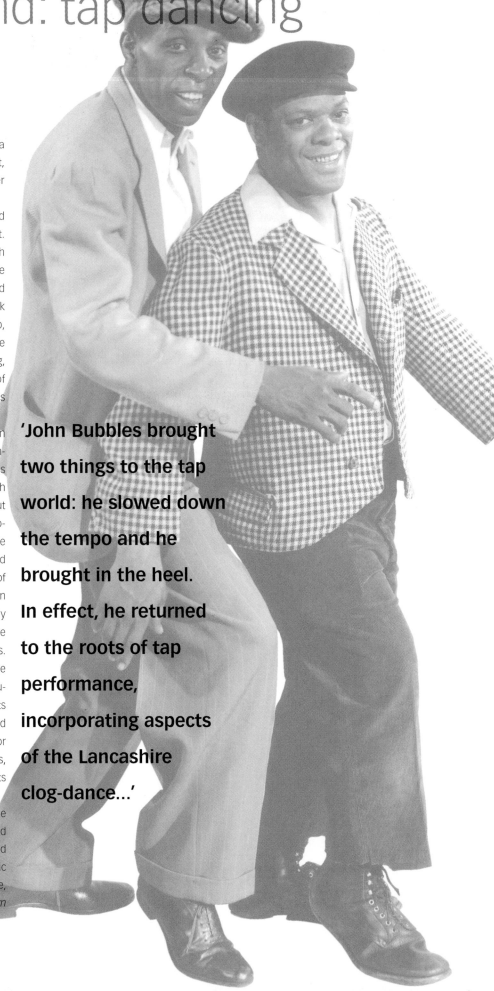

'John Bubbles brought two things to the tap world: he slowed down the tempo and he brought in the heel. In effect, he returned to the roots of tap performance, incorporating aspects of the Lancashire clog-dance...'

Follies two of the best known and instantly recognizable steps in the repertoire – over the top and through the trenches. These early flash steps anticipated later flash acts, such as the Nicholas Brothers and the Berry Brothers, but the young John 'Bubbles' Sublett, who watched and learned from Davis and Rector in the Hoofer's Club, was about to take the art in a different direction.

Heel and toe

John William 'Bubbles' Sublett (1902–86) was born in Louisville, Kentucky, and by the time he was 10 years old he was already ensconced alongside Ford Lee 'Buck' Washington (1903–55), who was his partner for most of his career. Initially the Buck and Bubbles act lacked any dance and consisted only of Bubbles singing along to Buck's accompaniment. However, Bubbles had an urge to dance, and he set about learning. His first attempts met with derision, but he later won the admiration of his peers.

John Bubbles brought two things to the tap world: he slowed down the tempo and he brought in the heel. In effect, he returned to the roots of tap performance, incorporating aspects of the Lancashire clog-dance. He had been greatly influenced by the eccentric dancing of Harland Dixon, whom he had seen performing as a child, and he realized that he could get extra beats by incorporating the heel into his routines. This, along with the slowing of the tempo, allowed him more time to fill the music with extra steps and more complex rhythms. The combination came to be known as rhythm tap, and with it tap dancing came of age.

Buck and Bubbles became a fixture in the New York variety circuit. In their prime, in the 1930s, they were starring in the *Ziegfeld Follies* and at the same time appearing uptown in the Lafayette Theater. Their clowning and artistry crossed the cultural divides of the era. Perhaps most famously, Bubbles was snatched from vaudeville to create the part Sportin' Life in Gershwin's ground-breaking opera, *Porgy and Bess* (1935).

Above: Buck and Bubbles were amongst the greatest of the 1930s vaudeville acts, and starred both in the *Ziegfeld Follies* and at the Lafayette Theatre.

'For white tap dancers, such as Ruby Keeler, George Murphy and Buddy and Vilma Ebsen, there was one opportunity that remained closed to their black counterparts – Hollywood.'

Tap goes to the movies

By the mid-1920s, the 'iron' laid down by the tap pioneers was beginning to bear fruit throughout the entertainment industry. No show was complete without at least one tap routine or one tap artist – preferably both. For white tap dancers, such as Ruby Keeler, George Murphy and Buddy and Vilma Ebsen, there was one opportunity that remained closed to their black counterparts – Hollywood.

A revealing example of the harsh realities of the movie business at this time can be found in the early career of Eleanor Powell (1910–82), one of the greatest female tap dancers of her generation. Powell's Hollywood career was nearly stopped in its tracks by Louis B. Mayer himself. On the look-out for a leading lady, Mayer was very taken with Powell's first screen performance in *George White's 1935 Scandals*, but announced that he

Above: *Broadway Melody of 1938* **was one of MGM's responses to Warners' Gold Diggers series, and all starred the singing and dancing Eleanor Powell.**

Far left: A winsome Eleanor Powell in a publicity photograph from the early 1940s, when her film career was at its height.

could not use her because she was 'coloured'. Somebody in the cutting-room corrected him (she later admitted that she had been heavy on the make-up), and one of the great Hollywood dance careers was saved. Nevertheless, it is a revealing indictment of the prejudices of the time.

A shy child, Eleanor Powell had found an emotional outlet for herself in dancing, which she was doing professionally by the time she was 12 years old. She only began to tap after her Broadway debut in 1928, however. Realizing the need for tap in a dancer's repertoire, she enrolled at Jack Donahue's dancing school, but ironically, she initially found the style difficult. Fortunately, Donahue recognized something in the girl and persisted.

Powell always insisted that she danced like a man – close to the ground – and this she attributed to Donahue's teaching. 'The first thing he did,' she said, 'was sit on the floor in front of me and

hold my ankles, explaining that tapping is done with the feet and not with the whole body. At the next lesson he turned up with some kind of army belt and two sandbags. He hung the bags on either side of the belt and I was riveted to the floor.' The methods may have been eccentric but the results were sensational. Eleanor Powell became a Broadway and then a Hollywood star.

Powell found herself at MGM just when the studio was beginning to establish its musical credentials. Her films included *The Great Ziegfeld* (1936), *Rosalie* (1937) and *Ship Ahoy* (1942), and in *Honolulu* (1938) she blacked-up and danced a tribute to Bill Robinson. (Fred Astaire paid his own tribute to Bojangles in the 1936 movie, *Swing Time*). Heavily influenced by the success of the Berkeley style, these musicals were normally built around Powell's dancing skill and featured at least one lavish number that overshadowed anything offered by the competing studios. In

Born to Dance (1936), for instance, Powell danced to Cole Porter's 'Swinging the Jinx Away' on the decks of a huge battleship, with sequinned cannons and a whole army of singing sailors and chorus girls behind her. The need for dazzling effects meant that Powell, always her own choreographer, made fewer films than her contemporaries during her seven-year contract with MGM. She did, however, feature in a series of backstage musicals that all shared the title of *Broadway Melody*, and it was in the *Broadway Melody of 1940* that MGM finally gave her a partner whose skill and grace could match her own – Fred Astaire.

The impact of Fred Astaire in the century's dance history is second to none. More than a mere tap dancer, Astaire was a magpie, eager to grab any style, any effect, that could be incorporated into a routine and that could offer the public something new. The root of Astaire's genius was that he saw no barriers between different dance forms: tap, ballet, ballroom, all were grist to his mill, and for this reason he was labelled in some quarters as an eccentric dancer. Astaire recognized that every dance routine tells a story.

In 1940 Astaire had just broken free of his iconic partnership with Ginger Rogers and was looking to branch out on his own. His pairing with Eleanor Powell was not, perhaps, what he had in mind for himself, for he recognized that she was an artist of some standing herself and could not be moulded to his will. Both were

'The root of Astaire's genius was that he saw no barriers between different dance forms: tap, ballet, ballroom, all were grist to his mill, and for this reason he was labelled in some quarters as an eccentric dancer.'

Above: Fred Astaire was undoubtedly the most accomplished dancer of his generation, and drew on a variety of dance forms to complement his creative abilities.

Left: Powell here partners Fred Astaire for a routine performed to Cole Porter's 'Begin the Beguine' in *Broadway Melody of 1940*.

Right: The flamboyant Ann Miller was destined to play supporting roles, but her tap dancing routines could often steal the show.

accustomed to being the dominant creative force, and their rehearsals were formal and subdued. The result of their work may have lacked the spark that made Astaire and Rogers such a powerful combination, but Powell and Astaire's dancing to Cole Porter's 'Begin the Beguine' in *Broadway Melody of 1940* is one of cinema's most memorable moments.

Marriage and the arrival of a family brought Powell's career to an early close (although she did briefly reappear as a cabaret star in the mid-1960s). Her natural successor was Ann Miller (b.1919), who shared the same agent and for some time laboured in her shadow. Miller was an entirely different proposition from Eleanor Powell. Her frank hoofing was the very antithesis of Powell's grace and romance, and for this reason she never really became a leading lady. Her down-to-earth personality always led to the less romantic, supporting roles, allowing her to lay down some taps while leaving the romance to her co-stars. Fred Astaire and Ginger Rogers danced as an expression of their love, but Ann

Miller danced as if she had to persuade her beau that she was worth it. The result was fast, dazzling and electric.

In an interesting reversal of the usual Hollywood career, Ann Miller went to Los Angeles when she was very young, and, bar one appearance in New York in 1939, she appeared on Broadway only after her Hollywood career was over. Born in Houston, Texas, she was originally named Lucy Ann Collier, but her parents decided to call her Ann Miller as they became aware of her ability. When she was 11 years old she was already working the nightclubs of California, and she made her celluloid debut in *New Faces of 1937* for RKO when she was 14 years old.

Even at this age, the machine-gun tapping style that would become her trademark was already in place, but it took a trip to Broadway in 1939 before RKO became fully aware of the talent they had in their ranks. In that year Miller appeared in *George White's Scandals* on Broadway, and her success led to her return to RKO with a secure reputation and a considerably better con-

ANN MILLER FACTFILE

Born: 12 April 1923

Real Name: Lucy Ann Collier

Early career: Met Bill Robinson when she was 10. Robinson encouraged her, and she was dancing professionally in Los Angeles at the age of 11.

First film: *New Faces of 1937* for RKO.

Film hits: *Stage Door* (1937), *Easter Parade* (1948), *On the Town* (1949), *Small Town Girl* (1953) and *Kiss Me Kate* (1953).

Stage musicals: Ironically, Ann Miller secured her reputation as a top class dancer in the wake of her Broadway debut in George White's *Scandals of 1939*. Other shows included *Sugar Babies*, in which she was still appearing, aged 66, in 1989.

Secret of success: With a vibrant personality and a sassy charm, Ann Miller possessed a fast and vigorous tap-dancing style. Her trademark was 'machine gun' taps.

Fact: Once officially recognized as the fastest tap dancer in the world (recorded at 500 taps per minute).

Left: Miller, here dressed for a Latin American routine, achieved success on Broadway before the film industry recognized her talents as a dancer.

'Miller was an entirely different proposition from Eleanor Powell. Her frank hoofing was the very antithesis of Powell's grace and romance ...'

tract. Before she went to New York many of her parts had been in non-musicals, including some classics of their kind – particularly *Stage Door* (1937) and *Room Service* (1938) with the Marx Brothers – but she returned from Broadway as a dancing star.

During her film career Ann Miller worked for most of the major Hollywood studios, but her work for MGM, the most famous of all musical film producers, was her best known. It was for MGM that she made *On the Town* (1949), in which her 'Prehistoric Man' rou-

tine is a highlight. In *Kiss Me Kate* (1953) she danced alongside Bobby Van, Tommy Rall and the young Bob Fosse (see pages 176–179) and created at least two thrilling numbers – 'Too Darn Hot' and 'From this Moment On' – alongside Hermes Pan. Perhaps her greatest routine is the 'I've Gotta Hear That Beat' number from MGM's *Small Town Girl* (1953). In this number many aspects of twentieth-century dance history came together: it was directed by Busby Berkeley (see pages 123–126), danced by Ann Miller and choreographed by Willie Covan. Together they fashioned one of the most dynamic and visually stunning tap routines ever put on film.

Alongside the great screen stars such as Astaire, Miller, Powell and Kelly, Hollywood also drafted in the great cabaret and theatre acts of the tap circuit. Although prejudice meant that few of these acts could ever hope to play a leading part in a musical, their talent meant that room could usually be found for cameos. Thus, the likes of the Four Step Brothers and the Berry Brothers could supplement their income by appearing in films – the Four Step Brothers, for example, were in *Greenwich Village* (1944) and the Berry Brothers were in *You're My Everything* (1949) -– while the Nicholas Brothers, whose skilful mix of flash, ballet and

Below: The semi-acrobatic movements of the Nicholas Brothers, here in *Sun Valley Serenade* in 1941, were a new approach to the conventional tap routine.

THE NICHOLAS BROTHERS FACTFILE

**Harold Nicholas
Born:** 27 March 1921

**Fayard Nicholas
Born:** 20 October 1914

Claim to fame: One of the most innovative and popular tap-dancing acts of the twentieth century. Their ability to mix jazz, ballet and acrobatics into their choreography allowed them to take 'flash' dancing to new heights.

Origins: Sons of professional musicians, they began dancing as the Nicholas Kids in 1930.

Stage appearances: As well as regular appearances at the Cotton Club throughout the 1930s, their stage work included *Blackbirds of 1936*, *Ziegfeld Follies*, and *Babes In Arms* (1937).

First film: *Pie, Pie Blackbird* (1932) with Eubie Blake.

Hollywood: Discovered by Sam Goldwyn at the Cotton Club. Over 50 film appearances, including *Kid Millions* (1934), *Sun Valley Serenade* (1941), *Stormy Weather* (1941) and *The Pirate* (1948).

Awards: Kennedy Center Honor for contribution to American culture; American Black Lifetime Achievement Award.

Fact: The Nicholas Brothers were the first tap act to perfect the mid-air splits.

rhythmic tap made them the best known brother team of the era, also made numerous film appearances. The sensational *Stormy Weather* (1943) is, perhaps, the best record of their vivacious talent.

The Nicholas Brothers and the Berry Brothers are both examples of what became loosely known as 'flash' acts. Athletic and acrobatic, these acts relied as much on physical effects as on tap skill. Their rivals on the tap scene were the 'class' acts, which emphasized elegance and grace, ease and style, instead of splits and leaps. The greatest class act of them all was the precision dance team of Honi Coles and Cholly Atkins. Their trademark number was that perennial favourite, the soft shoe, performed at a pace so slow as to be unimaginable to Primrose and his contemporaries. However, by the mid-1950s Coles and Atkins were the last of a dying breed. Tap, for so long the staple of the musical diet, was going out of fashion.

There were a number of reasons this waning of popularity. For a start, jazz music, which had been an inspiration for the explosion of tap dance in the 1920s, had moved into a new sphere. Only the extremely talented – or the extremely persistent – could find a way to tap to bebop. Second, jazz itself, for so long the cen-

'By the beginning of the 1960s many of the great tap artists were either getting old or seeking alternative employment.'

(1921), had always mixed music with tap, and coming as it did in the wake of another Broadway celebration of a jazz great - Fats Waller in *Ain't Misbehavin'* - *Eubie* offered a nostalgic trip back into the heady days of the jazz age. Realizing that Blake and Noble's shows had always featured an invigorating mix of music and tap, the producers of *Eubie* recognized that they, too, had to place tap at the heart of their show. This they did, thanks to the choreography of Henry LeTang and Billy Wilson and the virtuosity of LeTang's protégé and the show's star, Gregory Hines.

Gregory Hines's career lies at the very centre of the tap revival. Born in 1946, he was only in his early thirties when he appeared in *Eubie*, yet he is one of the very few dancers whose career spans both the glory days of the 1950s and the brave new world of the tap revival. Hines started dancing before he was three, learning alongside his elder brother, Maurice, under the supervision of Henry LeTang. By the time he was just five years old, he and Maurice had turned professional. Billed as the Hines Kids, they followed in a long tradition of child tap teams, and they became fixtures on the then very lucrative variety and theatre

Left: The Nicholas Brothers made cameo appearances in a number of films, including *Down Argentine Way* (1940), which also starred Betty Grable and Carmen Miranda.

Below: Gregory Hines, whose solo career has seen him bring dance back into films, including *Tap* in 1988.

trepiece of popular culture, was being usurped by those young upstarts, rock and roll and rhythm and blues, neither of which was conducive to the tap dancer's art. Finally, the rise of classical dance in stage and screen choreography had overtaken the vernacular tradition of tap entertainment. Leading Broadway choreographers, such as Agnes de Mille (see pages 157–158) and George Balanchine (see page154–156), did not choreograph tap routines. (Coles and Atkins later revealed that when they worked for Agnes de Mille in the Broadway production of *Gentlemen Prefer Blondes*, de Mille left them to their own devices and was wrongly credited with their choreography, a story de Mille was later brave enough to verify.) By the beginning of the 1960s many of the great tap artists were either getting old or seeking alternative employment. However, although many would lie low for more a decade, within a generation tap was being reborn.

The tap renaissance

In 1978 a new musical opened in New York that communicated to a new generation the tap heritage of the past. *Eubie* celebrated the life and work of Eubie Blake (1883–1983), who, together with Noble Sissle, had been a leading light in the Harlem renaissance of the 1920s (see page 55). Blake's work, not least in *Shuffle Along*

circuit. They were later joined by their father, who played the drums, and they became known as Hines, Hines and Dad. However, in a move symptomatic of the climate throughout the entertainment industry, Hines turned his back on tap dancing and ploughed his talents into new forms of music (he formed the jazz/rock band Severance).

These early years, however, brought Hines into direct contact with some of the tap greats of the earlier golden age. During their travels, the Hines Kids came into contact with the likes of the Nicholas Brothers, Honi Coles, Bunny Briggs, Teddy Hale, Jimmy Slide and Baby Lawrence. Many of these were stars of the swing band circuit, and they told the Hines boys tales of Bojangles, John Bubbles and other early tap legends. By the time Gregory Hines returned to New York and to dancing, he was well aware of the tradition of tap.

After *Eubie*, Gregory Hines became a fixture on Broadway. By 1981 he was appearing in *Sophisticated Ladies*, a musical tribute to Duke Ellington, for which he achieved his third Tony nomination in nearly as many years (the others were for *Eubie* and *Comin' Uptown*.) Recognized as a singer and straight actor, as well as a consummate dancer, Hines made the inevitable move into movies, often appearing in straight dramatic roles. However, some of his films have allowed him to utilize all his talents, and consequently throughout the 1980s and 1990s he returned the tap routine to the popular cinema on several occasions. In 1984 he starred in Francis Ford Coppola's *The Cotton Club*, a dramatic reworking of the story of the Harlem cabaret club in which many of Hines's mentors had begun their careers. The following year he was dancing alongside the Soviet ballet star, Mikhail Baryshnikov in *White Nights*. Then, in 1988, everything came together when Hines starred in *Tap*. Filmed on location in New York and Los Angeles, *Tap* featured full tap production numbers, breaking new ground in its imaginative use of tap dancing alongside contemporary rock and funk musical styles. The story of a second generation tap dancer and a paroled jewel thief, *Tap* allowed Hines to act and dance alongside Sammy Davis Jr and the young Savion Glover (see pages 116–117), not to mention other tap legends, such as Harold Nicholas and Bunny Briggs.

Tap is an extremely good example of what the tap revival is all about – a new interpretation of the tap dancer's art, inspired by a profound respect for the artists of the past. In this, Gregory Hines has been a major ambassador for his art, continuing to promote tap dancing alongside his singing and acting commitments. In

'After *Eubie*, Gregory Hines became a fixture on Broadway. By 1981 he was appearing in *Sophisticated Ladies*, a musical tribute to Duke Ellington, for which he achieved his third Tony nomination ...'

Above: Gregory Hines's solo career has been extremely varied, but he is primarily known for inspiring the tap revival and linking it to contemporary pop styles.

Left: Maurice Hines (left) joins brother Gregory in the finale of *Sophisticated Ladies*, at the Lunt Fontanne Theatre in 1982.

'Searching for new techniques in the world of modern jazz gave Bufalino renewed determination to give tap the artistic respect she believed it deserved.'

1989 he won an Emmy for his television film *Tap Dance in America*. However, as some of Hines' documentary work has shown, tap today is viewed differently from the way it was in the 1940s and 1950s. Today tap is seen not only as invigorating and exciting entertainment, but also an art form in its own right, and a major figure in this journey from the stage to the concert hall has been Brenda Bufalino.

Bufalino is another dancer whose career traverses the dark days of tap's decline. Born in 1937, Bufalino began her career working for a traditional white tap troupe known as the Strickland Sisters. By the time she was 15 years old she had encountered the jazz sounds of Charlie Parker and Dizzy Gillespie and knew that she wanted to incorporate these new rhythms into her dancing. In the mid-1950s she joined forces with the influential tap teacher Stanley Brown and became one of the few tap dancers – others were 'Baby' Lawrence, Bunny Briggs and Jimmy Slyde – to be able to survive in the complex world of bebop. Searching for new techniques in the world of modern jazz gave Bufalino renewed determination to give tap the artistic respect she believed it deserved. (The idea of tap dance in a concert environment was not totally new. Paul Draper had pursued the idea of classical tap in the 1940s and 1950s, before his career was cut short by Senator Joseph McCarthy's investigations into 'un-American activities').

By the early 1970s Bufalino was playing an increasingly important part in the revival and celebration of tap. In 1973 she was instrumental in bringing together the surviving members of the 'copasetic club' to teach and perform. These included Honi Coles of the Coles and Atkins class act, and by 1978 – the same year that Gregory Hines was thrilling Broadway in *Eubie* – Bufalino and Coles were presenting whole evenings of tap dancing in some of New York's concert halls. In addition, she helped put together a number of influential documentaries on the life and work of many of the tap dancing greats, not least the award-winning *Great Feats of Feet*. Gradually, the likes of Coles, Jimmy Slyde and Chuck Green returned to teaching – as well as giving the odd personal appearance – and the skills of the past began to trickle down to a new generation.

Above, left: The complex rhythmic structure of modern jazz was fertile territory for Brenda Bufalino's innovative developments in tap.

Bufalino's concert appearances led her on a journey towards the establishment of the American Tap Dance Orchestra (ATDO), which she began in 1986 alongside Tony Waag and Honi Coles. The American Tap Dance Orchestra – which, in the same way as a regular orchestra, is made up of an ensemble of dancers, all of them offering different sounds and rhythms that come together in one harmonious whole – also allowed Bufalino to pursue her interest in choreography. In a dance form that is so dominated by the solo performer, the concept of group choreography is relatively new, and the likes of Bufalino's ATDO, the Jazz Tap Ensemble (directed by Lynn Dally), the Chicago Human Rhythm Project (Lane Alexander) and the National Tap Ensemble have pursued this development with success and vigour.

What was needed to complete tap's revival and to re-establish it as an ever-present part of contemporary culture, however, was an undisputed master from the new generation. Savion Glover seems to fit the bill. He not only matches the masters of the past but may even surpass them. At the end of the century, even Gregory Hines agrees that Savion Glover is 'possibly the best tap dancer that ever lived'.

Above: The cast of *Bring In Da Noise, Bring in Da Funk* led by 21-year-old Savion Glover, one of the new generation of tap dancers that thrilled modern Broadway audiences.

'*Bring in Da Noise, Bring in Da Funk* ... took the history of African American musical styles, wove it into a tapestry of dramatic and satirical routines and created a tribute to both black culture and the art of tap.'

Above: Glover pictured on the last night of *Bring in Da Noise, Bring in Da Funk*, a musical that covered a range of social issues through the medium of African American dance.

Savion Glover was born in 1974, in Newark, New Jersey, and when he was very young his mother realized that he had an unusually advanced sense of rhythm. She had the sense to enrol him into a dance school were he studied jazz and ballet. When he was seven years old he saw an exhibition of rhythm tap by Chuck Green and Lon Chaney and was so impressed that he began to study tap himself. It soon became a vocation, and five years later, when he was only 12 years, old he was appearing on Broadway in the show *The Tap Dance Kid*. His subsequent stage appearances have included *Jelly's Last Jam*, alongside Gregory Hines, and *Black and Blue*, for which, at the age of 21, he became the youngest person ever in Broadway history to receive a nomination for a Tony award.

The director of *Jelly's Last Jam* was George Wolfe, an experienced musical director, who recognized in Glover a new embodiment of an old vernacular. Inspired by the prodigy, Wolfe decided to create a show that would celebrate the struggles and legacy of African-American history. The result was *Bring in Da Noise, Bring in Da Funk*, which opened in November 1995 at the Public Theater in New York. As successful commercially as it was critically, *Bring in Da Noise, Bring in Da Funk* established Savion Glover as the new tap superstar.

Bring in Da Noise, Bring in Da Funk, with a book by the poet Reg E. Gaines, as well as direction by Wolfe and choreography by Glover, took the history of African American musical styles, wove it into a tapestry of dramatic and satirical routines and created a tribute to both black culture and the art of tap. It was at once a musical entertainment, a social history and artistic investigation, all driven by the phenomenal talent of the show's young star. Indeed, Glover himself is on record as stating that he is as driven as much by a need to educate and innovate as to entertain. As he

Riverdance

Throughout the century the ancient precursor of modern tap, the Irish jig, never completely died out. Not only in Ireland, but elsewhere around the globe, wherever the Irish diaspora spread, Irish dancing took root and survived. In 1969 the World Irish Dancing Championships (*Oireachtas Rince na Cruinne*) was established, and over the years dancers from the United States, Canada and Australia as well as Ireland have taken the honours at these championships.

It was a multi-million pound television extravaganza, however, that transformed Irish dancing from a footnote in social dance history into a mass-marketed, fully fledged, global entertainment. In 1994 the Republic of Ireland hosted the Eurovision Song Contest – an annual European combination of music and kitsch – and keen to promote the country to a pan-European television audience, the national television company, RTE, hit upon the idea of celebrating the national culture through its indigenous dance styles. Produced by Moya Doherty, whose idea the show was, and with music by Bill Whelan, who had experience of

has said: 'My mission is to ... to funcktify everybody ... just to let them know that tap isn't this corny, washed-up art form ... it's new, and it's raw. It's today.'

Glover already possesses a list of credits that would assure him a place alongside the greats if he were to stop dancing today. He is the youngest man ever to receive a National Endowment for the Arts grant for choreography. He has danced a tribute to Gene Kelly at the Oscars. His feet have felt the beat on stages as far afield as the Moulin Rouge in Paris and the Carnegie Hall in Manhattan. Nevertheless, he remains a dedicated teacher and popularizer of tap, wedded to the principles of its history and development.

Bring in Da Noise, Bring in Da Funk originally possessed a subtitle: 'A Tap/Rap Discourse of the Staying Power of the Beat.' The 'staying power of the beat' would be a good description of the resilience of all percussive dancing throughout the century. By the mid-1990s, after decades of struggling to survive in a hostile climate, international percussive dancing shows broke out around the world. *Bring in Da Noise, Bring in Da Funk* was a major influence on this development, but in terms of international success and mass popularity it could not compete with some of the others, not least the global phenomenon that was *Riverdance*.

Above: That *Bring in Da Noise, Bring in Da Funk* was so highly influential, and spawned a number of respectful imitations, was due primarily to its star, Savion Glover.

Right: Also relying on a percussive, tap style, are the musicals *Riverdance* and *Lord of the Dance*, featuring the Irish style of Chicago-born Michael Flatley.

Above: Flatley achieved worldwide fame through *Riverdance*, but felt frustrated by his lack of influence within the company, and left to create the rival *Lord of the Dance*.

mixing multicultural rhythms with traditional Irish music, the resulting routine was a sensation and quite overtook the event for which it was planned.

Almost immediately, the producers realized they had created something more than a simple heritage industry package. One of the keys to its success were the dancers Doherty chose to star in the show. One was Jean Butler, an Irish-American dance cham-

pion in her own right. Another was Michael Flatley. Flatley, it would become apparent, possessed a flair for publicity that matched his dancing skill, and by the end of the century Flatley had become Irish dancing's first (maybe, only) international star. Michael Flatley grew up in a working-class neighbourhood of Chicago, the second son of a large family. The Flatleys were proud of their Irish heritage, which included competitive Irish

'Flatley, it would become apparent, possessed a flair for publicity that matched his dancing skill, and by the end of the century Flatley had become Irish dancing's first (maybe, only) international star.'

set up a show of which he was the undisputed star – *Lord of the Dance*. Using the same techniques of mixing Celtic themes with vigorous Irish tap, *Lord of the Dance* (and its successor, *Feet of Flames*) has proved equally lucrative and has taken Flatley to venues more used to rock bands than traditional Irish dancers. Flatley himself is received on stage more in the manner of a pop star than a stage dancer.

At the end of the century, the tap extravaganza has become big business. Shows like *Stomp*, *Blast* and *Tap Dogs* have more in common with the pop concert than the theatre. The work is vigorous, brash and athletic, and even if it lacks the skill and subtlety of the great tap acts of the past (or of the work of Savion Glover today), it somehow represents, with its great intensity, something of the speed, danger and heartbeat of life in the post-industrial age.

Below: *Stomp*, here seen at the Roundhouse in London, may not have been subtle, but it was certainly an exciting development in modern tap.

dancing, and when he was 17 years old Michael became the first American to win the World Irish Dance Championships. In the early 1990s he was performing on tour with the Irish folk band, the Chieftains, when he was spotted by Doherty and brought to Dublin to dance for the then President of Ireland, Mary Robinson. This led directly to his involvement in the original Riverdance routine for Eurovision. Flatley's charisma was irresistible. When it became apparent that the Riverdance concept could be made into a full-scale theatrical event, Flatley was the inevitable choice to star, as well as being the show's principal choreographer.

Like *Bring in Da Noise, Bring in Da Funk*, *Riverdance* is the story of a culture and how it has developed and evolved over time. The show tells the story, in dance, of Irish history from the dawn of time to the great migrations of the nineteenth century (the river in the title referring to the river of time). The live show cemented the reputation it established on television, and it went on to become an international success, thrilling audiences in Britain, the United States, Australia, Germany and Canada, as well as its native land.

As the *Riverdance* phenomenon grew, so did Michael Flatley's stardom. Because *Riverdance* was (in theory, at least) an ensemble production, its producers and management found themselves on a collision course with Flatley's dominant personality. Amid much acrimony Flatley broke free of *Riverdance* and

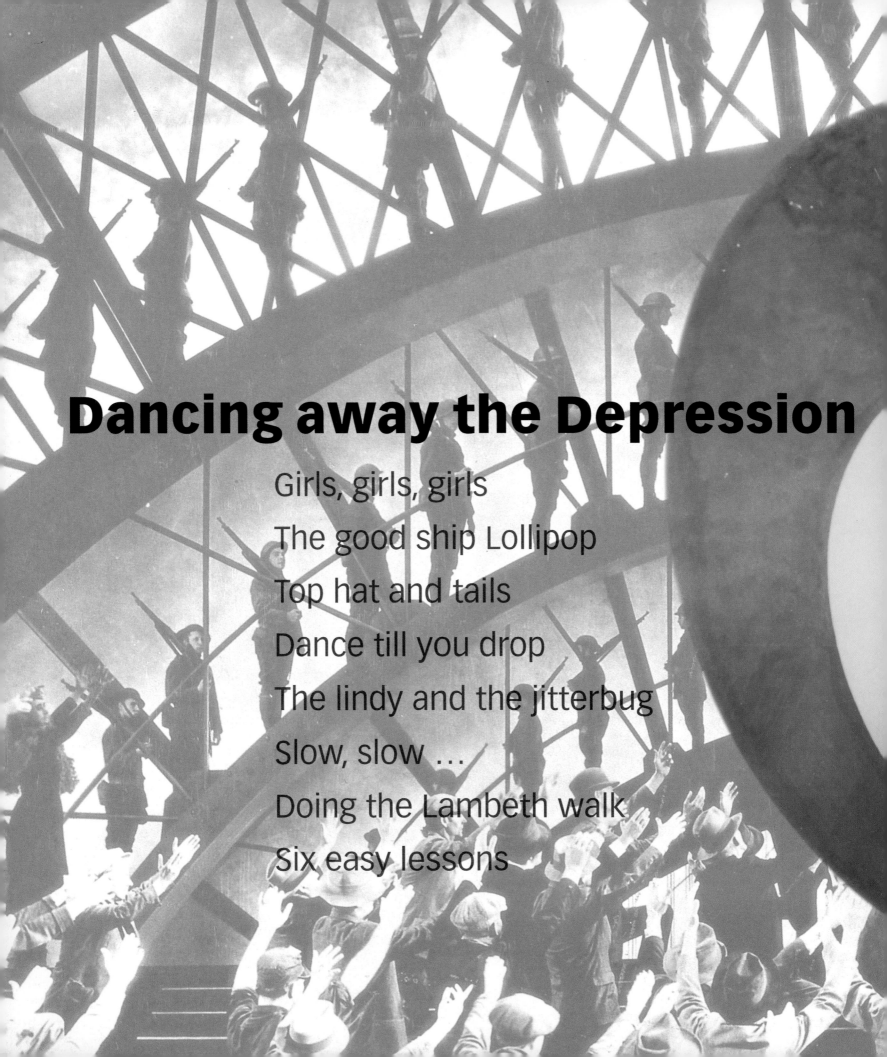

Dancing away the Depression

Girls, girls, girls

The good ship Lollipop

Top hat and tails

Dance till you drop

The lindy and the jitterbug

Slow, slow …

Doing the Lambeth walk

Six easy lessons

In 1929 the edifice of hope, prosperity and faith in the future that America had built up during the jazz age came crashing down. With it went the simple *joie de vivre* of the dance world. Between 1929 and 1933 the gross national product of the United States was halved, and by 1933 one-third of the labour force was unemployed. In the wake of economic catastrophe in the United States and the looming spectre of fascism in Europe, dance ceased to be a simple celebration of fun and frivolity. No longer participants at the party, the public joined together to dream about it instead.

Below: The film musical arrived just in time to stave some of the Depression blues; the first 'talkie' featured the music of Al Jolson.

Dancing away the Depression

'Musicals, so long excluded from celluloid because of the limitations on sound, were now able to expand into the synchronized world.'

For the first time the movies could offer a means of escape. The cinema, which for 20 years had been gradually eating into the vaudeville and musical circuit, finally took over as the primary shop window for song-and-dance. Musicals, so long excluded from celluloid because of the limitations on sound, were now able to expand into the synchronized world. Indeed, the most famous expression of the new technology – Al Jolson bursting into song in *The Jazz Singer* in 1927 – announced to the world that the musical had arrived.

The musical films that followed the innovation were clumsy in the extreme. A whole host of Broadway shows were transferred to film with little imagination and even less understanding of the new medium. Numbers were filmed exactly as they were performed on stage, with only the occasional cut-away as a means of narration. What was needed was someone able to harness both the dancers and the new medium. The special talent who was able to do this was Busby Berkeley. Like many dance directors of the period Berkeley was barely able to dance himself, but he made up for the skills that he lacked in his feet with his eye.

Left: The director and choreographer Busby Berkeley in a shot characteristic of his film style, framed by some of his dancing girls' legs.

Below: The famous bananas sequence in *The Gang's All Here* (1943), filmed in colour unlike many of Berkeley's most well-known musicals, and starring Carmen Miranda.

Girls, girls, girls

William Berkeley Enos (1895–1976) came with a theatrical pedigree: his father, Franci Enos, was a theatrical director, and his mother, Gertrude Berkeley, was an actress. Berkeley's father died when he was only eight years old, and although he remained extremely close to his mother for the rest of her life, she soon realized that the life of a touring actress was not conducive to a young man's education. He was enrolled at the New York Military Academy, and, surprisingly for a creative artist, the army came to play a key part in Berkeley's development.

Not long after graduating, Berkeley signed up and entered the First World War. Eventually becoming a second lieutenant, he found himself in France, responsible for over 200 men. One of his principal duties was to teach and conduct military drill, something for which he soon discovered he had a flair, and a discipline that would become very evident in his later choreography – *Gold Diggers of 1937*, for example, features a routine that consists of 70 girls dressed as soldiers and marching with flags and drums.

After the war Berkeley used a mixture of his mother's influence and his own hard work and strong self-belief to develop

Right: A career in the military gave Busby Berkeley the ability to co-ordinate precisely drilled dance routines, as here for *Gold Diggers In Paris* from 1939.

Opposite: The overhead shot with the dancers executing a routine reminiscent of the image at the end of a kaleidoscope was Berkeley's trademark.

BUSBY BERKELEY FACTFILE

Born: 29 November 1895

Died: 14 March 1976

Real name: William Berkeley Enos

Early career: The son of a director and an actress, Berkeley came from a theatrical pedigree but it was his experience training soldiers during the First World War that had the greatest impact on his subsequent career.

Stage musicals: Made his name choreographing *A Connecticut Yankee* (1927). Worked on more than 20 musicals before going to Hollywood.

First film: *Whoopee* (1930) for which he provided the choreography.

Film work: His most notable films were the Depression musicals of the 1930s: The 'Gold Diggers' series (1933–39) and *42nd Street* (1933). Other films included *Babes in Arms* (1939), *Strike Up the Band* (1940) and *For Me and My Gal* (1942).

Key to success: During a period of great economic hardship, Berkeley offered visual extravagance through technical innovation and imaginative direction.

Fact: Like many dance directors of his generation, Berkeley possessed no dancing ability of his own.

'Apart from the obvious "feel-good" factor supplied by a hundred tapping feet or a cascade of grand pianos, backstage stories offered the prospect of overnight success against all ... odds.'

a reputation as a choreographer on the New York stage. The success of his choreography in the 1927 smash hit *A Connecticut Yankee* secured his reputation, and by the end of the decade he was well enough known as a dance director and 'show-doctor' (someone called in to rescue ailing shows) for Samuel Goldwyn to invite him to Hollywood.

Although he arrived on the west coast at a time when the Hollywood musical was almost dead in the water, he recognized immediately the possibilities of the medium. In his very first assignment, the musical *Whoopee* (1930), he produced the overhead shot that was to become his trademark. It was in 1933, however, at the lowest point of the Depression, that his status was secured. Alongside the arrival of Franklin Roosevelt and the New Deal, Berkeley offered the general public a dream of wealth, happiness and collective success in the quintessential productions *42nd Street* and *Gold Diggers of 1933*. These were unique combinations of predictable plot and wildly extravagant choreog-

raphy. The complete package was crass, flamboyant and hugely popular, and Berkeley and his collaborators went on to repeat the formula for the rest of the decade.

The 'backstage' musical was a useful structure on which to hang a Hollywood musical. In practical terms it provided a reason for the presence of huge dance routines with no function in carrying the plot. In addition, the backstage template provided the perfect metaphor for an audience sunk in the Depression and dreaming of a way out. Apart from the 'feel-good' factor supplied by a hundred tapping feet or a cascade of grand pianos, backstage stories offered the prospect of overnight success against all economic and social odds. In these films chorus girls are discovered overnight, penniless composers create hits despite everything being stacked against them and, at the last gasp, true love wins out over temperamental sugar daddies. It is show business as life, and it told the audience that they must never give up. Furthermore, quite apart from the message of the movies, all of Berkeley's films offered a vital example of huge teams, all pulling together to create something new, bold and enterprising.

Incredibly, all this was achieved by a man with no formal training. It is perhaps not surprising, therefore, that Berkeley's ingenuity was not in the steps that he choreographed, but in the eye with which he shot them. Berkeley was the first to realize that the camera was not only a mere observer of the action but could actually become a participant in the routine. Released from its static limitations, Berkeley allowed the camera – and, by extension, his audience – to fly over, under and through the glorious routines that he devised.

In his best films there is often a tension between the dramatic action, more often than not filmed by another director, and the Berkeley routines alongside it. Consequently, a plodding piece of action can suddenly lead into a full expression of Berkeley's 'instinctive surrealism', as producer Arthur Freed described it. Visual puns, special effects, cinematic styles, vernacular dance and military drill all joined in a kaleidoscope of images that found a place not only in the history of popular dance but also, recently, in the lecture halls of film schools.

By the mid-1940s Berkeley's star was on the wane. Heavy drinking, tax debts and the loss of his beloved mother all took their toll, and at one point he was committed to a psychiatric institution. He did go on to direct *Take Me Out to the Ball Game* (1949) with Frank Sinatra and Gene Kelly (see pages 164–167), and in the 1950s he directed a few vehicles for Esther Williams (see page 161), but he would never again be the force that he had been during the 1930s. The film world had moved on. The writing had been on the wall even back in his prime, when alongside his most successful films, Astaire and Rogers (see page 128–133) were showing what could be done with dancing skill and more integrated story lines. In a revealing counter to Berkeley's cinematic style, Astaire once said: 'Either the camera will dance, or I will; but both of us at the same time - that won't work.' Astaire's success would prove that the public admired superb dancing as least as much as flamboyant directing, and for many years Berkeley's work faded into memory. However, his reputa-

'Enduringly cute, or unbearably saccharine, depending on your taste, little Shirley Temple (b.1928) conquered the world during the Depression ... she could also tap – and tap well.'

tion experienced a positive revision at the end of the twentieth century, while his pioneering work in music-driven, montage-based film-making survives in the vibrant music videos of the contemporary music world.

The good ship Lollipop

Many of the biggest names in musical comedy featured in Berkeley's movies. He made stars of Ginger Rogers and Ruby Keeler, and in his direction of the early MGM 'backyard' musicals he collaborated with the young Mickey Rooney and Judy Garland. At various times in his career he worked with Gene Kelly, Frank

Above: Shirley Temple in *Stand Up And Cheer*, the film that made her a star, and in many ways justifiably, because her acting, singing and dancing were highly accomplished.

Sinatra, Ann Miller and Eleanor Powell. In spite of all these illustrious names, though, the most celebrated tap dancer of the 1930s was a little girl from Santa Monica, California – Shirley Temple.

Enduringly cute, or unbearably saccharine, depending on your taste, little Shirley Temple (b.1928) conquered the world during the Depression. Between 1935 and 1938 – when she was still only 10 – she was the biggest box office star in Hollywood, beating off competition that included Clark Gable, Bing Crosby and Fred Astaire. She made as many as 24 films between 1934 and 1940, and her success did much to ensure the survival of Twentieth Century Fox. Most of these films were musicals, and

the reason for their success lay in her feet. Shirley Temple may have had a cute little smile and an endearing personality, but she could also tap – and tap well.

Temple started dancing when, at the age of three, she became a pupil at the Ethel Meglin Dance studio. Renowned throughout Hollywood for the quality of her child dancers, Meglin contracted out her 'Kiddies' throughout the business, and it was no surprise that Shirley should find herself dancing in the 1934 Fox musical *Stand Up and Cheer*. Her appearance was brief, but the audience was hooked, and Fox was persuaded to develop films in which she could shine.

Above: Temple with her tap dancing teacher, none other than Bill Robinson, in a poster for the film *The Littlest Rebel* (1935).

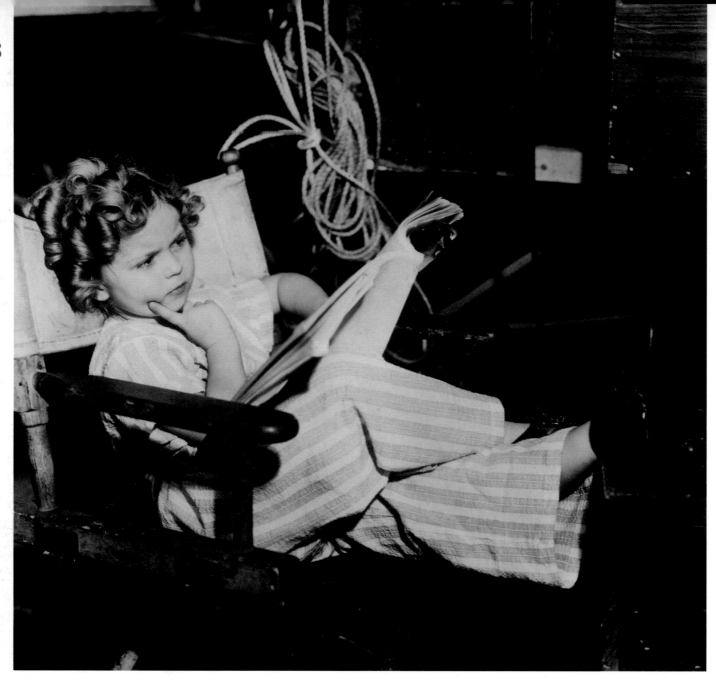

Above: A thoughtful Shirley Temple on a film set in 1935; to some she may have been resistably cute, however for others she brightened up a gloomy era.

More often than not Temple's musical films made use of the backstage format. With titles like *Curly Top*, *Dimples* and *Little Miss Broadway*, they shamelessly played on her innocent charm and usually involved her bringing youthful sunshine into a dark and often malevolent world. This was usually done with a song, a smile and some tap dancing.

Even more than the other great dancers of her generation, Shirley Temple encouraged others to dance. Enrolment at dance schools was said to rocket through the roof in the aftermath of her new movies, and she certainly offered anxious parents a healthy role model of how innocent the world of dance could be. But although suburban parents may not have recognized it, Temple's dance skill was bolstered by the quality of partner she was given. Alongside the 'little bundle of joy' (to use John Boles's song

lyric) were some of the greatest names in the tap dancing world. Buddy Ebsen, George Murphy and Bill Robinson all danced alongside her, with Robinson in particular becoming not only a dancing partner but also her friend and teacher. She called him 'uncle Billy', he called her 'darlin'', and by her own admission, she could not have had a better teacher.

Top hat and tails

If Busby Berkeley and Shirley Temple offered two cinematic visions of how song-and-dance could overcome the vagaries of the Depression, the best known and most enduring 'escape' musicals were coming out of the new and struggling RKO studio. Two dancers from Broadway, Fred Astaire (1899–1987) and Ginger Rogers (1911–95), were starring in a series of musicals

'Fred Astaire and Ginger Rogers ... were a partnership that became a byword for elegance, and they created an intimacy in screen dancing that will probably never be matched.'

that, in their use of style, plotting and song, were breaking new ground. The Hollywood musical would never be the same again.

Despite the choreographer Le Roy Prinz's comment that 'in screen dancing, we cater to the masses, not to the classes', in the 1930s Fred Astaire and Ginger Rogers offered class above all else. Between 1933 and 1939 they were a partnership that became a byword for elegance, and they created an intimacy in screen dancing that will probably never be matched. As the dance critic Arlene Croce has said: 'In their movies, dancing was transformed into a vehicle of serious emotion between a man and a woman ... Astaire had some good dancing partners, but without Rogers it is a world of a sun without a moon.'

Although they both came to Hollywood via vaudeville and Broadway, it was the differences in their styles that made them

Above: Fred Astaire originally made his name with his sister Adèle on stage on both sides of the Atlantic, but he eventually found his forte, the film musical.

Left: Astaire's first and most famous dancing partner in movies was Ginger Rogers, who was already a star through her appearances in Busby Berkeley musicals.

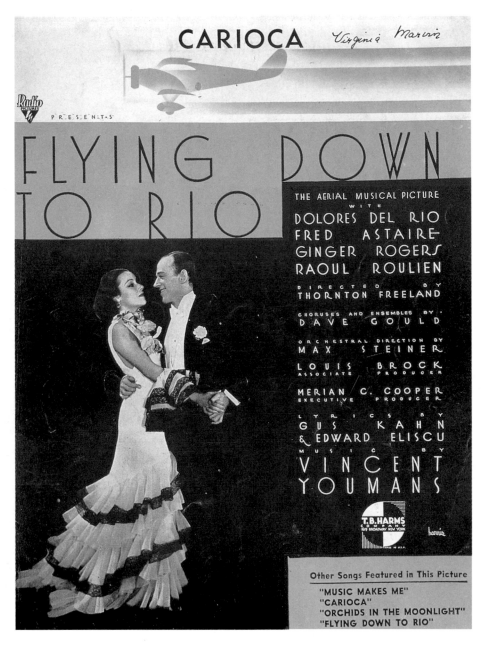

'This mix of rumba and Brazilian rhythms caused such a stir that RKO glimpsed a financial lifeline in economically difficult times and paired them throughout the next decade ...'

extravaganzas and the classically trained dancers that were to become so popular in post-war Hollywood.

Astaire, on the other hand, was the picture of insouciance. Suave and elegant, his demeanour owed much to Vernon Castle (see pages 34–35) a generation before. But Astaire was much more than an elegant ballroom dancer. For more than 25 years he had worked in the theatre alongside his sister Adele in a dance act. For much of this time he danced in her shadow, learning, observing and honing his style. Together they had appropriated the rich diversity of dance styles on offer in the vaudeville world, and ballet, ballroom and tap all featured in their routines. One story suggests that Ned Wayburn himself (see pages 34–35) recognized the young man's talent and taught Astaire tap. Whatever the truth of the story, one thing is certain: Astaire's name featured prominently on the advertising for Wayburn's schools.

Astaire and Rogers's first film together was *Flying Down to Rio* (1933). Billed as a 'giant musical extravaganza', it aimed to cash in on the success of the Warner Brothers' musicals of the same year, *Gold Diggers* and *42nd Street*. A pale imitation of Busby Berkeley's brash style, the film met with little critical success, except for one sequence in which Astaire and Rogers danced to 'The Carioca'. This mix of rumba and Brazilian rhythms caused such a stir that RKO glimpsed a financial lifeline in economically difficult times and paired them throughout the next decade (despite their continual protests). The films were hugely popular and enormously lucrative: a legend was born.

Above: Astaire and Rogers were not the stars of their first film together, *Flying Down to Rio* (1933), but it made their name as a partnership.

Right: The most enduring Astaire/Rogers musical was *Swing Time*, choreographed by Hermes Pan.

such a unique combination. With her wisecracking personality and a background as the 'queen of the Charleston', Rogers had something of the air of the 1920s flapper about her. 'Cigarette me, big boy' – a line she uttered in her screen debut in the *Young Man of Manhattan* (1930) – became a catchphrase. Her lack of pretension, however, evident both on and off the screen, should never be allowed to detract from her considerable skill as a dancer. She once said, characteristically: 'I did everything Fred did, only backwards and in high heels.' In effect, Ginger Rogers is the link between the massed showgirls of the Busby Berkeley

Dancing away the Depression

FRED ASTAIRE FACTFILE

Born: 10 May 1899

Died: 1987

Real name: Frederick Austerlitz

Stage musicals: Astaire made his debut on Broadway dancing with his sister, Adele, in 1917. His stage hits included *The Passing Show of 1918*, *Lady Be Good* (1924) and *Smiles* (1930).

First film: *Dancing Lady* (1933) in which he had a small part opposite Joan Crawford

Film hits: Include *Flying down to Rio* (1933), *Top Hat* (1935), *Swing Time* (1936), *You'll never get rich* (1941), *The Sky's the Limit* (1943) and *Easter Parade* (1948).

Secret of success: Astaire skilfully improvised dance numbers with a charming easy-going style. Most of all he shot to fame through his inspired pairing with Ginger Rogers in ten of his films.

Awards: Fred Astaire received a special Academy Award for his contribution to films in 1949. He was also nominated for the Oscar for best supporting actor for the *Towering Inferno* (1974).

What they said about him:
'Can't act. Slightly bald. Can dance a little.' – verdict of his first Hollywood screen test.

'The Carioca' lacked the sudden changes in tempo and the dramatic shading that would later become associated with their work, but it bore many of the trademarks of Astaire and Rogers's routines: it was choreographed by Astaire and Hermes Pan (1905–90), the assistant dance director on *Flying Down to Rio*, who became Astaire's collaborator; it was filmed nearly entirely in long shot and in one continuous take so that the audience could see the full movement of the dancers' bodies; and, in spite of the setting, Fred and Ginger danced with a togetherness and intimacy that looked both spontaneous and easy.

The spontaneity of the routines was, of course, an illusion – they rehearsed for weeks before filming a sequence – but, then, the RKO musicals were all about illusion. The harsh economic realities of the 1930s were never allowed to impinge on the party. Astaire and Rogers made 10 films together in total, of which *Swing Time* (1936) and the quintessential *Top Hat* (1935) are,

Left: Astaire, here with his collaborator, Hermes Pan, took his work extremely seriously, and the apparent ease with which he performed resulted from many months of preparation.

'The spontaneity of the routines was, of course, an illusion – they rehearsed for weeks before filming a sequence – but the RKO musicals were all about illusion.'

perhaps, the most enduring. All followed a similar plot, in which boy meets girl, nearly loses girl and wins girl back, with every stage marked by a dance choreographed by Astaire and Pan and songs written by the greatest lyricists of the day.

Although Astaire and Rogers came together in 1949 to film MGM's *The Barkleys of Broadway* (Rogers replacing Judy Garland at the last minute), to all intents and purposes the partnership came to an end in 1939. Their last film together for RKO was, suitably, *The Story of Vernon and Irene Castle* (1939), but even before the film was made, Astaire had committed himself to leaving RKO and pursuing his career as a freelance.

Rogers went on to a successful career as a straight actress, while Astaire continued to develop his talent with other partners and projects. In time, he would stake his claim as the pre-eminent jazz dancer of the century. But despite this, the public would never let them forget their timeless partnership, which brought joy to a 'dishonest decade' and romance to a brutal world.

Above: Although the individual performances of Astaire and Rogers were central to their musicals, they were often complemented by a large-scale chorus, as here in *Top Hat*.

Left: Astaire and Rogers in the 'Pick Yourself Up' routine from *Swing Time*, made in 1936 when their partnership was at its most successful.

Dance till you drop

In stark contrast to the Hollywood dream, the harsh realities of economic depression were making themselves felt in the dance-halls and ballrooms of the USA. The stage and dance floor, so closely connected during the halcyon days of the jazz era, were becoming distant cousins. Fred Astaire and Ginger Rogers executed steps of which the average dancer could only dream and in an environment to which they could only aspire. If Fred and Ginger danced for love, thousands of men and women across the United States and beyond danced for money. An era of dance marathons had arrived.

Ironically, for what would become an American phenomenon, the first dance marathons appeared in Britain in 1923. The United States, however, had already acquired a taste for the public endurance test and recognized in the British marathons a recipe for mixing dance with more prosaic entertainments. In the same year, the Audubon Ballroom in New York led the way with a 27-hour marathon, in which it was said that Alma Cummings, the celebrated New York hostess, wore out six partners.

For those who could afford it, however, the novelty of marathon dancing soon wore off. As the marathons became longer and the demands became greater, dance marathons took on all the characteristics of a fully fledged spectator sport. The public would pay to watch contestants dance non-stop for as long as they could, the winners being the last couple left standing at the end of the marathon. As with regular sports, rules were established. Contestants were allowed a two-minute toilet break and a 10-minute rest break every hour (although sleep was forbidden). Every 12 hours a shower was mandatory. Despite these apparent health and safety precautions, the emphasis was not on safety but on entertainment.

Audiences required ever more outrageous and demanding marathons. When a marathon at the Roseland Ballroom in New York City was raided by the police after three days, the remaining couples were transferred to a waiting truck and from there to a waiting boat. Three miles out to sea, beyond the city boundaries, the marathon continued until the dancers became too seasick to continue. The longest marathon on record was held in Pittsburgh, Pennsylvania, and lasted for 24 weeks and 5 days before the local authorities put a stop to it.

Many of the leading dancers acquired notoriety as well as financial reward. Some turned professional, and local businesses would sponsor those contestants most hotly tipped to win. MCs would help whip up support, and spectators would return day after day, enjoying the soap opera characteristics of the event.

Popular support could not hide the exploitative nature of the events, however. The prize money was meagre and the suffering immense – one man died after dancing for 48 days – and eventu-

'The prize money was meagre and the suffering immense – one man died after dancing for 48 days – and eventually there were calls for the marathons to be banned.'

ally there were calls for the marathons to be banned. In 1933 they officially became illegal, but not before a dancer called George 'Shorty' Snowden had made history in one at the Manhattan Casino, New York.

It was in June 1928 that the Manhattan Casino hosted a rare, non-segregated dance marathon. Among the contestants was a young black dancer from Harlem, Shorty Snowden. Shorty's dancing caused quite a stir, and before long local journalists, including the young Ed Sullivan, began to draw attention to his ability. Snowden had taken to relieving the tedium of repetitive steps by occasionally flinging his partner away and filling the 'break' with improvised steps. When Fox Movietone News hurriedly descended on the Casino to film the 'break-away', they naturally wanted to interview its creator as well. Shorty was asked what he was doing with his feet during the break-away. He replied, 'the lindy', and swing dance had arrived.

Below: The dance marathon phenomenon was harrowingly portrayed in the 1969 film *They Shoot Horses, Don't They?*, starring Jane Fonda and Michael Sarrazin.

The lindy and the jitterbug

Whether or not Snowden really had invented the lindy is open to conjecture –Ray Bolger (see page 42) always claimed that he had invented it in 1927 – but Snowden was presenting to an astonished world what had been evolving over the years in that great incubator of popular dance, Harlem. This northern neighbourhood of Manhattan had been setting the pace in dance development throughout the first quarter of the century, and now its dancehalls were proving as influential as its theatres and cabarets.

The most important dance venue in Harlem was the Savoy Ballroom. There were other ballrooms in the district – the Alhambra and the New Star Casino, for instance – but it was the Savoy that played a pivotal role in the development of swing dance. Snowden was one of the stars of the Savoy Ballroom, and he had even attempted to gain sponsorship from its proprietor, Charles Buchanan, before his 1928 appearance at the Manhattan Casino marathon. Buchanan, ever sensitive to his dancehall's reputation, declined, although in the aftermath of the marathon Snowden was given a lifetime pass to the Savoy. Buchanan had

Below: The Savoy dance theatre in Harlem, one of the most important venues in New York for the development of dance in the 1920s and 30s.

CAB CALLOWAY
COLUMBIA RECORDS exclusively

Left: Some Columbia Records artwork for the great Cab Calloway, the king of hi-de-hi, whose jump big band style had the crowds lindy hopping and jiving as never before.

THE GREAT DANCE BANDS

Benny Goodman – 'The King of Swing'. The most famous purveyor of the swing sound, learned from the work of Fletcher Henderson and his orchestra. His 1938 Carnegie Hall concert was a classic.

Glenn Miller Orchestra – Became a legend after Miller's wartime disappearance. Quintessential sound of the Second World War. Hits included 'Chattanooga Choo Choo', 'In the Mood', and 'Moonlight Serenade'.

Louis Jordan and his Tympani Five – Best known of the smaller 'jump band' units that became popular after the Second World War. Hits included 'Choo Choo Ch'Boogie', 'Five Guys Named Mo' and 'Caledonia'. Precursors to rhythm and blues and rock and roll.

Paul Whiteman Orchestra – 'The King of Jazz'. Pioneer of the big band sound. Laid the groundwork for the swing era at his legendary 1924 Aeolian Hall concert, New York. Musicians included Bix Beiderbecke (trumpet) and Bing Crosby.

Tommy Dorsey Orchestra – 'The Sentimental Gentleman of Swing'. Particularly strong in generating mood and putting over ballads. Influential in establishing Frank Sinatra.

also indirectly aided the development of the lindy by banning the Charleston (see pages 59–61) in his establishment on grounds of decorum, and dancers, eager to break the ban, developed a running Charleston, which allowed them to escape the eagle-eyed bouncer, and this gradually fed into the lindy.

On its double bandstand the Savoy played host to many of the leading lights in the development of swing – Fletcher Henderson, Chick Webb, Cab Calloway, Don Redman, Dizzy Gillespie, Count Basie and Benny Goodman all played at the Savoy at one time or another – and on any given night, two bands would alternate their performances, often giving way to a friendly rivalry that itself did much to push back the boundaries of what could be achieved with the new sound.

The great jazz bandleader Paul Whiteman (1890–1967) was the first to realize the potential of the large jazz orchestra. Per-

'Harlem ... had been setting the pace in dance development throughout the first quarter of the century, and now its dancehalls were proving as influential as its theatres and cabarets.'

'The strict code of gang life was carried on to the dance floor, and the rules of behaviour within the Savoy Ballroom were intricate.'

haps because he lacked the improvisational skills of the jazz pioneers, Whiteman understood that jazz could be written down and orchestrated, and his work led to his being known as the 'King of Jazz' (he appeared in a film with that name in 1930), but he could not have appreciated how his ideas would evolve into swing.

Swing is the perfect way to define the difference in sound between the old jazz bands and the new dance orchestras. The rhythm had more momentum and, literally, swung. The traditional jazz sound encouraged staccato, up-and-down style dances, which made up for a certain loss of grace with an abundance of energy. Swing was a more 'horizontal' sound. It was still energized, but it gave the dancers a more flowing momentum. The dancers at the Savoy Ballroom felt the change and danced accordingly. Musicians and dancers at the Savoy inspired each other. Every time Dizzy Gillespie played a crazy lick, the dancers would try to match it with a step, and vice versa. The Savoy was a jazz laboratory, and the regulars were proud of it.

The star dancers at the Savoy, of whom Snowden was one, came off the street. Many belonged to street gangs, which played as significant a part in the development of the lindy as they would in the development of break dancing 40 years later (see page 236). The strict code of gang life was carried on to the dance floor, and the rules of behaviour within the Savoy Ballroom were intricate. The northeast corner of the Savoy became known as Cat's Corner. This area of the floor played host to unofficial dance contests, in which rival pairs would cut in on other dancers in an attempt to top what was already being presented. This was a

Right: Paul Whiteman pioneered the orchestral form of jazz, notably with his performances of George Gershwin's great work, Rhapsody in Blue, featured in the film *King of Jazz*.

Opposite: The lack of inhibition of African Americans compared to their white compatriots gave impetus to the new form of dancing.

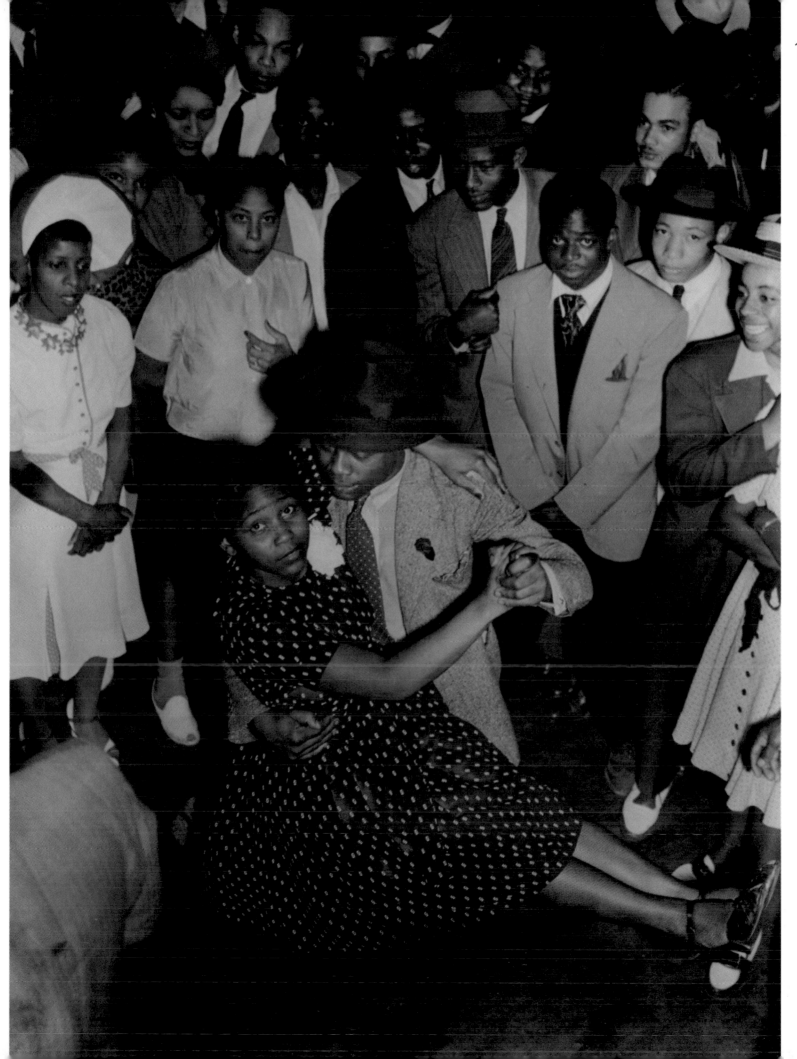

kingdom, and at first Shorty Snowden ruled there. Any attempt to steal the steps seen there or to muscle in on the scene, could earn the offender a good kicking - gang members established a way of dancing the Charleston that allowed them to kick an interloper's shins. Territorial it may have been, but it was in Cat's Corner that the lindy came to life.

The lindy or lindy hop was a direct answer to the swing sound emanating from the bandstand. The lindy has one basic step, a syncopated two-step, with the offbeat accented, which is repeated before the break-away in which the dancers do pretty well what they like. It owed much to the Texas tommy, which had been made famous by Florence Mills more than a decade before (see page 55). In the beginning the improvisations of the break-

away concentrated solely on footwork, but in the mid-1930s, just as the lindy was gaining mass appeal, air-steps began to make an appearance.

It was a young dancer called Al Minns who first challenged the authority of Cat's Corner by introducing air-steps. Although initially causing a rift within the movement – Shorty Snowden always regretted the evolution of air-steps – these moves eventually became most firmly rooted in the public's imagination as the lindy crossed the world.

An ex-bouncer with dubious underworld connections called Herbert White began to spread the lindy's reputation out of the Savoy and into public consciousness. White established performing troupes of lindy dancers with names like the Savoy Hoppers

Below: The Savoy continued to foster the talents of local dancers, and soon the groups formed there were touring the country giving demonstrations of the lindy hop.

and Whitey's Lindy Hoppers. Made up largely of dancers from the Savoy Ballroom, these troupes appeared across the United States, often receiving little financial reward for their pains; Herbert White was a man who knew how to hold on to his money. Whitey's Lindy Hoppers appeared in the Marx Brothers classic, *A Day at the Races* (1937), while another lindy troupe caused such a stir when they appeared at the Radio City Music Hall that they immediately had their contract curtailed by a confused and threatened management.

The management of Radio City was only voicing a concern that was being felt across the United States as the lindy moved into the mainstream. In what was now time-honoured fashion, the moral guardians of the nation took to lamenting the lost direction of the 'jitterbugging youth', the lindy having acquired a new name as it swept all before it. The name 'jitterbug' may have come from the 'jittery' manner of performance, or it may have derived from jazz slang, but whatever the dance's provenance, nobody could deny its raw appeal. Brash, athletic and, above all, new, jitterbugging became not so much a dance as a state of mind.

The jitterbug came to Europe fairly late in its life – American GIs introduced it, together with Betty Grable, Glenn Miller and chewing gum – but it proved no less popular, and soon the dancehalls of Europe were clearing space to make way for the lindy hoppers. Britain, however, was also proving the saviour of more traditional dancing pleasures.

'Brash, athletic and, above all, new, jitterbugging became not so much a dance as a state of mind.'

Right: Whitey's Hopping Maniacs, one of the lindy hop groups that helped spread the word about the latest dance, posing for the camera at the Cotton Club.

Slow, slow ...

The jitterbug, with its brash athletics and cocky virtuosity, illuminated the way social dancing would develop in the future. It broke all the rules of traditional ballroom dancing by placing as much emphasis on solo improvisation as on couples dancing together, and it pioneered air-steps, which were considered anathema by the traditionalists, and downright dangerous by the majority. It may have paved the way for the solo dances of the rock and roll era, but it was not to everyone's taste, and dance teachers in Britain, quickly recognizing that traditional ballroom dancing had to regroup and reorganize in the face of this youthful impostor from across the Atlantic, took steps to save its more sedate charms.

In 1924 a Ballroom Branch of the Imperial Society of Teachers of Dancing was formed. Within the world of highly regulated ballroom dancing this is a landmark date, for it marks the beginning of the standardization of ballroom steps, and the origins of what would become known as the 'English style'. It also marks the point at which modern ballroom dancing, with its characteristics of high level competition and pursuit of excellence, broke away from the everyday world of recreational dancing for good. Ballroom dancing survived to a large extent not because it tried to compete with the wild dance styles that were flooding in from across the Atlantic, but because it strictly defined and codified itself, and then sought excellence within a number of specialized styles. The fact that ballroom dancing continues to be so popular today, long after the ballroom has ceased to exist, is proof of the strategy's success.

Throughout the 1920s conferences of dance teachers defined and codified the speeds and steps for the main four dances of the ballroom genre: the waltz, the foxtrot, the tango and the quicktime foxtrot and Charleston (which would eventually become known as the quickstep). The Ballroom Branch of the Imperial Society further defined the dances by laying down a minimum standard of performance necessary to join the ranks of dance teachers. One of the members of the committee of the Ballroom Branch, Victor Silvester (1900–78), wrote in his classic book on ballroom dancing that the formation of the Ballroom Branch of the Imperial Society had 'as great an influence on ballroom dancing as did the founding of the Académie Royale by Louis XIV of France on Ballet'.

By the time of his death, Silvester was in a position to recognize the importance of the standardization of steps that had

'Ballroom dancing survived not because it tried to compete with the wild dance styles that were flooding in from across the Atlantic, but because it strictly defined and codified itself ...'

Above: Public ballrooms in the pre-war years were sometimes huge affairs, but they were very often filled with people as couple dancing was extremely popular.

Opposite: Ballroom dancing in Britain around 1935, apparently owing something to the influence of the films of Fred Astaire and Ginger Rogers.

Dancing away the Depression

Above: In war-time the dancehall became the main focus of recreational activity, and even the Royal Opera House, Covent Garden was opened up for dancing.

taken place in 1924. He had played an integral part in the growth and development of modern ballroom dancing throughout the middle years of the century. As well as being a teacher, dance historian and administrator, Silvester was also a successful orchestra leader. In the inter-war years he had recognized that British dancers demanded more traditional dance bands as well as the jazz and swing bands that were visiting Britain from the United States. Understanding that there was a need for music played at the correct tempo for ballroom dancing, he began to play and record music to fill the gap. By the time of his death, the records made by Victor Silvester and his Orchestra had sold more than 75 million copies.

Silvester also developed a chain of dance studios, which he opened in collaboration with the Rank Organization, a British entertainment company more generally known for its development of British film. Rank's involvement reflected the growing interest in dancehalls by the entertainment industry, and throughout the 1920s and 1930s the ballroom industry grew. At the beginning of the century there had been a few public dancehalls around the country, not least in the great British seaside resorts, but now, what had been the exception became the rule. The Palais de Danse in Hammersmith, London, was perhaps the best known ballroom venue in Britain, but in the 1940s its pre-eminence was challenged by dances held at the Royal Opera House, Covent Garden. After the war, Covent Garden returned to its high art roots, but its brief stint as a 'palais de danse' reflects the enormous popularity of ballroom dancing during the dark days of the Second World War.

An employee of the company that was paid to provide the catering at Covent Garden at this time was C.L. Heimann. He recognized the huge potential of providing local dancehalls to provincial populations, and he urged his company to acquire and promote other dancehalls. In time, Heimann became chairman of the board, and his company, the Mecca Organization, became a byword in social dance entertainment throughout Britain.

Into these new dancehalls, dancers, unsettled by the brash improvisation of swing dancing, could relax within the context of more traditional ballroom styles. Couples danced together, with the man leading, following the rules laid down by the Ballroom Branch. Based on natural movement and with a strictly codified technique, the English style was relaxed, subtle and dignified, the exact opposite of the swinging hips and overt physicality of the lindy dancers. Personified in the dancing of Jack Buchanan (1891–1957), the leading British film dancer of the era, the English style offered elegance instead of power, and grace instead of speed. It is a style indebted to the nation's image of itself.

'... with a strictly codified technique, the English style was relaxed, subtle and dignified, the exact opposite of the swinging hips and overt physicality of the lindy dancers.'

Left: The leading film dancer in Britain was Jack Buchanan, whose suave and elegant style was in sharp contrast to the brashness of imported American dances.

Above: Buchanan in 1922 with Lily Elsie, who had taken the title role in the first London production of Lehár's waltzing operetta *The Merry Widow* in 1907.

With such strict criteria for correct performance and with such subtle shades of right and wrong, it was inevitable that ballroom dancing should introduce a level of competition. Again, the ballroom world returned to the breezy seaside town of Blackpool, where, in 1931 the first British Open Championships were held in the Empress Ballroom of the Winter Gardens. Other competitions had been held before this – Blackpool itself had hosted a dance festival since 1920 – but the British Open Championships remained the pinnacle of competitive ballroom dancing achievement until the end of the century. Until the mid-1960s the Championships were a largely domestic affair, but since then the growing international flavour of the event has mirrored the rise in popularity of competitive ballroom dancing across the globe.

Over the years the range of competitive dances has stretched and broadened. Latin American and formation dancing have joined the 'standard' ballroom quintet of waltz, tango, foxtrot, quickstep and Viennese waltz. In fact, it could be said that all recreational dances that appeared in one venue or another through the century eventually made their way into the competitive arena – even the most unruly and rebellious dance styles are eventually tamed, standardized and performed in the competitive dancing world.

7284.

L.S. & P.

By the end of the century, however, competitive dance had moved a long way from its social dancing roots. With its rigid discipline, which requires hours of practice and real financial commitment, modern ballroom dancing has more in common with professional sport than nightclub frivolity. Indeed, in the 1990s the International Dance Sport Federation, the world governing body for ballroom dancing, officially dropped the word 'ballroom' from its title. The English style is today enmeshed within what is known as 'standard' dances, performed by international dance stars at competitions around the world. What used to be known as modern ballroom dancing has become a fully fledged Olympic sport.

'With its rigid discipline, which requires hours of practice and real financial commitment, modern ballroom dancing has more in common with professional sport than nightclub frivolity.'

Opposite: The entrance and dome of the Winter Gardens in Blackpool, one of Britain's premier ballroom dancing venues, and the location of the first open championships.

Right: Today, ballroom dancing is almost regarded as a sport, separate from amateur participatory dancing, but still retaining a glamorous image through its costumes.

Dancing away the Depression

'The British contributions to the decade's novelty crazes were the Lambeth walk and the mock-cockney hokey-cokey.'

Doing the Lambeth walk

Inevitably, as new ballrooms and dancehalls began to appear throughout the suburbs of Britain during the 1930s, the majority of dancers failed to reach the heights that were demanded by the modern ballroom rules, but then neither did they attempt the athletic physicality of the lindy crowd. Most were happy to while away the hours shuffling around the dance floor, dancing an approximation of the waltz, foxtrot or tango. The predictability of these dance programmes was broken up by a rash of novelty dances, which proved as popular in the 1930s as at other times in the century.

The British contributions to the decade's novelty crazes were the Lambeth walk and the mock-cockney hokey-cokey. The Lambeth walk came from the British musical *Me and My Girl* (1937) and was a fun pastiche of the older coster walk. The hokey-cokey – or hokey-pokey as it is known in the United States – survives today only at children's parties and informal celebrations, but it was a huge craze throughout the 1930s and 1940s.

The conga, which endures everywhere from seaside resort to sports stadium terrace, was another product of the period. Hailing from Cuba and inexplicably named after the Congo, the conga consists of a line of dancers, each with their hands on the hips of the dancer in front, snaking around the dance floor and beyond, with every third step eliciting a kick and a yell. It is fun and silly.

In terms of dance history, however, the most important novelty dance of the period was the big apple. This is not because of its enduring appeal or the ground-breaking manner of its execution, however. The big apple is important today because it was the vehicle that launched the career of Arthur Murray, the man who taught the United States – and the world – to dance.

Six Easy Lessons

By 1937 Arthur Murray had already established a successful dance teaching business, but it was continually buffeted by the economic climate. A product of the great dance boom of the ragtime era, Murray had trained at Castle House, the dance school

Opposite: British dancing was not without a sense of humour, perhaps illustrated best by the Lambeth walk, from the musical *Me and My Girl*, and here the hokey-cokey.

Right: Arthur Murray and partner dancing the Charleston in about 1920 before he embarked on his mission to educate the masses in the finer points of ballroom dancing.

run by Irene and Vernon Castle (see page 34), before becoming an instructor at their summer school in Massachusetts.

Murray had a keen entrepreneurial sprit. He had been one of the first to recognize the popularity of ballroom dancing and the large, untapped market for dance instruction that went with it. He also recognized the potential in magazine advertising and pioneered the concept of mail-order dance instruction. According to legend, the opera singer Enrico Caruso, a pupil of Murray's, suggested the idea of sending the 'footprint' of a dance step through the mail, thereby allowing anybody anywhere to learn his method – the dancing 'footprints' became Murray's trademark. For a while the mail-order business went well, but the rising cost of magazine advertising and the vagaries of the Depression meant that by the late 1930s his business had shrunk to a two-floor teaching concern on East 43rd Street, New York City.

In the summer of 1937 Murray read an article in the *New York Times* describing a novelty dance current in North Carolina. The report was vague, mentioning only that the dancers had been

seen in a nightclub called the Big Apple. Murray, ever eager to seize an opportunity, sent a teacher to North Carolina to investigate, and the report came back that the dance consisted of little more than a group of dancers forming a circle and following the calls of an elected leader. Murray saw an opportunity to promote the new dance and enhance his reputation at the same time. The steps called out by the leader during the big apple were invariably taken from current dance trends, such as the shag or the Suzie Q. Murray gave these steps new names, including 'peel the apple' and 'cut the apple', and wove them into his publicity.

'According to legend, the opera singer Enrico Caruso, who was a pupil of Murray's, suggested the idea of sending the "footprint" of a dance step through the mail, thereby allowing anybody anywhere to learn his method ...'

As the craze grew, the management of the chain of Statler Hotels asked Murray to send teachers to their hotels to teach the dance, which he duly did. The teachers sent a percentage of what they made back to Murray and kept the rest, and so began the Arthur Murray franchise system. By the end of the century there were more than 200 dance studios across the globe, and Arthur Murray is still the biggest name in dance instruction anywhere in the world.

Arthur Murray did for ballroom dancing in the USA what Victor Silvester did for the movement in Britain: he took away the mystique and made dancing accessible. Both men laid down the foundations that allowed ballroom dancing to endure long after the social climate that fostered them had changed. In truth, the dancehall culture that bred them was in terminal decline as early as the late 1940s. The arrival of be-bop in the late 1940s marked the beginning of the end for the big band sound, and the new form's rhythmic complexity and lack of melody made it a difficult sound to dance to. In addition, the United States, which for so long had been the incubator of dance creativity, imposed a federal tax of 20 per cent on the nation's dance floors, and venues that had previously provided a mixture of dance and musical entertainment, ripped up their dance floors and left the jazz kings to work out their new sounds alone. Jazz music, for so long something to be danced to and celebrated, became something passive. Now it was to be listened to, wrestled with and digested. All this, plus the arrival of television, meant that for a brief period, the dance world rested its feet.

Above: Arthur Murray's school in Covent Garden, London, in 1955, where the comedian Max Wall is being given a lesson.

Opposite: Arthur Murray demonstrating some new steps to some of his students at one of his first schools in the 1920s.

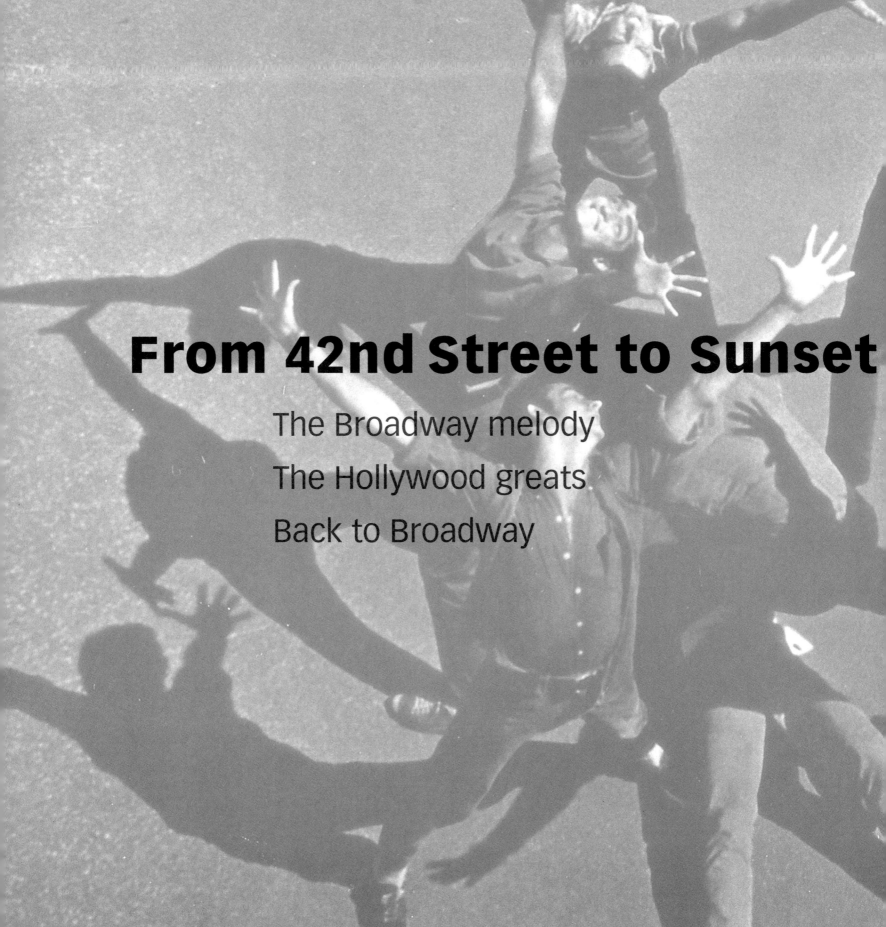

From 42nd Street to Sunset

The Broadway melody

The Hollywood greats

Back to Broadway

Boulevard

The evolution of dance on film had done much more than simply present a mass market with extravagant routines. Pioneer movie choreographers, like Busby Berkeley or Fred Astaire and Hermes Pan, had offered audiences dancing of a skill and on a scale previously unimaginable. The Astaire and Rogers vehicles, in particular, had pushed back the barriers of what was possible within the musical form. Audiences were demanding ever more sophistication, and this was as true in the theatre as elsewhere. By the early 1940s dance as simply a pleasant diversion within a musical comedy was dead. People were no longer rushing from the theatre to ballroom to try out the latest steps or flocking to Broadway to discover the latest craze. Instead, dancing in the theatre had became a tool with which to tell the story.

From 42nd Street to Sunset Boulevard

The Broadway melody

The first indication of the radical transformation that show musicals were going to experience was in the Rodgers and Hart musical *On Your Toes*, which was produced on Broadway in 1936. Rodgers and Hart had returned to Broadway from Hollywood the year before, and the plot of *On Your Toes* was based on a film musical originally pitched to Fred Astaire, who was too busy to take it on (this is an interesting twist on the 1950s trend that will see Broadway taking the lead and bringing ideas to Hollywood; see page 171). In a subtle signal of a change of direction for Broadway musicals, George Balanchine was credited in the programme as the 'choreographer' of the show. The previously ubiquitous term 'dance director' no longer seemed suitable.

Balanchine (1904–83) brought to musical theatre the rigours and discipline of classical ballet. Born in Russia, he trained with the élite Russian Imperial Ballet School in St Petersburg and

'George Balanchine was credited in the programme as the 'choreographer' of the show. The previously ubiquitous term "dance director" no longer seemed suitable.'

Above: Richard Rodgers and Lorenz Hart, creators of *On Your Toes*, which brought serious dance into the popular mainstream, combining ballet with jazz dance.

Right: The classically trained Russian dancer George Balanchine, who choreographed *On Your Toes*, in rehearsal with Tanaquil LeClerq and Francisco Moncoin.

ST. JAMES THEATRE
44th ST. W. of BROADWAY   MATINEES THURS. & SAT.

'De Mille's choreography was also notable for its expressiveness: each movement appeared to elucidate an aspect of character.'

danced with some of the foremost ballet troupes of his time, including Serge Diaghilev's Ballets Russes. He emigrated to the United States in 1933, where he quickly became established as one of the leading ballet choreographers. For *On Your Toes*, which takes place backstage at a ballet company, Balanchine worked with both classical and vernacular styles of dance to create a number of notable dances – the title number, for instance, alternated tap and classical ballet –- and as part of this cross-fertilization, Balanchine used the movements of classical ballet in combination with the positions of jazz dance, omitting the turn-out typical of ballet.

The number that attracted the most attention at the time was 'Slaughter on Tenth Avenue', danced in the original Broadway production by Ray Bolger (see page 43) and the prima ballerina Tamara Geva. Rather than being a separate set piece, as ballets (the term used to connote a set-piece dance, irrespective of style; a ballet in a musical is not necessarily danced in the style of a classical ballet) had always been on Broadway, 'Slaughter on Tenth Avenue' is firmly linked to the production's plot and conveys an important aspect of the narrative: the character learns during the course of the dance that he is to be murdered at its end, and therefore, although he is exhausted, he must keep dancing until help arrives. Beginning simply, the dance grows more frenzied and desperate, and the dancer becomes more tired and terrified. This integration of story and dance was commonplace in ballet but new and exciting when seen on the popular stage. Nevertheless, it was important to Balanchine to appeal to his new audience at the same time as offering a major innovation, and to make sure that the dance he was creating was stylistically appropriate for the popular stage, Balanchine worked with tap dancer Herbie Harper to inject authenticity into his jazz dance style.

Balanchine continued to choreograph for the popular stage for several years, contributing dances to hit shows such as *Song of Norway* (1944) and *Where's Charley?* (1948), which also starred Ray Bolger. He worked briefly in Hollywood, on *The Goldwyn Follies* (1938) and the film version of *On Your Toes* (1939), but soon the classical ballet occupied his full attention when he became artistic director of the New York City Ballet.

Many dance historians consider *On Your Toes* to be a turning point in the history of musical theatre, seeing it as making crucial step towards the integrated musical. 'Slaughter on Tenth Avenue' may have been the first dance routine integral to the plot

Above: The staging of *Oklahoma!* in London just after the war, with its integration of dance into plot and the dream ballet, proved revolutionary for the home-grown musical.

Left: The poster for the first production of *Oklahoma!* stresses the dance in one of the most successful musicals ever.

of the show that contained it, but *Oklahoma!* (1943) was the show that transformed the nature of theatrical choreography for good.

Oklahoma! was choreographer Agnes de Mille's first musical comedy. Like Balanchine, Agnes de Mille (*c.*1905–93) also came from a classical background – among other things she had created *Rodeo*, acclaimed as the first truly American ballet. To music by Rodgers and Hammerstein, she created the dance sequences for *Oklahoma!* in a very balletic and technically demanding style, and her work would revolutionize musical comedy for good.

Oklahoma! was ground breaking. For one, the chorus did not appear until 45 minutes into the first act, moving away from the 'girls, girls, girls' spirit of previous musicals. Most importantly,

however, *Oklahoma!* was the first truly integrated musical. Each song and each dance contributed to the plot and demanded that the performer remain in character. The prime example of this is in the dream sequence, 'Out of my Dreams', in Act I, in which information about one character, which is not available to the other characters, is conveyed to the audience. De Mille's choreography was also notable for its expressiveness: each movement appeared to elucidate an aspect of character. In addition, the dance seemed to arise organically from matters of plot and character. She worked with the dancers, allowing them to interpret their characters through movement and using aspects of the dancers' personal styles to facilitate the process. Consequently,

Above: A stage shot from the original Broadway production of *Oklahoma!*, dating from 1943.

the choreography was very personal to each dancer, which subsequently made it difficult for new dancers to take on the roles.

Oklahoma! also introduced a new aspect of seriousness to musical theatre. It featured a negative character, Jud Fry, who dies onstage at the end of the play, falling on his own knife after threatening the life of Curly, the romantic hero. The show's success was phenomenal. In the three years following *Oklahoma!*'s arrival on Broadway, more than half the musicals in New York included a ballet, and more than 20 included derivative dream sequences. For more than 10 years *Oklahoma!* toured the United States and abroad, breaking records around the world. Eventually, in 1955, it was taken up by Hollywood, but the film somehow lacks the energy and excitement of the original stage version.

Agnes de Mille had a number of other successes to her credit. On *Carousel* (1945) she worked with the same production team as she had on *Oklahoma!*, and, along with Rodgers and Hammerstein's impressive score, she took the integration of dance and character even further. With *Brigadoon* (1947), which was set in Scotland, her innovative choreography, which included highland flings, silenced the critics at the time who had been complaining bitterly that they were tired of the use of ballets in musical theatre. In this show as well, dance was used effectively to further the plot: one scene consists of a chase that is totally dramatized in dance.

For one dance tradition, however, *Oklahoma!* failed to provide good news. In the aftermath of *Oklahoma!*, tap dancing ceased to

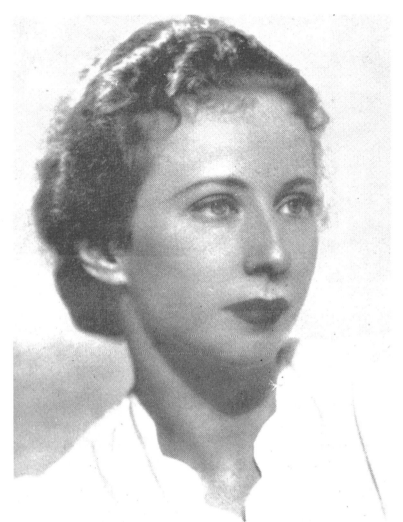

be the primary dance form on the musical stage. It was replaced by a form of expressive dance customized to the demands of musical theatre and incorporating aspects of jazz, folk, ethnic, ballroom, classical ballet and myriad other dance idioms – together making up the best of what has come to be known as jazz dance. The new style was technically demanding, but choreographers during the 1940s and 1950s could take advantage of the fact that classical ballet was not as prevalent as it is today: ballet companies were smaller and fewer in number, and virtuoso dancers were eager to turn to the Broadway stage to supplement their income.

As the move to integrated musicals continued during the 1940s, the plots of the shows themselves became more sophisticated. Although musicals based on stock situations remained popular with audiences, many shows – including *Carousel* – were based on more complex and realistic stories. The emphasis on plot construction and the integration of the music within the story meant that a show like *South Pacific* (1949) could be a major critical and popular success, even though it had no chorus line and made minimal use of dance routines.

'In the aftermath of *Oklahoma!*, tap dancing ceased to be the primary dance form on the musical stage. It was replaced by a form of expressive dance ...'

Above: Agnes de Mille, the choreographer of *Oklahoma!* and other Broadway musicals of the 1940s and 50s including *Carousel*, *Brigadoon* and *Paint Your Wagon*.

Right: The souvenir programme for the first run of Rodgers and Hammerstein's *Carousel* at New York's Majestic Theatre in 1947.

The Hollywood greats

If Broadway was slowly turning musicals into a serious art form, in Hollywood in the 1940s plot and character continued to take a backseat to glamour. Movies remained big business and, as in the 1930s, successful formulae were copied ... and copied. While the stock plot of a 1930s musical saw a plucky hero or heroine emerging from difficult circumstances by strength of character, in the 1940s the most popular plots were romances, with the action set in theatres and nightclubs and with the emphasis firmly on glitzy costumes and sets, all enhanced by the vivid colours afforded by the new technology of Technicolor.

Producers were always looking for ways to innovate while remaining firmly within the successful formula. Twentieth Century Fox discovered a goldmine when it introduced Sonja Henie (1912-69), the Norwegian-born Olympic figure skater. Her films were musicals, with typically thin plots, but the attraction was her skating, which gave the studio the opportunity to have exciting

'Some of Hollywood's top choreographers worked on the synchronized swimming routines that added curious and captivating dance interludes to Esther Williams' romantic films.'

Left: Ice-skating star Sonja Henie, here in a publicity still for *Happy Landing* (1938), was the inspiration for many spectacular ice dance routines.

SONJA HENIE
DON AMECHE
HAPPY LANDING
JEAN HERSHOLT
ETHEL MERMAN
CESAR ROMERO

variations on typical dance routines. Although Henie's acting and singing abilities were limited, the quality of her skating was unquestionable, and when she worked with talented choreographers, such as Hermes Pan on *Sun Valley Serenade* (1941), the skating routines could be dazzling. Meanwhile, at MGM, Esther Williams (b.1923) dove and swam through musicals with names like *Bathing Beauty* (1944) and *Neptune's Daughter* (1949) for more than 14 years. Some of Hollywood's top choreographers worked on the synchronized swimming routines that added curious and captivating dance interludes to her romantic films.

One of the biggest stars of 1940s musicals was Betty Grable, famous for her million dollar legs (the amount for which they were said to have been insured by Lloyds of London). Throughout the 1930s, Grable (1916–73) had struggled in Hollywood, playing bit parts as a contract player. She did not come to prominence until 1940, when she appeared in *DuBarry was a Lady* on Broadway. She was called back to Hollywood by Daryl Zanuck at Twentieth Century Fox for her first starring role in *Down Argentine Way* (1940), a movie also notable as the debut of the exotic Carmen Miranda (see pages 76–78). She was an immediate hit and proceeded to star in top-grossing, dance-oriented musicals throughout the decade. Most of her films followed what became a tried-and-true formula, pairing Grable with any of the decade's leading men: Don Ameche, Dan Dailey or Douglas Fairbanks Jr. The plots were slight, the ending happy, and the real focus was on Betty's dancing. Hermes Pan choreographed 10 of her films and appeared with her in four, including *Moon Over Miami* (1941) and *Pin-Up Girl* (1944).

It was not until after the Second World War that Hollywood began to offer more finely crafted musicals to an eager public. Many of the best came from MGM producer Arthur Freed (1894–1973). Freed, a lyricist turned producer, teamed the top talents of Broadway and Hollywood to produce such musicals as *The Wizard of Oz* (1939), *Meet Me in St Louis* (1944), *An American in Paris* (1951), *Singin' in the Rain* (1952) and *The Band Wagon* (1953). By bringing Broadway directors and writers to Hollywood, Freed set the stage for the creation of 'integrated musicals' in the movies. He fostered many major talents: the director Vincente Minnelli; choreographers Michael Kidd, Gower Champion and Bob Fosse; writers such as Betty Comden and Adolph Green and Alan Jay Lerner; song-writers such as Irving Berlin, Cole Porter and Jule Styne; and performers such as Gene Kelly (whom Freed encouraged as a choreographer/director) and Judy Garland.

Above: Betty Grable, star of numerous lightweight musicals in the 1940s, dancing with the choreographer Hermes Pan, as Evelyn Poe tries to intervene.

Left: The MGM producer Arthur Freed brought together the best of Broadway and Hollywood directors, songwriters and choreographers for a remarkable series of film musicals.

ARTHUR FREED FACTFILE

Born: 9 September 1894

Died: 12 April 1973

Real name: Arthur Grossman

Claim to fame: Freed's work at MGM made him the most successful musical producer in the history of motion pictures. The Arthur Freed unit became synonymous with musical excellence.

Early career: A vaudeville performer, Freed moved to Hollywood in the wake of the sound revolution and established himself as a lyricist (usually working alongside Nacio Herb Brown).

Songs: Freed and Brown's compositions include 'You are my Lucky Star' and 'Singin' in the Rain'.

First film: *The Wizard of Oz* (1939). His ability to spot and develop talent was revealed in his championing of Judy Garland for the lead role.

Films: Among the legendary musicals he produced are *Meet Me in St Louis* (1944), *Easter Parade* (1948), *Singin' in the Rain* (1952), *The Band Wagon* (1953) and *An American in Paris* (1951).

The stable: Those Freed brought to MGM included Gene Kelly, Fred Astaire, Busby Berkeley, Vincente Minnelli and Stanley Donen.

Freed broke with tradition in many ways. Although his films had stars, they were not star vehicles, as had been true of many of Hollywood's musical offerings. His goal was to create films of the highest quality, and he was respected for his ability to put together talented teams who worked together to create a unified product. Freed's use of choreographers also marked a change with established Hollywood practice. With a few exceptions (including Hermes Pan), the dance directors on Hollywood films were not dancers themselves. They had a technical understanding of filming and an artistic vision of the scene as a whole, but they did not necessarily choreograph the dances, leaving that to the dancers themselves. However, the choreographers used on Arthur Freed's films, who honed their skills on the stage where they could not exploit the artifice of film, placed more emphasis on the dance itself.

Some of Hollywood's established artists did some of their best work for Freed's unit: Judy Garland and Fred Astaire both produced superb performances, particularly in films directed by Vincente Minnelli. In several Freed films, such as *The Band*

'Garland was a true performer: she could deliver a song like no other singer of her generation ... She wasn't a dancer, but she could pick up a step instantly.'

Wagon (1953), Astaire found a partner in Cyd Charisse, whose long legs and balletic style complemented his own elegance.

Judy Garland (1922–69) is one of the artists most closely associated with the MGM musicals of the period. Like other successful performers of the time, she was born into a theatrical family and made her vaudeville debut when only a child. She made her film debut, for MGM, when she was 14 years old. After a series of all-singing, all-dancing 'Andy Rooney' films, in which she co-starred with Mickey Rooney, she made her star appearance in *The Wizard of Oz* (1939), produced by the Arthur Freed unit. She went on

Above: A 'couple of swells' – Fred Astaire and Judy Garland heavily disguised for the popular dance routine in the 1948 film *Easter Parade*.

opposite: Judy Garland (with Ray Bolger) in *The Wizard of Oz*, an early success for Arthur Freed, starting a long working relationship between the actress and producer.

Left: Fred Astaire and Cyd Charisse in *The Band Wagon* (1953), one of Freed's greatest films, with a magnificent score and choreography.

to make many other films for Freed, including *Girl Crazy* (1943), *Meet Me in St Louis* (1944) and *The Pirate* (1948), and married Vincente Minnelli, director of some of Freed's best musicals.

Garland was a true performer: she could deliver a song like no other singer of her generation; and as Gene Kelly said, after they worked together on *For Me and My Gal* (1942): 'I was amazed at her skill. She knew every mark and every move … She wasn't a dancer, but she could pick up a step instantly.'

Easter Parade (1948) brought together Astaire and Garland, under the director Charles Walter, himself a former dancer and choreographer. Walter ensured that the dance numbers in the film, which were choreographed by Robert Alton, were conceived with the camera in mind. Astaire was actually a replacement for Gene Kelly, who broke his ankle one month into rehearsals, and the film features Astaire and Garland's ever-popular 'Couple of Swells' comic dance routine, in which they are dressed as two tramps, as well as some rapid-fire tapping by Ann Miller (see pages 107–109), who was making her first appearance in an MGM film, playing Garland's rival for Astaire's attention.

Right: Perhaps the most famous action shot of Gene Kelly, with the possible exception of the 'Singin' In The Rain' routine, from *An American In Paris* (1951).

Below: The groundbreaking sequence in *Anchors Aweigh* in which Gene Kelly performed with the 'Jerry' the mouse from the cartoon series Tom and Jerry.

'Kelly (1912–96) was a unique talent: he combined balletic form with an athletic style and acrobatic ability in an unmistakable whole.'

Although he missed out on *Easter Parade*, Gene Kelly's films for The Freed unit are among the best musicals that were ever made. Kelly (1912–96) was a unique talent: he combined balletic form with an athletic style and acrobatic ability in an unmistakable whole. Like many of the other big names in the Freed unit, Kelly began his career, both as a dancer and a choreographer,

on Broadway, where he came to fame in *Pal Joey* (1940). After arriving in Hollywood in 1942, he made his mark in a series of films for MGM, but his role in *Cover Girl* (1944), starring Rita Hayworth (see page 169), was the first that showed the depth of his talent. Kelly did some of the choreography himself, and the 'alter ego' dance, in which he dances with his reflection, is one of his more memorable cinematic moments. Kelly received his first Hollywood credit as a choreographer for *Anchors Aweigh* (1945), in which he danced with Jerry (the cartoon mouse of Tom and Jerry fame). After this film, Kelly joined the Navy and left Hollywood for two years.

When he returned to MGM, Kelly was a natural for the Arthur Freed stable, with which his first film was *Ziegfeld Follies* (1946), in which he danced 'The Babbitt and the Bromide' with Fred Astaire, their only screen appearance together. Kelly always disliked this routine, feeling that their dance styles did not harmonize and that he appeared the lesser dancer for that. He summarized their differences: 'Astaire represents the aristocracy when he dances – I represent the proletariat.'

Above: The two greatest dancers in Hollywood films, Gene Kelly and Fred Astaire, in a rare appearance together for *Ziegfeld Follies*.

Above: Gene Kelly and Leslie Caron in *An American in Paris*, which like *Oklahoma!* featured a lengthy dream ballet, choreographed to the music of Gershwin.

Opposite: Perhaps the most well-known dance sequence of all time, Gene Kelly's 'Singin' in the Rain' routine from the film of the same name.

Kelly gave one of his most rounded performances in *On the Town* (1949), perhaps because he had achieved his ambition to direct – he was co-director with Stanley Donen, himself a former dancer and choreographer. The movie was loosely based on a Broadway show of the same name, which had opened in 1944 with music by Leonard Bernstein and choreography by Jerome Robbins (see page 173). Little of Bernstein's score was retained in the Hollywood remake, and the dance numbers were re-choreographed by Kelly and Donen. *On the Town* broke new ground in terms of movie musicals, in that many of its scenes were filmed on location in New York City, a feat of technical wizardry. Kelly also included a de Mille-style ballet number, 'A Day in New York', which encompasses themes from the rest of the film.

A popular ballet was to feature even more significantly in *An American in Paris* (1951), which was directed by Vincente Minnelli and had music by George Gershwin. The film is considered by many to be Gene Kelly's masterpiece, and it closes with a 17-minute-long dream-sequence ballet set to Gershwin's symphonic piece of the same name. Each segment of the dance

'Kelly's dance to the title song, which sees him tapping through puddles, is one of the most joyous moments in movie musical history.'

GENE KELLY FACTFILE

Born: 23 August 1912

Died: 2 February 1996

Real name: Eugene Curran Kelly

Early career: Along with his brothers and sisters, began his career as one of the Five Kellys, a local vaudeville act. For a while, Gene and his brother Fred ran a dancing school in Pittsburgh, Pennsylvania.

Stage musicals: Made his name creating the part of 'Pal Joey' in the 1940 Broadway musical of the same name.

First film: *For Me and My Girl* (1942). Co-starred with Judy Garland.

Film credits: Among his most famous are *Cover Girl* (1944), *Anchors Aweigh* (1945), *On the Town* (1949) and *An American in Paris* (1951).

Singin' in the Rain: Co-directed and co-choreographed by Kelly, *Singin' in the Rain* (1952) was named the best musical of all time by the American Film Institute. Kelly's performance of the title song has become a seminal movie moment.

What he said: 'Astaire represents the aristocracy when he dances – I represent the proletariat.'

Above: Donald O'Connor and Gene Kelly in *Singin' in the Rain*; O'Connor nearly outshone Kelly with his own acrobatic routine 'Make 'em Laugh'.

was inspired by a different painting. In the Toulouse-Lautrec segment, for example, the movement was inspired by the image of the American jockey in the poster 'Du Chocolat', and other segments were inspired by various paintings by Utrillo, Manet, Rousseau, Van Gogh and Dufy. Although the dance style is balletic, it is also informed by Kelly's particularly American and athletic style.

Although the dance in *An American in Paris* is a cinematic classic, *Singin' in the Rain* is undoubtedly Kelly's most popular film, because a sense of fun pervades the whole. His dance to the title song, which sees him tapping through puddles, is one of the most joyous moments in movie musical history. *Singin' in the Rain* also features Donald O'Connor's superb comic routine, 'Make 'em Laugh'.

O'Connor was born in 1903 and his parents were circus and vaudeville performers. He joined the family act when he was only three years old, making his Hollywood debut when he was 13 years old. His comic gift was appreciated by the studios, and he worked steadily, including on a series of films in which he co-starred with a talking mule named Francis. O'Connor improvised the entire 'Make 'em Laugh' number, in which he is partnered by a headless dummy. Replete with acrobatic feats, which see him dancing off the walls and off planks carried through the set by stage-hands and being wrestled to the ground by the dummy, the routine is a comic masterpiece, instantly loved by audiences over the years. Ironically, the first version of the number was spoiled

'... O'Connor's "Make 'em Laugh" number ... is a comic masterpiece, instantly loved by audiences over the years.'

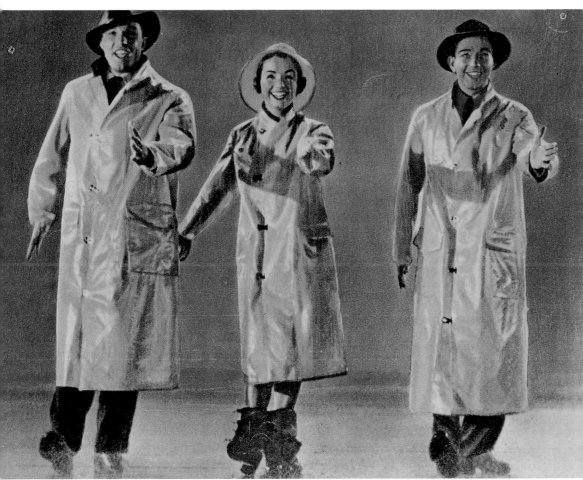

by second-rate film stock, and the version we see today is O'Connor's second take, which was made three days later.

One of the few 1940s musical stars not working in the MGM/Freed stable was Rita Hayworth (1918–87). The daughter of a Spanish dancer, she made her first stage appearance when she was six and her screen debut aged 16. Like Judy Garland, Hayworth could dance, but she was not a dancer *per se*: it was her star presence that set her films apart. The musicals she made for Columbia Pictures were distinguished by her erotic aura, and her siren image was encapsulated by the only dance number in the otherwise non-musical *Gilda* (1946), when Hayworth dances 'Put the Blame on Mame', choreographed by Jack Cole. Cole worked with Hayworth several times, bringing out the dangerous elements of her persona; when she worked with Hermes Pan, on the other hand, Hayworth could appear gentler and more romantic.

Above: Gene Kelly, Debbie Reynolds and Donald O'Connor in a publicity poster shot for *Singin' in the Rain*.

Right: Rita Hayworth in *Tonight and Every Night*, a tribute to London's Windmill Theatre, which 'never closed' throughout the Second World War, but which could barely be recognized in Hollywood's version.

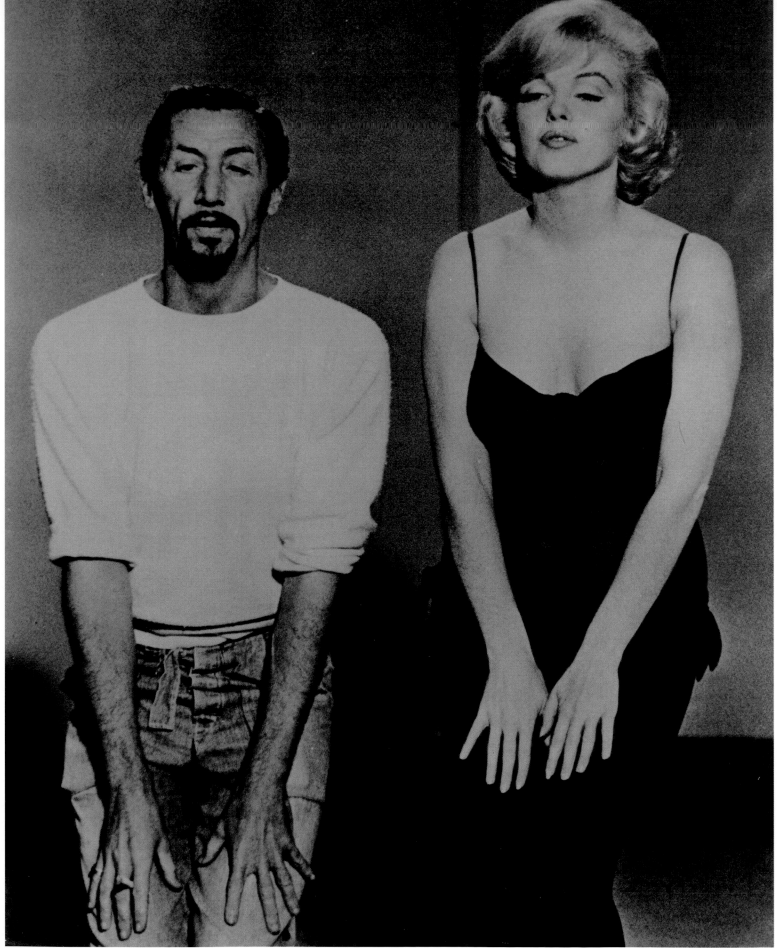

'... **by the 1950s even MGM's musicals were beginning to lose their fizz. After doing so much original work, the studios turned to making film adaptations of successful Broadway musicals ...'**

Cole (1914–74) was under contract at Columbia from 1944, running a permanent dance troupe for the studio. His dancers, who were also under contract, took classes for six hours a day, which kept them in top condition, and their energy and technical ability enlivened the dance routines in Columbia's otherwise mundane musicals. Cole's training programme included classical ballet as well as Eastern forms of dance, and his choreographic style was very dramatic, controlled and demanding, and he is sometimes credited with developing the first form of jazz dance ideally suited to musical theatre. In many ways, his work was rooted in vernacular dance, because he was strongly influenced by popular dance and folk dance and frequently said that all jazz dance was based on the lindy (see page 140), but his genius lay in his ability to take common movements and make them theatrical. His style, sensual and almost feline, was influenced by the rhythms of swing music, and there is a feeling of compressed energy behind the movement, which often erupts suddenly and dramatically yet nonetheless remains smooth and flowing.

Although Jack Cole was an important choreographer, admired by dancers and choreographers alike, he never became a household name, perhaps because he never had a huge hit to his credit. Nonetheless, his style lived on the work of the dancers he trained, including Gwen Verdon (see page 176), and his influence can be seen in the work of later choreographers, including Bob Fosse and Jerome Robbins. He imposed a high level of discipline upon his dancers and also stressed the importance of the motivation behind the movement, both qualities that made his dancers sought after by other choreographers. In addition to working frequently with Rita Hayworth, he was Marilyn Monroe's preferred choreographer, again bringing out the eroticism in her persona in dance numbers in such films as *Gentlemen Prefer Blondes* (1953) and *Let's Make Love* (1960). His emphasis on eroticism also shaped his choreography for a number of Broadway shows, including *Kismet* (1954).

Despite all this energy, by the 1950s even MGM's musicals were beginning to lose their fizz. After doing so much original work, the studios turned to making film adaptations of successful Broadway musicals, such as *Brigadoon* (1954), *Kismet* (1955) and *Kiss Me Kate* (1953). This last was notable as a star vehicle for Ann Miller(see page 109), but despite her abundant talent, Miller came to prominence in Hollywood musicals only after their heyday was passed.

Above: *Brigadoon* teamed Gene Kelly with Cyd Charisse in a fantasy about a Scottish ghost village, which just about manages to avoid Hollywood's clichéd view of the country.

Opposite: Jack Cole in 1960 coaching Marilyn Monroe for a dance sequence in the star's final film *Let's Make Love*.

Back to Broadway

Although Hollywood musicals were in the doldrums in the 1950s, that decade saw Broadway flourishing. Curiously, the first show of the decade was a musical that left the idea of integration far behind and returned to an earlier style of musical that favoured big, entertaining production numbers. *Gentlemen Prefer Blondes*, which opened at the Ziegfeld Theatre in December 1949, was a huge hit and made a star out of its leading lady, Carol Channing. Choreographer Agnes de Mille had thoroughly researched the vaudeville entertainments of the 1920s, and she presented skilful and appealing pastiches of the dances of the period: one show-stopper was a Gilda Gray-style shimmy (see page 38), another was a samba routine.

'Guys and Dolls ... opened in 1950 to universally rave reviews, with the critics uncharacteristically unable to find fault with any aspect of the show.'

Above left: Leading man Robert Alda helps fellow cast member Isabelle Bigley put her name in lights for the 1951 opening of *Guys and Dolls*.

Left: The all-star line up for the 1955 Hollywood version of *Guys and Dolls* with (left to right) Marlon Brando, Jean Simmons, Frank Sinatra and Vivian Blaine.

Right: Jerome Robbins demonstrating one of the most enduring images from the musical *West Side Story*, which he choreographed both on stage and in film.

Other shows continued the progression towards integration that marked the 1940s, however. *Guys and Dolls* was one such show, and the success not only of the original but of its many revivals testifies to its astute construction. Based on stories by Damon Runyon, the popular chronicler of New York City life, the show had music by Frank Loesser and choreography by Michael Kidd. It opened in 1950 to universally rave reviews, with the critics uncharacteristically unable to find fault with any aspect of the show. The dances worked to great effect to maintain the pace and flow of the plot: the first scene, a ballet portraying many aspects of New York City life, painted an indelible picture of the locale in which the show is set, and the nightclub dances made an essential contribution to the comic force of the show.

Michael Kidd (b.1919) was a leading Broadway and Hollywood choreographer with a string of successes to his name, including the Broadway hits *Finian's Rainbow* (1947) and *Can-Can* (1953), the show that launched Gwen Verdon (see page 176) to stardom. Kidd's choreography was credited with making a success of *Lil Abner* (1956), a musical based on a popular cartoon strip. In Hollywood he choreographed the film versions of such Broadway musicals as *Where's Charley?* (1952), *The Band Wagon* (1953), *Seven Brides for Seven Brothers* (1954), *Guys and Dolls* (1955) and *Hello Dolly!* (1969). His style was typically highly energetic and his dances always communicated a great deal of information about character or setting.

Another show that opened at the beginning of the decade, *The King and I* (1951), was a major success for the ground-breaking Broadway choreographer, Jerome Robbins (1918–98). The show became famous for the opulence of its sets and costumes, which in their glamour harked back to the earlier days of Broadway. Robbins's choreography was notable for its beauty and grace as well as its gently comic elements.

Robbins himself trained as a dancer and had performed in the chorus of several Broadway shows before turning to choreography. Throughout his career he worked both for the ballet and for the popular stage, and his work was marked by a cross-fertilization of ideas from the two forms. In fact, his first ballet, *Fancy Free* (1944), the story of three sailors on shore leave during the Second World War, was the impetus behind the Broadway musical *On the Town*, which became the hit film starring Gene Kelly.

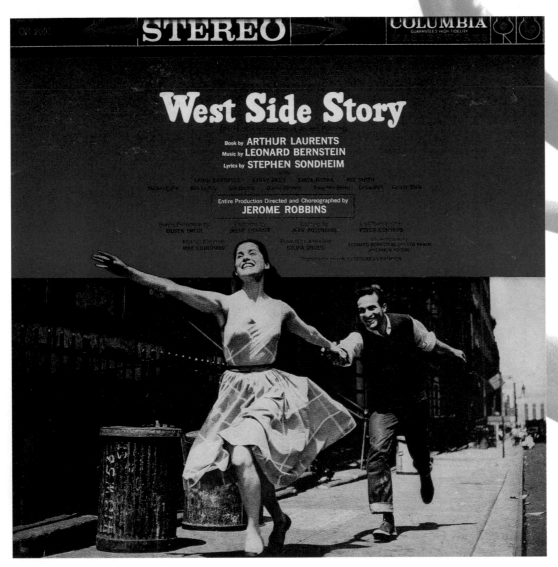

'The dances in *West Side Story* created an image of the American teenager of the period – loose-limbed but tightly coiled, wary but studiously casual at the same time – that has long endured.'

above: The album cover for *West Side Story*, a reworking of Romeo and Juliet, with music by Leonard Bernstein and lyrics by Stephen Sondheim.

Robbins worked on a number of Broadway musicals, including *Wonderful Town* (1953) and *Fiddler on the Roof* (1964), but his most enduring contribution was his choreography for the landmark show, *West Side Story* (1957).

West Side Story's dances created an image of the American teenager of the period – loose-limbed but tightly coiled, wary but studiously casual – that has long endured. In addition, the dances have been rightly credited not only with advancing the plot, but also in creating the atmosphere of excitement and tension essential to the piece, a contemporary take on Shakespeare's *Romeo and Juliet* that presented a doomed love affair between two young people allied with rival New York City street gangs. Combining elements of ballet as well as contemporary popular dance, including the mambo and be-bop, the dance movements

were vigorous and brutal, expressive of the edgy life of the street gangs, and the fight scenes, conveyed in dance form, electrified the audience. In fact, the dances, as well as the songs, contained so much information that the book (the spoken word content) of the show is quite short compared with that of other musicals.

Robbins was an exacting and demanding choreographer. He insisted that his dancers produce work of the highest quality, not only in terms of dance technique but also in expressiveness – that is, they had to act as well as dance. But his high standards paid off, as contemporary critics hailed the dances as the high points of the show, which was criticized by many for portraying the seamy side of New York City life in a realistic manner.

West Side Story made the move to Hollywood, reasonably unscathed, in 1961, perhaps because Robbins was co-director.

He was co-director or director on other successful Broadway shows, including *The Pajama Game* (1954) and *Gypsy* (1959).

The transformation of choreographer to co-director or director was a logical extension of the idea of the integrated musical. As song-and-dance routines played an increasingly important role in conveying information about plot and character and in driving the plot, it became natural for the choreographer to have a great deal of control over the whole work, not just the dance segments, in order to ensure that the show was truly 'integrated'. This was an aspect of the musical that Gene Kelly (see pages 164–167) recognized early in his career, and he did more and more directing, both in Hollywood and on Broadway, later in his life. The choreographers who made the greatest impressions in the second half of the century, particularly Bob Fosse, generally made a point of obtaining a large degree of creative control over their projects.

Robbins was one of the driving forces who brought Broadway musicals to a new level: from the integrated musical to the concept musical. In an integrated musical the song and dance

Below: A shot of the original 1957 stage production of *West Side Story*. The spectacular dance sequences ensured its success and it still continues to be revived more than forty years on.

JEROME ROBBINS FACTFILE

Born: 11 October 1918

Died: 29 July 1998

Real name: Jerome Rabinowitz

Claim to fame: Along with George Balanchine and Agnes De Mille, pioneered the fusion of classical ballet and American Jazz dance in musical theatre.

Dance career: Began career dancing on Broadway. In 1940 he joined the (American) Ballet Theatre. Roles included 'Petrouchka'.

Classical choreography: Choreographed *Fancy Free*, his first ballet, in 1940. With music by Leonard Bernstein, *Fancy Free* became the template for the popular stage and screen musical, *On the Town*. Continued to choreograph for New York City Ballet throughout his life.

Stage musicals: *High Button Shoes* (1947), *The King and I* (1951), *The Pajama Game* (1954) and *Fiddler on the Roof* (1964).

Film: His numerous film credits include the groundbreaking *West Side Story* (1961), for which he won an Academy Award.

Legacy: His insistence on overall control of his projects allowed for greater integration between narrative and dance. Paved the way for director-choreographers like Bob Fosse.

'... think about Fosse and you immediately conjure up images of sexy women with heavy eyeliner, jutting hips, raised shoulders and limp wrists, and bowler hats ...'

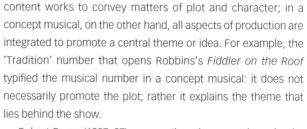

Below: Another great choreographer of stage and film was Bob Fosse, here leading the dancers in rehearsal for *Pleasures and Palaces* in 1965.

content works to convey matters of plot and character; in a concept musical, on the other hand, all aspects of production are integrated to promote a central theme or idea. For example, the 'Tradition' number that opens Robbins's *Fiddler on the Roof* typified the musical number in a concept musical: it does not necessarily promote the plot; rather it explains the theme that lies behind the show.

Robert Fosse (1927–87) was another choreographer who, by maintaining absolute control of all aspects of his work, took dance musicals to a new and exciting level. His choreographic style remains one of the most distinctive – think about Fosse and you immediately conjure up images of sexy women with heavy eyeliner, jutting hips, raised shoulders and limp wrists, and bowler hats.

Having studied dance, including tap, when he was at school, Fosse was influenced by his experiences performing in burlesque houses and strip clubs as a young man. After a spell performing in shows for the US Navy, he took chorus work in several touring productions before making his Broadway debut in 1950 in the revue, *Dance Me a Song*. He spent three years in New York, working in theatre, television and nightclubs, before venturing to Hollywood. In his third film, *Kiss Me, Kate* (1953), he was given the chance to choreograph a dance for himself and Carol Haney. This caught the eye of George Abbott, a writer and director who was putting together the team for the Broadway production of *The Pajama Game* (1954), and Abbott and co-director Jerome Robbins enlisted Fosse as choreographer. Fosse's routines were rapid and intricate, and one in particular, 'Steam Heat', was a real show-stopper. The show was a critical and popular success and set Fosse's career in motion.

Fosse's next job was as choreographer for the Broadway production of *Damn Yankees* (1955), a musical-comedy version of the Faust legend. It was on this show that he met Gwen Verdon, who was to become his first wife. (Although the marriage did not last, they remained close throughout their lives: in fact, Fosse died in Verdon's arms.) Verdon came to prominence through the Broadway production of *Can-Can* (1953). Although she only had a supporting role, she stole the show, particularly with her high-kicking Apache dance. The dances Fosse created for her in *Damn Yankees*, both the Broadway production and the Hollywood film, show her to her best advantage, and the two forged a remarkable creative partnership. Fosse choreographed or directed all of Verdon's shows from then on, and Verdon was

Left: Fosse with Gwen Verdon in *Damn Yankees*, a musical based on the Faust legend, that he directed in 1955 on Broadway.

Below: A poster for Fosse's film *Sweet Charity*, starring Shirley Maclaine, a musical that he had earlier directed on the Broadway stage.

his muse. She had worked for years with Jack Cole (see page 171), benefiting from his exacting training, and in her work with Fosse, she brought an understanding and mastery of dance technique to his creative vision.

From the late 1950s on, Fosse both directed and choreographed all the shows that he worked on with one exception, *How to Succeed in Business without Really Trying* (1961), which was directed by Abe Burrows, who had worked on *Guys and Dolls*. Fosse's tight control over his work was a key factor in his success, as he was able to impose fully his creative concept. In fact, his work, both in film and theatre, is remarkable for its depth of vision – a Fosse show is immediately recognizable as such. He

BOB FOSSE FACTFILE

Born: 23 June 1927

Died: 23 September 1987

Early career: Toured with his own dance act, the Riff Brothers, when still only 13. His early burlesque experiences heavily influenced his choreographic style.

Dance career: Worked on Broadway and in Hollywood. Film appearances included *Damn Yankees* (1958) and *Kiss Me Kate* (1953).

First choreography: Choreographed the original production of *The Pajama Game* (1954). His innovative presentation of the number 'Steam Heat' introduced the suggestive style that became his trademark.

Stage musicals: Redefined the role of director/choreographer with shows like *Damn Yankees* (1955), *Sweet Charity* (1966), *Pippin* (1972) and *Chicago* (1975). The tribute show *Fosse* was a Broadway smash in 1999.

Film musicals: With *Sweet Charity* (1969) Fosse became the first choreographer since Busby Berkeley to have complete control over production. Won an Academy Award for *Cabaret* (1972).

All That Jazz: His last musical film, *All That Jazz* was thought to have been an autobiographical examination of his working practices and his personal relationships.

remains known for his portrayal of the wrong side of town, of the denizens of smoke-filled dance clubs and nightclubs. His staging was full of razzle dazzle, but behind that, the dance was captivating in its own right.

The benefits of the dual role of director-choreographer were evident in Fosse's Broadway staging of *Sweet Charity* (1966), which starred Gwen Verdon as a New York City dancehall hostess who longs for love and marriage but ends up with a broken heart. The dance routines were electric and atmospheric – in creating them, Fosse was able to call upon his experiences of performing in strip clubs. The show was an unqualified success, but the film version of *Sweet Charity* (1969), Fosse's first experience as a film director, was panned, being criticized for over-acting and indulgent camera work. Shirley MacLaine starred in the role that Gwen Verdon had originated, but she lacked Verdon's force of presence. Nonetheless, at a time when film musicals were in the doldrums, Fosse injected an element of excitement and innovation.

In his later film work as a director, Fosse was more disciplined, and his dance numbers were, as a result, allowed to shine. *Cabaret* (1972), his second film, returned Fosse to Hollywood's good books; the film won eight Oscars, including one for Fosse as best director. Again set in the sleazy show-business world familiar to Fosse, this time in Berlin, *Cabaret* boasted some of Fosse's most enduring dance imagery. The film *All that Jazz* (1979), a portrait of Joe Gideon, a workaholic, heavy smoking, heavy drinking choreographer (played by Roy Scheider), was assumed to be autobiographical. The hard-driven dance numbers, many featuring Ann Reinking, another of Fosse's leading ladies, were remarkable in their imagination and force.

Fosse also had some notable successes on Broadway, particularly with *Pippin* (1972) and *Chicago* (1975). On the former Fosse

'... at a time when film musicals were in the doldrums, Fosse injected an element of excitement and innovation.'

Right: Ann Reinking in *All That Jazz*, directed by Bob Fosse in 1979 and believed by many to be autobiographical.

Above: Liza Minnelli's most famous role in Fosse's most famous film, *Cabaret*, made in 1971 and set in the decadence of 1920s Berlin.

Right: *Chicago*, which Fosse brought to the stage in 1975, was one of his later successes and again starred Gwen Verdon, here with Chita Rivera.

was credited as director and choreographer, but it was said that he also wrote much of the script as well. *Pippin*'s construction was similar to that of a vaudeville show, with the life story of Pippin (or Pepin, son of French king Charlemagne) told in a series of song-and-dance routines, introduced by the Leading Player. Fosse was co-author, director and choreographer of *Chicago*, and the star was his favourite leading lady, Gwen Verdon. This show, which concerns the sleazy underbelly of Chicago, bore many similarities to his great success, *Cabaret*. It, too, was constructed like a vaudeville revue, with great song-and-dance routines, such as 'All That Jazz' and 'Razzle Dazzle', held together by a thin plot.

Fosse's sleazy, sensual style reflected how far show dancing had come since the innocent days of the 1950s. For so long the ultimate harbinger of romance, modern show choreography had to reflect something of the complexity, sexuality and anarchy of rock culture.

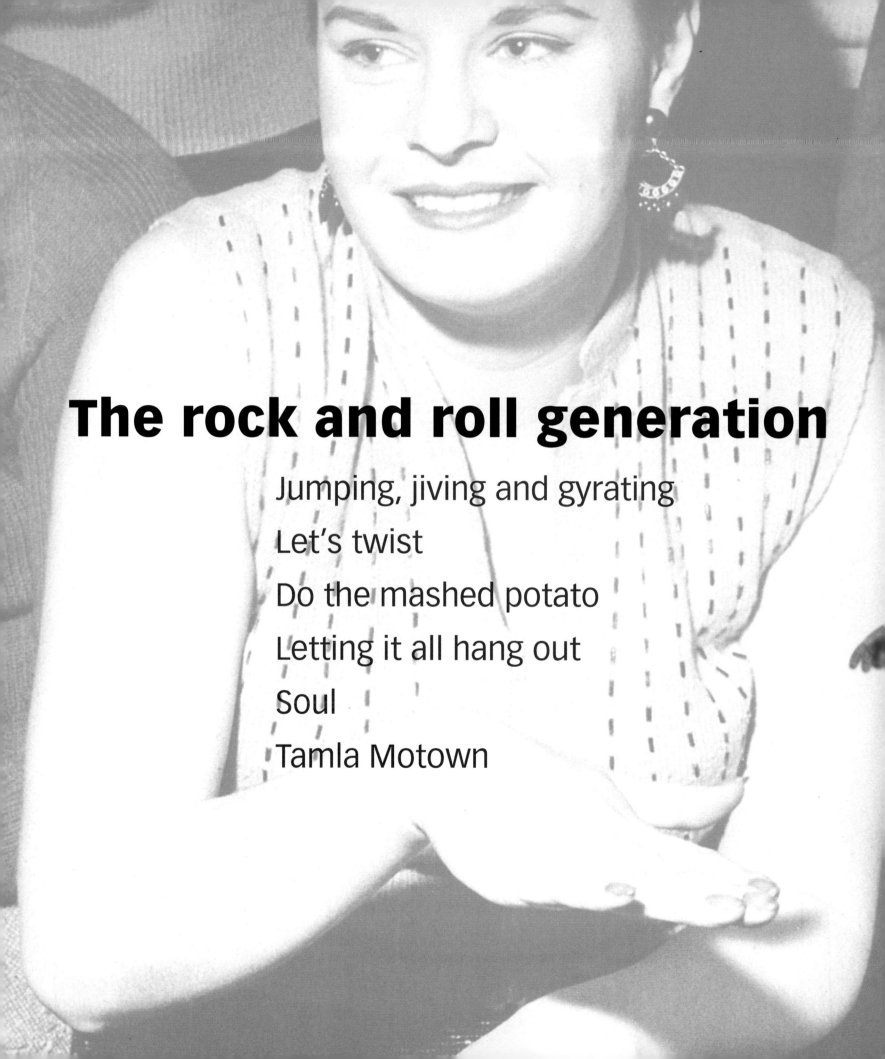

The rock and roll generation

Jumping, jiving and gyrating

Let's twist

Do the mashed potato

Letting it all hang out

Soul

Tamla Motown

Below: Even the well-respected Arthur Murray dance school business jumped on the rock'n'roll bandwagon in the Fifties.

The economic prosperity of the 1950s may have been a balm to the wounds of a generation forged in the furnace of two world wars and the most devastating economic depression the world has ever seen, but it was not an ideal environment for cultural innovation.

The rock and roll generation

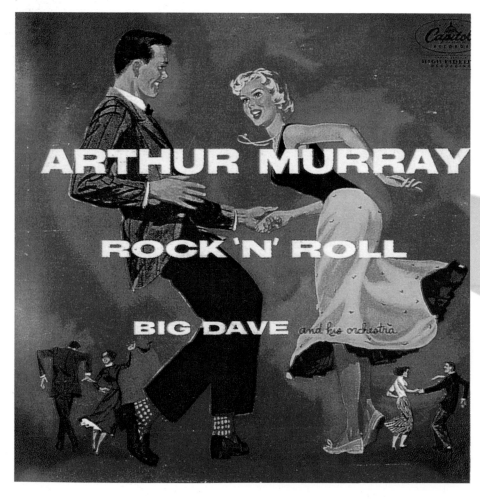

In North America, particularly, people were moving out of the urban centres into newly developed suburban sprawls, where back gardens took the place of the street and radio and television took the place of live entertainment. This suburban middle class was more prosperous than it had ever been before, and it wanted nothing to upset the bourgeois tranquillity, be it communism or jive. In this environment, where entertaining was more likely to happen in someone else's house than in the dancehall, dance music ceased to provide a soundtrack to most people's lives.

In the cities, too, dance was suffering from the complexities, and banalities, of the popular music scene. Bebop continued to plough its own furrow, and elsewhere the music scene was dominated by the treacly banalities of the popular crooners. On stage, traditionally the birthplace of new dance styles, cabaret was on the wane, and musical choreography was moving ever closer to the world of classical ballet. Social dancing, such as there was, had reached a degree of staleness and conventionality not seen since the days before the great ragtime boom. Within this stifling conformity a new voice was being heard, however. It was young, and (more importantly) it had economic clout. The 'teenager' had arrived.

Whatever the sociological reason, the post-war generation felt less pressure to ape the lifestyles of their parents. The concept of generational rebellion may not have been new – in dance it had always been an impetus in the evolution of new styles – but for the first time a large section of society had both the time and

Right: Cheap dance-driven exploitation movies didn't start with the rock'n'roll craze; this 1946 musical feature was a vehicle for Dizzy Gillespie and other jazz stars of the day.

Below: It seems strange that the apparently innocent, alcohol-free coffee bar and its juke box should have fostered rock and roll with its teen-rebellion image.

'Within this stifling conformity a new voice was being heard, however. It was young, and (more importantly) it had economic clout. The teenager had arrived.'

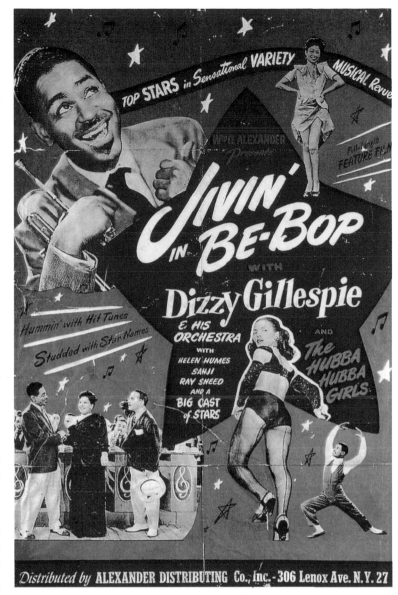

money with which to assert their collective identity. Furthermore, there was a variety of new media through which the young could celebrate their voice.

In the movies James Dean and Marlon Brando were immortalizing the image of broody teenage rebellion. On television *American Bandstand* and shows like it were beaming into every home the new styles and music, and anybody anywhere with a radio could tune into the hot sounds. For the first time new dance styles did not have to filter down from hotbeds of creative innovation such as the Savoy Ballroom or the Lafayette Theater in Harlem (see page 52). Rock and roll came into every home fully formed and professionally packaged. To be part of it you just had to be young and 'with it'.

Jumping, jiving and gyrating

Rock and roll did come from somewhere, of course – its roots lay in African-American culture – and swing had not suddenly ceased to exist with the arrival of Charlie Parker and 'Birdland'. Alongside bebop and the electrified blues of the industrial north, small rhythm and blues combos were plying their trade. Smaller and more compact, these bands began to offer brasher 'jump' blues, an energized combination of hard-driving rhythm sections and blues progressions, often featuring stomping horns or a wail-

ing sax. This was unapologetically dance music, and among the best known exponents of jump blues were Louis Jordan (1908–75) and 'Big Joe' Turner (1911–85), who originally wrote that seminal anthem of rock and roll, 'Shake, Rattle and Roll'.

Swing dance had not totally disappeared, either. It had evolved and cloned into a myriad of different forms and variations. The jitterbug, jive, boogie-woogie and the original lindy hop had all survived from the days of the big bands, but as a rule these styles required a fair amount of space in which to move. Now, these styles are grouped under the collective title of East Coast swing, but the decline of the large ballrooms, and the development of the smaller rhythm and blues bands resulted in the evolution of a tighter, more linear, dance style. This is West Coast swing, and it includes styles such as the push, the whip and the shag.

By the early 1950s nearly all swing dances had become loosely known as jive, a name that was used to refer to improvised swing dancing, much of it relying on individual expression as well as partnered steps. On the whole, this was a toned-down version of swing's boisterous past. The Madison was also

Above: Disc jockey and promoter Alan Freed, who pioneered the exposure of rhythm and blues and early rock and roll artists to a white teenage audience.

Right: Doing the Madison; rock and roll reaffirmed the role of dancing as part of the social ritual of boy-meets-girl, which had been the case in ballrooms and dancehalls since the turn of the century.

popular around this time. A unique set dance, that was performed in a line with its own distinct music, the Madison is one in a long line of novelty dances that sprinkle the century.

All these components then - jump blues, jive dance, teenage identity – came together to give birth to rock and roll. The father of rock and roll – or, at least the person credited with giving rhythm and blues a new title and selling it to white youngsters – was radio DJ Alan Freed (1922–65). When he was told by a local record producer that kids were buying rhythm and blues records in great numbers, Freed began giving the public what they wanted over the airwaves. On 11 July 1951 he began broadcasting 'Moon Dog's Rock and Roll Party' out of Cleveland, Ohio. According to legend, recognizing that the term rhythm and blues (which was still referred to in some quarters as 'race' music) might be off-putting, Freed gave his records the title 'rock 'n' roll'.

The origins of the term rock and roll are shrouded in myth. Ironically, for a phrase attempting to instil respectability, rock and roll was slang in the black community for sex, and this may have something to do with its suitability as a name for the new musical form. The visceral energy of the music was at least partly driven by testosterone. It may be that rock and roll was simply a phrase that cropped up in rhythm and blues music, such as Roy Brown's 'Good Rockin' Tonight' or 'Shake, Rattle and Roll', or it might be that rock and roll simply says it as it is – here was music to dance to.

It was impossible to stand still while listening to rock and roll: its strong accented beats practically demanded that those young fans who listened to it stood up and moved, whether they were in a dancehall, a cinema or simply their own bedrooms. The 'King'

'The "King" himself – Elvis Presley – always maintained that his pelvic gyrating was an honest response to how the music made him feel.'

Left: Elvis in 1956 in typical pose performing one of his many hits, songs that owed much to black American rhythm and blues music.

Above: For many, the man who epitomized the era of rock and roll was Elvis Presley, here dancing on stage with a member of the audience.

'The energy of Presley, Little Richard, Jerry Lee Lewis and the rest inevitably fed into the feet of those who danced to the new sound.'

himself – Elvis Presley – always maintained that his pelvic gyrating was an honest response to how the music made him feel. Others, of course, disagreed, and Presley appeared live on the Ed Sullivan television variety show filmed only from the waist up so as not to incite degenerate behaviour. With hindsight, it is possible to have some sympathy for Presley. Although those surrounding him were more than capable of harnessing teenage thrills for their own economic advantage, Presley was probably innocent of the accusation. 'Elvis the Pelvis' was instinctively reacting to how the music made him feel, as many musicians had done before – only this time, the musician, Elvis, was white.

By now, social dance had been flirting with the desire to drop the centre of gravity into the pelvis for more than 50 years. The mooche, Georgia grind and slow drag had been staples of African-American dance since well into the nineteenth century. Pelvic gyrations had been a principle part of Bert Williams's act 50 years before. He called it the mooche (see page 27). The mooche, and moves like it, had been present in the ragtime animal dance crazes (see pages 28–30) before the First World War, but they had been ironed out as the dances spread across sophisticated society. In the 1920s any visitor to the Cotton Club in Harlem could have seen an eccentric dancer who called himself 'Snake Hips' Tucker in honour of his act. Elvis Presley's dancing was not notorious because it was new – rather it was a physical manifestation

of what had happened in popular music. The black influence had ceased to be latent and had become overt instead.

The energy of Presley, Little Richard, Jerry Lee Lewis and the rest inevitably fed into the feet of those who danced to the new sound. Rock and roll dancing was basically swing dance, but with an audacity and sexual energy not seen since the early days of the lindy hop (see page 140). As with the early evolution of the lindy, the importance ceased to be in the footwork but in the air-steps. Dancers threw themselves around in what many thought outrageously provocative ways. Girls threw their legs around their partners' waists or slid between their partners' feet. The dancers would, literally, dance up, over and around each other, whole bodies gyrating. It was sexual, athletic and exhilarating.

Realizing that rock and roll was more than a passing craze and that it – and teenage rebellion – was here to stay, the entertainment industry set about taming it. From the outset, films such as *Rock Around the Clock*, *Don't Knock the Rock* and *The Girl Can't Help It* (all 1956) had helped to satisfy the appetite for rock and roll across North America and Europe, but without a doubt the major influence on the spread of its popularity was Dick Clark's television programme *American Bandstand*.

By 1956 popular records were played by radio stations across the country. In 1954 Texas Instruments had begun marketing the first transistor radio, and its size and portability meant that peo-

ple could listen to music at any time and anywhere. Most importantly, teenagers could get together and listen to the new sounds away from their parents. Television station WFIL in Philadelphia, Pennsylvania, hit on the idea of transferring this format to television. Presented by Bob Horn, a local disc jockey, *Bandstand* aired locally and featured an invited audience of local teenagers. The show proved successful, and in July 1956 another local DJ, Dick Clark, took over as the show's host. In 1957 it went nationwide, and such was the show's impact that Clark was still presenting *American Bandstand* more than 40 years later.

Unlike many of the popular music shows that followed in its footsteps, the local teenagers in *Bandstand* were not peripheral to the show, which was never simply a succession of bands plugging their latest records. Instead, the camera roved around the room, settling for a time on the teenagers as they danced, and many of the regulars become nationally renowned. Viewers looked for clues for romance as couples smooched to the slow number at the end of the show and watched for their favourites to see what they wore or how they did their hair. Dances and dancing was at the very heart of the programme.

Variant forms of swing dancing, including rock and roll, were the staple dances of *American Bandstand*, but in much the same way that street fashions were toned down for the show – jackets, pin ties and button-down shirts were de rigueur for the men – the

Above left: The set of the phenomenally popular *American Bandstand* television programme that brought the music of rock and roll to homes all over the USA.

Above: The presenter of *American Bandstand*, Dick Clark, seated with members of the audience during filming in 1960.

wild excesses of rock and roll dancing were also discouraged. Dick Clark, whose character in the show was that of the responsible elder brother, was a master of easing couples out of the limelight if necessary. (A satire of this can be seen in the 1970s musical *Grease*, see page 222, which has an amusing pastiche of Clark, his show and the dances that featured on it.)

The show regularly held dance contests, with simple rules that harked back to the dance marathons of the 1930s (see pages 134–135). The dancers were numbered, and the viewers cast their votes over several weeks, the winners being awarded a simple prize and piece of the limelight. The atmosphere was ripe for innovation, and over the years the show became an incubator for new styles and dance crazes. The bunny hop, the stroll and the calypso were among the dances that spread across the country from the studios in Philadelphia. The stroll is a good example of how a new dance could create a hit record. This was a slow line dance, inspired by the song 'C.C. Rider' by the 'King of the Stroll', Chuck Willis, and Clark suggested that songs be specifically created for the dance. The 1957 hit 'Lil Darlin'' by the Diamonds was a direct response to Clark's suggestion.

Let's twist

Dick Clark was much more than the compere of a TV show. He also used his influence on *Bandstand* to become a powerful player in a new and revitalized record industry.

More than even the transistor radio, popular music in the 1950s was transformed by the arrival of the 7-inch single. Hitherto popular music had been available only on clumsy 78 rpm records. The sound quality was poor, and the records themselves were fragile and did not lend themselves to being played at parties. The 45 rpm discs, on the other hand, were light, portable and extremely hard-wearing, and they could be popped into the bag of even the most rumbunctious teenager. More importantly, they were relatively easy to produce, and the cheap manufacturing process meant that a new, independent record company had a good chance of competing with the big boys of the industry. For all these companies, radio or television air-time was a vital component of a disc's success, and Dick Clark soon realized that he controlled access to the most important air-time in the business.

By the end of the decade Clark owned, or had interests, in some 33 companies related to the music business, and he used his position to promote and review records that he himself had

Left: Chubby Checker exploited the twist craze to the limit with what seemed like endless variations on the theme.

Opposite: Chubby Checker, whose version of 'The Twist' inspired the worldwide dance craze, the success of which owed much to how easy it was to perform.

helped to produce. In 1959 he admitted to having a 27 per cent stake in every record promoted on his show. He was not alone, and the resulting 'payola' scandal ruined the career of his contemporary, Alan Freed. Although Clark escaped from the Senate hearings with his reputation intact, he still had to relinquish more than $8 million worth of music-business investments. Clark was a shrewd operator, however, and he continued to promote acts and to lever them on to his show. One of these acts was a little known chicken-plucker from Philadelphia known as Chubby Checker.

Chubby Checker was born Ernest Evans on 3 October 1941 in Philadelphia. In 1959, while working in a poultry market, he made his first record, 'The Class'. It was after this that he became one of a series of artists who enjoyed the patronage of Dick Clark and the local independent label, Cameo-Parkway. Checker's moniker, Chubby – a deliberate allusion to Fats Domino – was even said to have been given to him by Clark's wife. Checker recorded a second single, 'The Twist', and was then duly 'discovered' on *American Bandstand*. The number had originally been recorded by Hank Ballard and the Midnighters, but Checker created a bright and breezy version of the song. In the tradition of

'... popular music in the 1950s was transformed by the arrival of the 7-inch single.'

CHUBBY CHECKER FACTFILE

Born: 3 October 1941

Real Name: Ernest Evans

Nickname: 'Chubby' is said to have been suggested by the wife of TV presenter Dick Clark.

Early career: An obscure chicken plucker from Philadelphia, Pennsylvania, Checker's first record, 'The Class' (1959) brought him to the attention of the impresario Dick Clark.

The twist: Checker recorded a cover of Hank Ballard's 'The Twist' (1960) and presented it on Clark's *American Bandstand* with his own unique performance. The record went to the top of the charts and sparked a dancing sensation. Its success led to a host of imitations.

Other records: Between 1959 and 1964 Checker had more than 20 Top-40 hits in the US alone. Among them were 'Boogie Woogie' (1962), 'Let's Twist Again' (1963) and 'The Hucklebuck' (1960).

Key to success: Checker's breezy performances mirrored the spirit and style of the dance.

Fact: 'The Twist' is the only record to reach No 1 in the US charts in separate years when performed by the original artist.

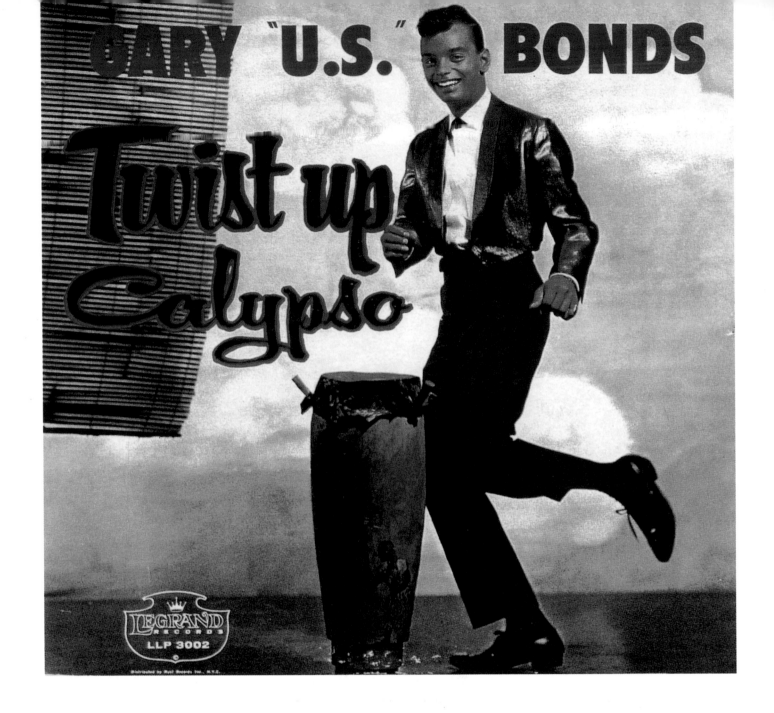

GARY "U.S." BONDS

Twist up Calypso

LEGRAND
RECORDS
LLP 3002

Above: Gary 'U.S.' Bonds, whose biggest hit was 'Quarter To Three', in 1961, attempted this twist-and-calypso cash-in.

the show, the record was designed to encourage a brief craze for the dance that went with it. Instead, the dance became a worldwide phenomenon.

The twist was the culmination of more than 50 years of social dance evolution. Throughout the century, countless dance styles had encouraged dancers to move away from close-couple holds and to express themselves individually. Always, however, a semblance of couple dancing had survived. Even rock and roll dancers held each other's hands, if only by the fingertips. Now, finally, a dance had arrived that did not require a partner at all. At no point during its execution did one dancer need to touch another. The twist could be danced alone.

The dance that Checker demonstrated on *Bandstand* in 1960 could not have been easier to do. With one foot forward, the

dancer swivels the foot as if stubbing out a cigarette, while simultaneously swinging the hips. The arms rock from side to side as if towelling the back after a shower. And that is it. It was easy, took no time to learn, and could be done by anyone at any time. The twist was the first dance that could be performed as easily in the privacy of the bedroom as in the busiest of dancehalls. The steps, the look, the sensation, would be exactly the same.

'The Twist' single reached the top of the US charts for two years running. In 1962 it crossed the Atlantic and proved nearly as successful in Britain. It was followed by 'Boogie Woogie' and 'Let's Twist Again', which cemented Checker's and the dance's reputation around the world. In the immediate pre-Beatles era, Chubby Checker became one of showbusiness's biggest draws, although other artists were producing twist records and feeding

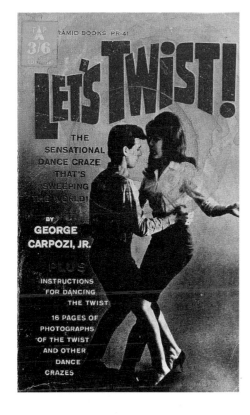

the international craze. Some of these records were simply old rhythm and blues records cleaned up and repackaged; others were original songs aiming to cash in on the craze. The Isley Brothers' 'Twist and Shout' and Sam Cooke's 'Twisting the Night Away' were, perhaps, the best known.

The twist was more than just a teenage fad. Checker's singles kept resurfacing in the music charts because the dance was taken up by successive generations. In fact, the twist marks a turning point in popular entertainment – from now on rock and roll music and dance would have mass cross-generational appeal. In this respect it prepared the ground for the Beatles and the beat invasion. The twist was a more hyped and commercially packaged dance craze than any that had gone before, and in addition to records, shops sold everything from twist ties to twist shoes. One paperback book, called *Doing the Twist*, sold 125,000 copies in 10 days. A New York club called the Peppermint Lounge became the centre of the phenomenon. Here, everyone from Arthur Murray to Greta Garbo came to twist their hips and, more importantly, to be seen doing so. Joey Dee and the Midnighters even had a hit single entitled 'Peppermint Twist'. Joey Dee was one of the club's nightly attractions.

'The twist was the culmination of more than 50 years of social dance evolution.... Now, finally, a dance had arrived that did not require a partner at all.'

Above left: In view of its simplicity, the dance seems unlikely subject matter for books, but that clearly didn't trouble writer George Carpozi Jr.

Left: Although they only made one twist record, a cover version of the Isley Brothers' 'Twist And Shout', the Beatles were not above doing it, as Ringo Starr showed in 1964.

**DANCE CRAZES OF THE
1950S AND 1960S**

The frug: Evolution of the Twist. The foot-work ceased and arm movements began to compensate for less movement in the hips. Also known as the surf, big sea and the thunderbird.

The hand jive: Widely practised by those who wouldn't or couldn't dance and made famous by Johnny Otis's 'Willie and the Hand Jive' (1958). It was also covered by British artists Cliff Richard and Eric Clapton.

The Madison: Best known 1950s 'group' or 'gang' dance. Couples danced in a line. Others included the bop, the jet and the locomotion.

The mashed potato: Another pan-tomimic offspring of the Twist. The name comes from the movement of the arms and hands. Some claim it is reminiscent of the Charleston.

The stroll: 1950s dance created by seminal US TV show 'American Band-stand'. Slow line dance inspired by the 'King of Stroll' Chuck Willis and the 1957 song 'Lil' Darlin'' by the Diamonds.

The twist: Chubby Checker's gift to the world. The most famous dance of the gen-eration. Couldn't be easier: twist your foot as if you are stubbing out a cigarette and pretend to towel your back.

Do the mashed potato

The twist inevitably spawned a host of similar dances, mimetic in quality and sporting animal or alliterative names, and with these the dance scene took on an uncanny resemblance to the animal dance craze seen before the First World War. (There was even a resurgence of the turkey trot; see pages 29–30) As simple and straightforward as the original, these dances had names that gave an indication of their performance. The mashed potato required imaginary mashing of spuds; the pony called for the knees to be raised in the manner of a trotting horse; the Marilyn was an imitation of Marilyn Monroe's wiggle. Others, such as the frug, the boogaloo, the slop and the watusi, were distinguished by variations so small as to be nearly negligible. Checker, too, tried to prolong the craze by cutting records to match his new dance ideas, but the likes of 'The Fly' (1961) and 'Limbo Rock' (1962) failed to catch the public imagination.

'Although the twist had led to a revolution in the way people danced, the music itself was nothing new.'

Although the twist had led to a revolution in the way people danced, the music itself was nothing new. However, the music scene was about to be taken over by the 'beat' generation and Checker's breezy records would be unable to compete. Solo dancing, however, was here to stay.

Critics decried solo dancing. They claimed that it was a manifestation of the individual's isolated position within a modern and fractured society. This was not, however, how the dancers saw it.

Practitioners of the twist and other solo dances believed they felt more aware of their peers than ever before (at least in the twentieth century). A couple dancing the waltz can dance together all night if they wish, oblivious to their surroundings. Someone dancing the twist cannot fail to be aware of the other dancers surrounding him or her. A dancer's loyalty was no longer to the partner but to the group.

Above: The hand jive, a 'dance' for those of a less energetic bent, was part of the solo dancing phenomenon influenced by the twist.

Opposite: The style of the twist, and its absurdity, led to a whole series of dances with peculiar names and movements, like the mashed potato.

Right: Slightly more durable than some of the early 60s dances was Little Eva's the locomotion, which sometimes gets an airing in discos even today.

Far right: From the mid-60s, a now-forgotten novelty was the swim.

Above: Although the Beatles made no real attempt to create dances themselves, unlike other groups of their era, their music was still eminently danceable.

'Ultimately, the style in which one danced to the Beatles was not as important as the simple fact that one was dancing at all.'

Letting it all hang out

Group identity was one of the defining qualities of the 1960s. People became defined by where they stood in relation to the group, whether it was a rock band, a generation or a political movement. Politics, sex and rebellion all became entwined, and ultimately, the style in which one danced to the Beatles was not as important as the simple fact that one was dancing at all. Rock bands did not simply offer dance music: they were the focus of dreams and rebellion. This may be a reason why the 1960s failed to produce a distinctive dance style. The British sound that led the decade certainly demanded physical expression, but it could be as unique and personal as the idols who created it. Like the pop artists of the time, pop groups took aspects of everyday culture and reworked and repackaged them in order to kick against the doors of con-

vention. Language, fashion, music and dance were all enlisted to sell the idea, and dancing, therefore, became a means of self-expression – as freeform as the music to which it was allied.

A dance like the shake is a good example of this progression. One of a host of dances that appeared in the wake of the twist, the shake was an ill-defined dance, requiring little more than a frenzied shaking of the whole body. It was, if anything, a modern incarnation of the shimmy (see page 38), and in the early 1960s it seemed as loose and unstructured as any dance could get. Yet by the end of the decade, although the dance remained, the name had been dropped. Revellers in the counterculture in San Francisco and members of the underground clubs of Paris and London still shook their bodies wildly, but they no longer thought of themselves as participating in a dance. They were simply responding to the sound in the moment. For the time being, dancers had given up imitating styles and become their own personal choreographers.

The LP, too, had taken over from the 45 rpm single as the premier means of expression in the music industry. Bands were pushing back the boundaries of what was possible within the format of the traditional single. Tracks were getting longer and longer. When the British band Cream went to the United States in the mid-1960s, for example, they fully intended to survive as a regular blues band. However, they ran straight into a counterculture that craved long, improvisational compositions, and they ended up stretching out numbers to more than an hour.

Left: By the end of the 1960s, there was no longer any form to dancing, and young people just moved their bodies to the music in whatever way they wanted.

Below: Rock fans inspired by the music to revive the ancient tradition of circle dancing while attending a festival near Stonehenge in 1978.

In this environment traditional rituals of social dancing no longer applied. You could dance for as long or as short a time as you wished. If you left the dance floor, the chances were that the same track would be playing when you returned. No one was dancing specific steps; everyone was improvising their own response. It was the ultimate free-for-all. (In fact, the great rock festivals of the era saw a brief flowering of medieval European folk dances, such as the carole, or chain dance, and the farandole, but this seems to have been an isolated phenomenon, a direct response to the conditions and emotions of the environment.)

In the event, the freeform dance styles that came with advanced rock culture would not have a lasting effect on social dancing. Far more influential was soul music and the black vernacular traditions within it.

Soul

Soul music was built on strong and proven musical traditions. Whereas rock and roll took rhythm and blues and mixed it with the blues and hillbilly music to produce its sound, soul music was the logical extension of mixing rhythm and blues with gospel and doo-wop. It was an undeniably black sound, and it was full of the pride and struggle of the culture. As the decade progressed, it became a primary means of raising black consciousness, and, as such, it came directly from the heart of the urban centres of the United States.

The most significant dance innovator to emerge from the soul scene is James Brown (b.1933). Along with his illustrious contemporaries such as Ray Charles and Otis Redding, Brown epitomizes the raw emotion of the southern Memphis sound. The gospel tradition present in soul music was present in Brown's stage act as well, and his stage persona was an exhilarating mixture of revivalist preacher and in-your-face entertainer. The physical exertion this former boxer brought to his act more than justified his sobriquet 'the hardest working man in show business'.

To songs such as 'I Got You (I Feel Good)' (1965), 'It's a Man's, Man's, Man's World' (1966) and 'Say It Loud, I'm Black and I'm

'James Brown owed as much of his success to the Nicholas Brothers and the Berry Brothers as he did to rhythm and blues.'

Left: The charismatic James Brown on stage at Buffalo Bill's Hotel Casino in Las Vegas in 1998, still giving his audience one hundred per cent.

Left: Soul singers and musicians often carried out energetic dance routines as they performed, as illustrated here by James Brown.

Below: Motown founder and supremo Berry Gordy (bearded, second right) with singing superstar Diana Ross in 1971.

Proud' (1968), Brown would dance with prodigious energy. He could slide across the stage on one foot, then spin and drop into the splits. He would drop on to his knees and implore the audience and the microphone to take pity on his soul. It was brash and theatrical and owed not a little to the acrobatic dance acts of the tap era – James Brown owed as much of his success to the Nicholas Brothers and the Berry Brothers as he did to rhythm and blues.

Brown's influence has been huge. His moves and attitude directly influenced performers from right across the rock spectrum, most notably Mick Jagger and Michael Jackson. His live performance of 'Get on the Good Foot' (1972) was so widely copied that a dance known as the good foot developed in New York City, and the early imitation of Brown's style, involving primitive drops, spins and knee bends, were to become the catalyst for the breakdancing culture of the 1970s and 1980s (see page 236). His stage act was ahead of its time. This mixture of raw emotion and intense physicality was both the key to James Brown's success and the reason for his failure to attract a mass audience. In the 1960s Middle America was still close enough to the civil rights debate to find James Brown threatening. Instead soul music found mass appeal through the lush, cultivated sound of Tamla Motown.

Tamla Motown

Ironically, the raw southern soul sound was presented to the public by way of white-owned record labels. Motown, which offered white America a smoother version of soul music, was a solely black enterprise. It was the brainchild of Berry Gordy Jr (b.1929), who believed as much in African-American hard work and self-reliance as he did in good music. He set in place a production line that discovered, packaged and distributed soul music to the world, and by the close of the 1960s Motown was the largest black-owned corporation in the United States.

Gordy built his success on a specific formula: the need for a song would be identified; the streets of Gordy's native Detroit, Michigan, would be scoured for talent; and an act or group would be developed. Once a song had been provided – often by the phenomenally successful writing team of Brian and Eddie Holland and Lamont Dozier – it was recorded with the help of Motown's

Below: Perhaps the most memorable of the Motown acts in the 60s were the Supremes, whose lead singer Diana Ross is still a major star.

in-house musicians. Then, while the song was mixed and produced, the talent was coached, trained and 'finished' in order to go out and perform the record with suitable aplomb. It was a production line, reminiscent of Tin Pan Alley or the Brill Building, and it was very successful.

Dance played a central part in Motown's finishing school. The Motown sound owed a great deal to the doo-wop tradition, in which a singer would offer an expressive vocal line (usually telling of love lost or love unrequited), and a collection of background singers responded with close vocal harmonies. Numerous doo-wop groups had sprung up in the 1950s, only to have one hit single and then disappear without trace. One of the reasons for this was the inability of many of the groups to present themselves onstage in an interesting fashion. Doo-wop, by its very nature, required the performers to be onstage alone. In the studio a recording can be helped with a little instrumentation, but on stage the singers had no guitars or pianos to hide behind. Doo-wop acts had to perform.

Gordy realized that his Motown acts, which were mostly vocal groups, required training to help them perform in the spotlight. The man he brought into his organization to help coach these new acts was Cholly Atkins, one half of the tap team, Coles and Atkins (see pages 110–111). Coles and Atkins were the doyens of tap's class acts, and they were unsurpassed in mixing grace, class and sophistication with precision dancing. Atkins brought these same qualities to Motown.

Moves, steps and ideas were resurrected, revamped, and worked into the acts. With this training, groups such as the Four Tops, the Temptations and the Supremes presented sophisticated stage acts that placed before a new generation many of the classic styles of African-American jazz dance. Background vocal-

Above: With hits like 'Can't Help Myself' and 'Reach Out I'll Be There', the Four Tops came to epitomize the Motown male vocal group.

Opposite: The Contours were an early name on the Motown-related Gordy label, whose 'Do You Love Me' made the No 3 spot in the US pop charts in 1962.

ists moved together with intricate precision steps, and the steps that accompanied their vocals were variations on, among others, the camel walk, suzy-q and trucking. To give one example of this, the suzy-q – which consists of clasping the hands in front of the knees, bending the body from the waist and moving sideways with your arms swinging in opposition – had been a staple of tap dance acts back in the 1930s. What was new was seeing the ways in which these jazz dance styles could adapt to soul music.

Another popular move with the Motown acts was the boogie-woogie. Again, this was a jazz dance from an earlier generation, but its signature move – knees together while the hips sway from side to side and the dancer moves forward – can be found in mambo and the cha-cha-cha. This is an important point, because the next leap forward in social dancing would be characterized by the combination of Latin with rock and roll dancing. Disco, that last great wave of the couple-dancing tradition, is a direct result of the fusion of Latin dancing with the African-American tradition.

'... the Four Tops, the Temptations and the Supremes presented sophisticated stage acts that placed before a new generation many of the classic styles of African-American jazz dance.'

Night fever

Although rock and roll was a revolution, it was largely a white, suburban revolution. The music may have borrowed elements of black rhythms and blues, but it was played by white musicians, and as it evolved, it became music that was listened to rather than music that was danced to. While all this was going on, however, rhythm and blues music survived intact, and in the urban centres of New York, Philadelphia and Miami the beat was strong, and the music, influenced by African and Latino rhythms, demanded that people got on to the dance floor.

Night fever

The disco scene

While hippies and rockers were doing their freeform thing at concerts throughout the late 1960s, glamour was reasserting itself in cities in the US and Europe. Jetsetters were pictured in newspapers and magazines moving in and out of the top clubs in major European and American cities, and in US cities teenagers, dressed in their finest, were going to discos and dancing the night away to soul music.

The term 'discotheque' was coined in Paris to be the name of a new club in the rue Huchette. It was a play on the word *bibliothèque* (library) because the new club relied on its library of records to provide the music rather than on live bands, and the term was popularized in the early 1960s by Chubby Checker's song of the same name. As the 1960s wore on, a number of discos in major cities came to prominence as the stomping grounds of the rich and famous: Arthur in New York City, Whisky A Go Go in London and Regine in Paris. These were plush, upmarket clubs, providing elegant dinners as well as dancing. But because there was no need to pay a live band to perform, the disco club format spread quickly: club owners found that the books were easier to balance, and club-goers anywhere and everywhere could dance to top-class music. This allowed everyone to enjoy a variation on the lifestyle of the rich and famous.

The music was shaped by DJs who combined records, sequencing them to create a rhythmically danceable unit so that

'Disco took its influences from across the spectrum of musical styles – jazz, rhythm and blues, soul, gospel and Latino – so there was a something to appeal to every audience, and as it spread, it inspired a sea-change in the music business.'

The Commodores blow the disco and its dancers into an all-new time zone – as only they know how!

THANK GOD IT'S FRIDAY.

A COLUMBIA PICTURES RELEASE

78007

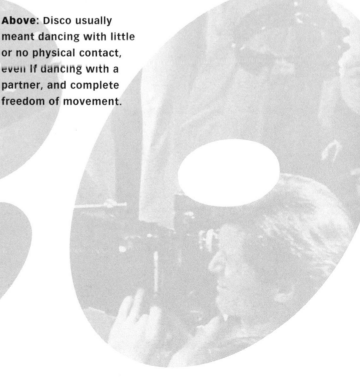

one record appeared to flow smoothly into another, to encourage dancers to stay on the floor for long periods. Each DJ had his own style, but the best could create a dance-oriented mix that was also thematically interesting. The mixes were hardly spontaneous, however, and DJs worked hard at their craft, trying out mixes during the day, scouring record shops and visiting each other's clubs to check out what the competition was up to.

By the early 1970s, as clubs started to proliferate, disco music began to carve out its own identity. Record labels began issuing longer versions of songs on 12-inch records, since the three-minute playtime of traditional 45s was too short to satisfy either DJs or dancers. The music was rhythmic and sensuous, often with lush orchestration, and the mood was uniformly upbeat. It was the antithesis of the popular rock and roll of the time and was based more on the music popular with minorities than with the white, middle-class mainstream.

Disco took its influences from across the spectrum of musical styles – jazz, rhythm and blues, soul, gospel and Latino – so there was a something to appeal to every audience, and as it spread, it

Above: Disco usually meant dancing with little or no physical contact, even if dancing with a partner, and complete freedom of movement.

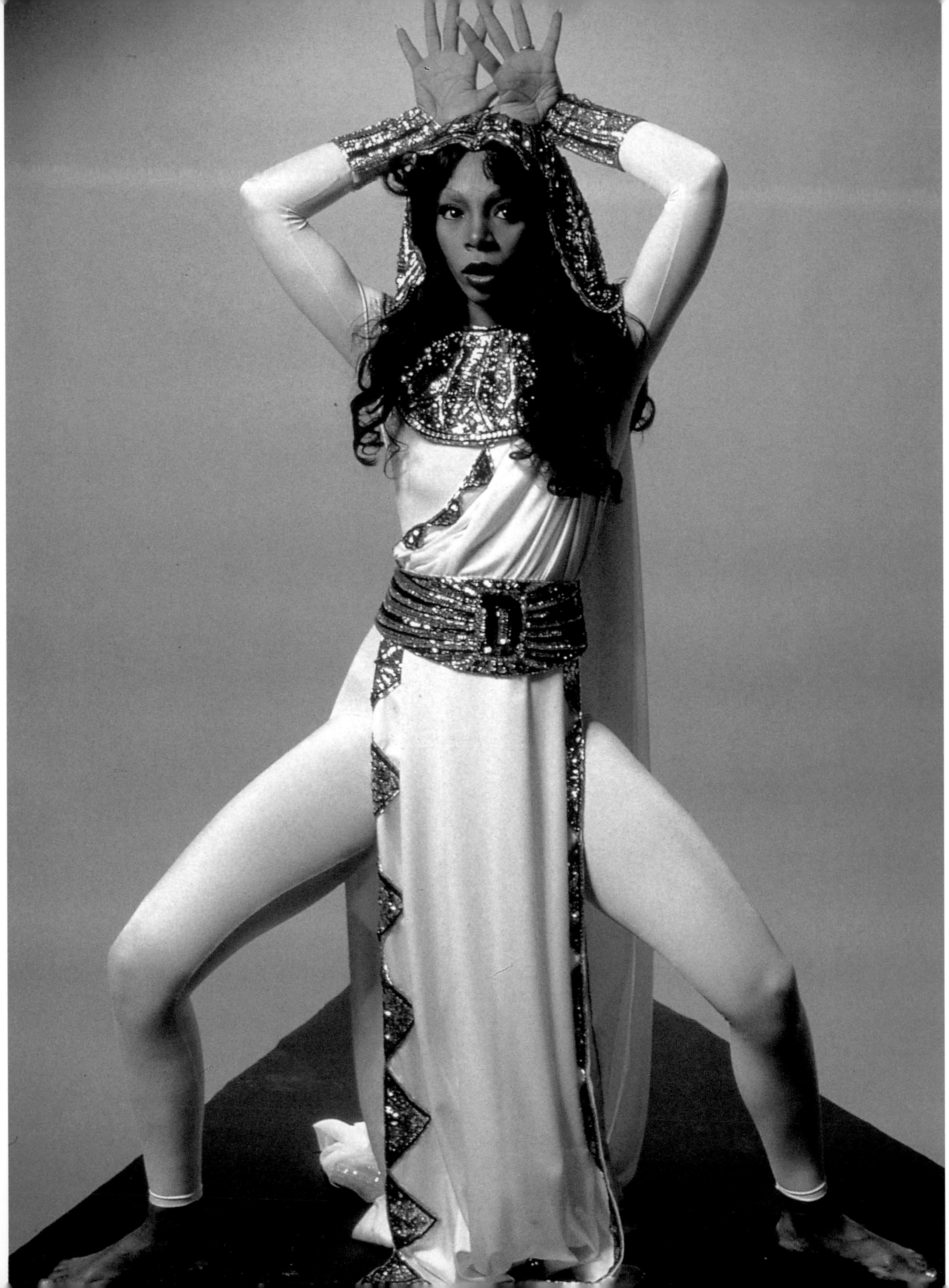

'... black sounds received little airtime on major stations ... record companies made little attempt to market it, firmly believing that such music would have only limited appeal.'

inspired a sea-change in the music business. Even as late as the 1960s, soul, rhythm and blues and other music by black artists was still being referred to as 'race music' in the record industry and the media, despite the fact that it was highly influential. As almost everyone knew, 'race music' had shaped the work of some of the most popular white musicians of the period, including Mick Jagger and Janis Joplin, but black sounds received little airtime on major stations, with the exception of those in urban centres or those with a major university as its listener base. The record companies made little attempt to market it, firmly believing that such music would have only limited appeal.

As disco became more popular, however, ethnic artists began to experience mainstream success. New labels emerged, such as Salsoul, which captured the Latino beat, and Philadelphia Sound for African-American artists. Gradually, these dance-oriented sounds began to emerge into the mass music market. By

Above: The Village People, creators of perhaps *the* disco record of the 1970s, 'YMCA', which took advantage of the acceptance of the gay music scene into the mainstream.

Opposite: The queen of disco in the 1970s, Donna Summer, had a string of hits with a driving beat deliberately aimed at the dance floor.

Night fever

1975 and the launch of the classic 'Love to Love You Baby', by 'disco diva' Donna Summer, the process was complete. Black disco artists such as Summer, Boney M and Grace Jones never knew what it was like to be marginalized. More established artists, such as Barry White, were no longer niche players but suddenly found their songs playing on major radio stations as well as in clubs across North America and Europe.

Even the gay music scene began to cross over to the mainstream, with Sylvester and the Village People achieving the highest profile. The gay community played a major role in shaping the disco sensibility, and the rise of disco was contemporaneous with the acceleration of the gay rights movement. Gay bars were illegal in New York City until 1965: it was against the law to serve liquor if there were more than three homosexuals present. Even after the law was changed, police harassment of gay clubs, as well as other clubs either owned or frequented by blacks and Hispanics, continued unabated. In reaction to this, in 1969 the Stonewall riots in New York City broke out, and in their aftermath the 1970s saw a new phase, when the gay rights movement shifted into a new and more activist phase and the gay community began to take a higher public profile.

During the 1960s, before Stonewall, there were many gay dance clubs, often with members-only policies to ensure that they were frequented by like-minded people. In the 1970s they no longer had to be secretive – although many remained exclusive by choice – and the gay clubs had well-deserved reputations for outrageous atmospheres: they were places you could party through the night and where nearly any behaviour was acceptable as long as it was fun. Dancing was often near the top of the agenda, and many disco artists won gay followings.

The hedonistic gay lifestyle shaped the disco scene, and a camp aesthetic pervaded disco from the start. Later, as disco hit the mainstream, this campness offended many people, encouraging the 'disco sucks', white, straight and largely male backlash.

Do the hustle

No matter who they were or where they were coming from, what all disco aficionados had in common was a love of dance. But this dance fashion was radically different from what their rock and roll contemporaries were up to. Rather than being wholly freeform and individualistic, much disco dancing relied on set steps and styles – and it marked a return to touch dancing.

Some of the most exciting dancing was taking place in the Latino clubs in New York City. Clear communication between partners was essential, and in a way not seen since the height of the lindy hop in the 1930s and 1940s (see page140) many hot dance couples spent hours practising together in private before taking to the dance floor.

Clubbers were dancing in this new style for some time before the new style was given a name. The story goes that in 1975 a New York City producer and musician, Van McCoy, was informed of a new dance fad by a DJ friend of his. As he watched a couple demonstrating the dance, McCoy was immediately inspired to write a song that suited the moves – this was the genesis of the song 'Do the Hustle', the formative track that gave the dance its name. The song, to a Latin beat with heavy rhythm and blues influences, became a hit in the US, rising to number one on the

Above: The hustler himself, Van McCoy, whose musical style owed a lot to the Latin American sounds that had been popular in the USA since before the Second World War.

DISCO HITS

'The Hustle': Van McCoy (1975). The track that started it all. Sold more than eight million copies and made the Hustle the biggest dance craze since the Twist.

'I Feel Love': Donna Summer (1977). The only disco diva to rival Gaynor's position at the top of the tree. 'I Feel Love' tapped into the growing electronic scene coming out of Europe and urban North America.

'I Will Survive': Gloria Gaynor (1979). Eternal anthem for the spurned lover. 'The First Lady of Disco', Gaynor's influences include Nat King Cole and Sarah Vaughan.

'Stayin' Alive': Bee Gees (1978). One of a clutch of Bee Gees classics that provided the spine to the *Saturday Night Fever* soundtrack, and linked the Gibb brothers with disco forever.

'YMCA': Village People (1978). Most famous representatives of the gay disco scene, 'YMCA' brought gay disco beyond the confines of the Sanctuary and Fire Island. Complete with de rigueur arm movements spelling out the letters.

'Structurally, the hustle is not unlike the lindy hop: it has a basic step structure, which is then enlivened by more elaborate improvised moves that are unique to each dancing couple.'

music charts and bringing the hustle before the general public.

The hustle was strongly influenced by the Latin dances that had been so popular earlier in the century, such as the rumba, the samba and the mambo. Structurally, the hustle is not unlike the lindy hop: it has a basic step structure, which is then enlivened by more elaborate improvised moves that are unique to each dancing couple. But its sensuality and rhythm give it a decidedly Latin feel. In addition, the man's moves can be as strikingly exhibitionist as the woman's, if not more so (think of John Travolta in *Saturday Night Fever*, overshadowing partner Karen Gorney), and this is, stylistically, more akin to the tango than the lindy.

Although there are many variants of the hustle – the New York hustle, the Latin hustle, the swing hustle, the tango hustle – the basic pattern of them all has certain structural similarities under-

Above: Couples dancing the freak, created in 1978 by a group called Chic with their song of the same name, and which was a development of the twist.

'Debate still rages among disco aficionados about which variation represents the purest form of the hustle.'

which the pattern was repeated.

Because there were set steps to many disco dances, dance schools began to offer lessons, and disco activity inspired a mini-renaissance in social dance teaching, which had gone into decline during the rock and roll years. In order to pass on instruction, teachers had to codify the dances, thus formalizing existing stylistic and regional variations. Debate still rages among disco aficionados about which variation represents the purest form of the hustle.

lying the stylistic differences. Essentially, the hustle is a three-count dance that is danced to four-count music, which means that the dance has to cut across the beat of the music, giving it great creative potential. Couples begin by dancing together in the traditional social dance position, with one partner the leader. Once a basic pattern is established, the fun can begin, as dancers elaborate the pattern, adding spins and lifts, separating and joining together again.

Other less intricate dances were also done. The bump was popular because, although it was a partner dance, involving physical contact and requiring communication between the two dancers, anyone could do it: it simply involved bumping against the partner on the beat, starting with the hips and moving to other parts of the body.

Not all disco dancing was partner-oriented, however. Single dancing was also common, which meant that anyone could get out on the dance floor to join an existing group of dancers or even to dance alone among the crowd. Some individual dancing was freeform, taking its inspiration from the music. There were also established individual dance styles, such as the freak (which was popularized by a 1978 song of the same name by the band Chic), which was a slow, grinding version of the twist (see pages 189–191).

Disco also spawned a number of line dances. Like the hustle, they were based on a formal step pattern, but they were much more populist: even mediocre dancers who might have felt intimidated by the elaborate set pieces performed by adept hustle dancers were able to take to the floor and learn the simpler steps of line dances. The bus stop was probably the best known of the disco line dances: it consisted of three steps backwards, a clap and foot tap, three steps forwards, another clap and foot tap, then a variety of side steps, culminating in a quarter turn, after

Below: Manhattan's Studio 54 probably had no better facilities than many other clubs, except that it was highly fashionable, and somewhere that you could rub shoulders with the famous.

Studio 54

Disco was more than dance and music, however. It was a total style, informed as much by international jetset glamour as by innercity chic. The environments of the clubs were an experience in themselves. They retained the lushness and exclusivity of the jetset clubs that achieved a high profile in the 1960s but took it all a step further. Modern, high-tech touches included dance floors illuminated by underfloor lighting, unbelievably powerful sound systems and spectacular light shows and plush furnishings. The top clubs were also defined as much by the people who

Opposite: The interior of Studio 54 in 1979; a somewhat arbitrary entry policy meant that an interesting mix of people were admitted.

frequented them as by the music they played, as each vied to attract celebrities and beautiful people.

The best known disco of the era was, without doubt, Manhattan's Studio 54. Like many of the people who frequented it, Studio 54 was famous for being famous. So much hype surrounded its exclusionary door policy – a barrier of velvet ropes marked the entrance, which was presided over by bouncers who had total discretion over who did and did not get in – that it became the place to be seen. These bouncers had the ultimate responsibility for ensuring that an exciting mix of people was admitted, maintaining a balance between men and women, gays and straights, famous people and those who loved to dance. Only the most attractive and dynamic among the eagerly jostling crowd got past the ropes, while the paparazzi documented the comings and goings of the famous. Celebrity alone did not guarantee admission: myth has it that the singer Cher was once turned away.

Studio 54 was opened in 1977 by two entrepreneurs, Steve

Below: The owners of Studio 54 were convicted of tax evasion in 1980, but it soon reopened even though they were in jail, only to close again finally in 1986.

Rubell and Ian Schrager, in a former TV studio at 254 West 54th Street, and they designed the club as the ultimate theatrical nightlife fantasy. The dance floor, 5400 square feet (502 square metres) of it, was electrified by 54 different but equally dramatic lighting effects throughout the night, and a huge figure of the Man in the Moon snorting cocaine from a silver spoon hovered over the expanse. Exoticism reigned, drugs and sex were rife, and an unforgettable time was had by all. This was the venue where, notoriously, a naked Bianca Jagger rode astride a white horse on her birthday, a much-published image that came to represent the outrageousness of the disco high life.

Rubell and Schrager were openly defiant of the law. There was no attempt to play down the fact that heavy drugs were used in the club, and the two frequently boasted about the money they were illicitly skimming from the club's heady profits. Their attitude was a challenge to the law enforcement authorities, which began a crackdown almost before the club opened. Studio 54

Left: Two of the glitterati dancing the night away at Studio 54, dancer and choreographer Mikhail Baryshnikov and Liza Minnelli, star of *Cabaret*.

'Exoticism reigned, drugs and sex were rife, and an unforgettable time was had by all.'

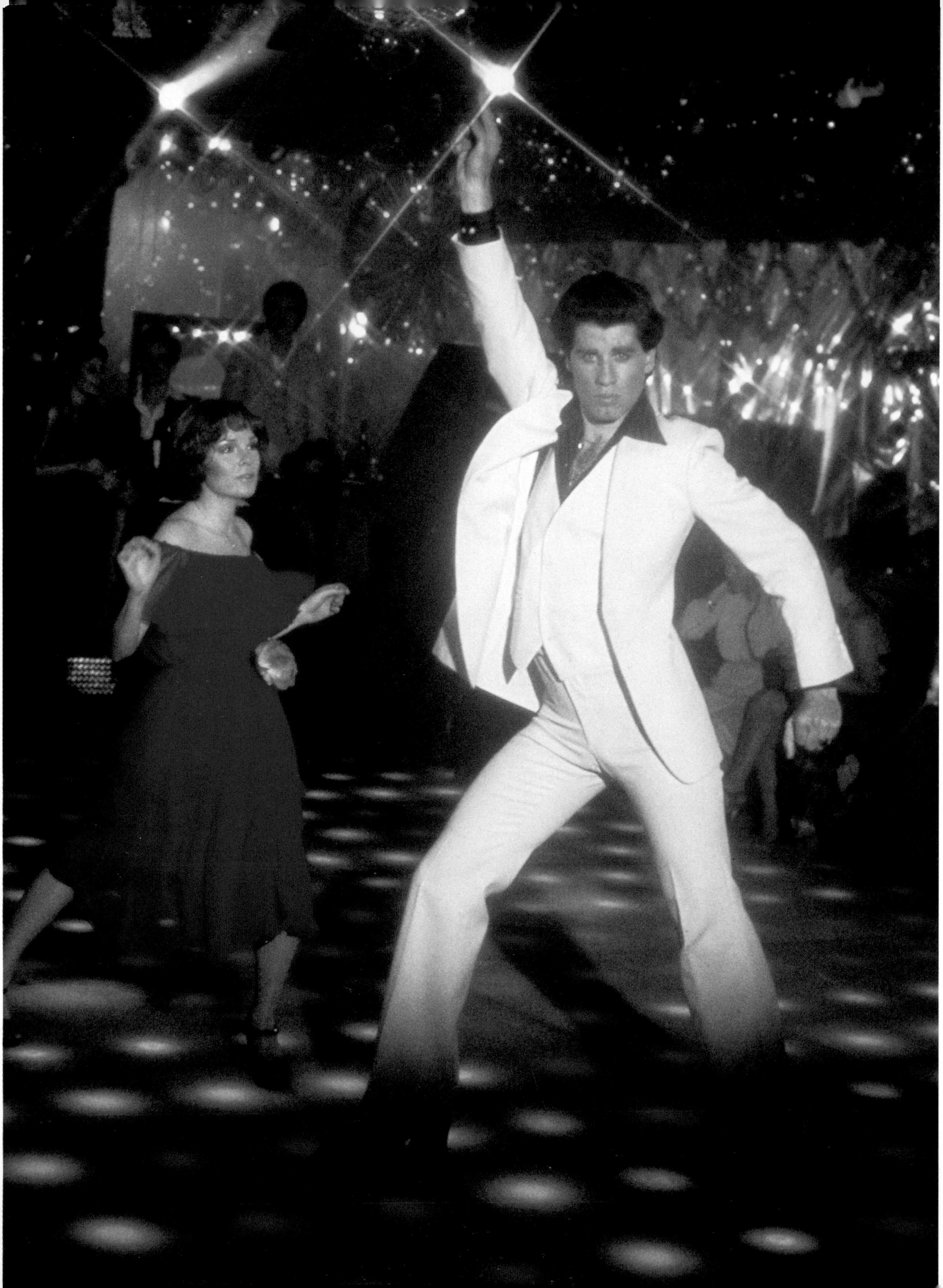

was never granted a permanent liquor licence – the owners had to reapply for 24-hour permits each day – and in 1980 the IRS raided the club, and Schrager and Rubell were jailed for tax evasion. The club remained in business while they were in jail, but its glory days were already past. It finally closed in 1986, although the building remains as a venue for concerts and private parties.

Other clubs arose as rivals to Studio 54, although none achieved quite the same star status: in London there were the Embassy, in Old Bond Street, and Heaven, under the arches at Charing Cross; in Manhattan there were the cavernous Infinity, with its startling lightshow, New York New York, top-heavy with celebrities, and Xenon, with its huge, mirror-coated spaceship hovering above the dance floor; in Paris (and with an offshoot in New York City), there was Regine's, which thrived on its aura of exclusivity.

To get into these clubs was the first hurdle; to be noticed once you were inside was the next challenge. Disco brought out the exhibitionist in everyone, and as dancers strove to devise more and more dramatic routines, their dress and make-up became ever more flamboyant and their drug use often excessive. A number of people became famous simply for being outrageous.

Saturday Night Fever

Disco itself really hit the mainstream in 1977 with the release of the film *Saturday Night Fever*. It was loosely based on a 1976 feature by rock journalist Nik Cohn in the then style bible, *New York Magazine*. In this article, entitled 'Tribal Rites of the New Saturday Night', Cohn documented the suburban disco scene, writing of young people in the outer New York City borough of Brooklyn, who stagnate in dead-end jobs during the week and who feel as if they come to life only at weekends on the dance floor (many years later, Cohn admitted that much of the article was fabricated). The film starred John Travolta as Tony Manero, who works in a paint store by day but stars on the dance floor at his local disco by night. Manero sees his dancing as his ticket out of his dreary Brooklyn existence, and by the end of the film he has left for the bright lights of Manhattan. (A second-rate sequel, *Staying Alive* (1983), traces his progress as he attempts a career as a professional dancer.)

Travolta (b.1954) was well known at the time because of a starring role in a television sitcom, *Welcome Back Kotter* (1975-78), but *Saturday Night Fever* made him famous for his strut and

'Manero sees his dancing as his ticket out of his dreary Brooklyn existence, and by the end of the film he has left for the bright lights of Manhattan.'

Opposite: John Travolta with Karen Lynn Gorney in *Saturday Night Fever* (1977), which firmly established disco in mainstream culture and made Travolta a star.

SATURDAY NIGHT FEVER FACTFILE

Claim to fame: Quintessential disco movie, credited with igniting Disco Fever worldwide. John Travolta and his white suit have acquired iconic status.

Source: Based on Nik Cohn's 1976 *New York Magazine* feature 'Tribal Rites of the New Saturday Night'.

Credits: Produced by Robert Stigwood. Directed by John Badham. Starred Travolta and Karen Lynn Gorney.

Travolta: The star was plucked from the cast of TV's *Welcome Back Kotter*. As a child he had taken dancing lessons with Gene Kelly's brother, Fred.

The hustle: In the wake of the film, dance school membership soared as dancers flocked to learn the hustle.

Soundtrack: The album has sold more than 30 million copies. Alongside the legendary Bee Gees tracks are performances by such classic disco outfits as Kool and the Gang and KC and the Sunshine Band.

Fact: The famous opening sequence of Travolta's feet strutting along the sidewalks of Brooklyn was actually performed by Travolta's stand-in Jeff Zinn.

Below: Patrick Swayze as the maverick dancing instructor with Jennifer Grey as his more than enthusiastic pupil in the 1987 movie *Dirty Dancing*.

Right: Travolta in the sequel to *Saturday Night Fever*, *Staying Alive* (1983), that followed Tony Manero's career in professional dancing.

for his dance flair. He had studied dance as a boy, enrolling in the dance school run by Gene Kelly's brother, Fred. The dance scenes in *Saturday Night Fever* were a virtual primer for inspired disco-maniacs throughout the world and live on to document the dance style. Many dance images from the film are icons of the 1970s.

The disco scene exploded in the wake of *Saturday Night Fever*, and it is estimated that the number of discos in the United States grew 10-fold between 1974 and 1978. More people were dancing than at any other period since the Depression, and there were even disco-dance marathons, reprising the 1930s fad. It spawned numerous fashions and crazes, some of which remained within the clubs, while others, like roller-skating, hit the mainstream.

After one Studio 54 disco habitué started appearing on roller-skates every night, roller disco became all the rage. For a few years in the late 1970s everyone seemed to be on roller-skates, and many skating rinks transformed themselves at night, adding light shows of their own and attracting bold and acrobatic skaters to dance the night away. Roller disco inspired its own songs and films, including *Skatetown USA* (1979), which featured Patrick Swayze, later to be better known for his role in the musical *Dirty Dancing* (1987), and *Xanadu* (1980), starring Olivia Newton-John and Gene Kelly.

By the 1980s the public had lost interest in disco. As it entered the mainstream, disco became mundane and lost the glamour, excitement and exclusivity that lit its early flames. As the major

'By the 1980s the public had lost interest in disco. As it entered the mainstream, disco became mundane and lost the glamour, excitement and exclusivity that lit its early flames.'

record companies rushed to cash in on the disco phenomenon, they mass-produced disco songs, which lacked the subtlety and flow of the earlier creations, and a rash of disco films, rushed out in the wake of the success of *Saturday Night Fever*, made the campness and glamour of disco style seem tacky rather than exotic.

Nonetheless, the flamboyance of the disco phenomenon continues to captivate. For people who love to dance, the best of disco music remains club classic. Around the world, there are hustle clubs that continue to evolve the dance styles from the 1970s, and dance clubs mount nights devoted to 1970s-style dancing, with the throbbing disco tracks still enticing people on to the dance floor. In the late 1990s a wave of movies revisited the craze: *Boogie Nights* (1997) was look at the disco era, focusing on a team of hardcore pornographers; *54* (1998) was a portrait of the fall of the club and the tainting of its glamorous lifestyle; and *The Last Days of Disco* (1998) was a witty and incisive look at 'yuppie' frequenters of a disco obviously modelled on Studio 54 and their coming of age in the competitive arena of Manhattan.

Above: The 1998 film *The Last Days of Disco*, which satirized the disco culture of the 70s and 80s, but not without sympathy for those involved.

The country and western revival

One lasting effect of disco was the 1970s and 1980s renaissance in country and western and line dancing. Although the two dance cultures were different in style, disco had inspired a resurgence in the popularity of both couple dancing and line dancing, and as disco's star was waning, a victim of its own success, country music's was on the rise.

Country music and country and western dancing are indigenous to the United States, and their origins lie in the country dances carried to the new country by British, Irish and German settlers in the seventeenth and eighteenth centuries and later combined with European imports, such as the minuet, the quadrille and the polka (see page 12).

From the early 1800s a peculiarly American form of dance developed. It was known as the contra and was largely based on British folk dances. In the contra two opposing lines of dancers faced each other, men on one side and women on the other, with partners opposite. The top couple would meet and dance down between the two lines in their own individual style. When they reached the bottom they would rejoin the others, and the next top couple would follow suit. (This form of dance, constantly reinvented, remains current in North America and Europe - think of the stroll; see page 188.) Square dancing arose from a combination of the contra and the minuet and quadrille, but the caller was an American innovation, a response to the complexity of patterns in the quadrille. Having a caller meant that anyone

Below: The Old Dodge City Cowboy Band, photographed here in about 1911, belonged to a musical tradition originating with the first settlers of North America and continued today in country and western.

'Square dancing arose from a combination of the contra and the minuet and quadrille, but the caller was an American innovation, a response to the complexity of patterns in the quadrille.'

could join the dance without having previously studied the dance form and also made sure that order was maintained on the dance floor.

During the 1800s, as settlers moved west across North America, dance played an essential social role. People would get together for barn dances, frequently travelling long distances, and the gatherings, often raucous affairs, could last for up to a week. Many of these settlers were recent European immigrants, and they brought together their disparate dance styles, creating a homogenous and altogether new form, which much later came to be known as country and western dancing. Some movements were inspired by the polka, others by the schottische, popularized by German immigrants. Still others were reminiscent of the movements of cowboys – for example, the 'double arms over' movement in country and western dancing is not unlike the arm movements required to tie off a calf.

Couple dancing in the country and western style emerged out of the square dance, as other dance styles, such as the polka and the waltz, were woven into the traditional square dance figures. In the 1930s and 1940s these 'round dances', as they were known, began to grow rapidly in popularity. Eventually, they broke free from their square dancing roots, and the twentieth-century style of country and western dancing was free to evolve.

It was from the 1930s on, with the spread of radio in the United States, that country and western music began to take influences from other musical forms of the day, and the country

Above: Joe Mouton playing music for the complex Louisiana form of dancing Zydeco at the Acadian Festival in 1997.

and western dance scene began to develop in its modern form. In the 1930s a musician named Bob Wills (1905–75), impressed by jazz and the big band sound, devised his own take on country and western music, and the genre known as western swing was born. This was a significant development, and contemporary country and western music and dance forms still have their roots firmly in country swing. After the Second World War country and western really hit the airwaves and spread beyond its roots in the western United States. Honky-tonks – the term used for bars with country and western dancing – grew busier and busier, and many musicians became household names. Hank Williams, Chet Atkins and Johnny Cash were among those who began to establish their reputations around this time.

Although it grew steadily in popularity, it was not until the late 1970s and early 1980s that country and western dancing hit the mainstream. In a broad cultural sense, disco had paved the way, re-establishing a tradition of couple dancing and set dances. And again it was a film that created a dance fad. As he had with disco, John Travolta brought country and western to a mass audience, this time with the film *Urban Cowboy* (1980), in which he co-starred with Debra Winger. Like *Saturday Night Fever*, *Urban Cowboy* was based on a magazine article, this time investigating the country and western dance club scene. In the film Travolta plays a country boy who moves to the big city, Houston, Texas, and comes of age in its honky-tonk dance clubs. Although the film was not a huge money-maker, it inspired a craze for country and western, and it seemed that suddenly everyone threw away their disco glitter and donned cowboy boots and stetsons instead. Country and western dance clubs appeared to replace discos almost overnight. The film also popularized a style of pop-like country and western music, epitomized by singers like Dolly Parton and the Oak Ridge Boys. Although this fad, like others, eventually subsided, country and western dancing has retained a large and loyal following around the world.

Country and western couple dancing relies on pre-determined dances, set either to specific songs or to specific tempos, and because the dances are often inspired by popular songs, dance styles have evolved to follow the trends in country and western music. In general, however, most dances are based on a two-step pattern, similar to the foxtrot. By the end of the twentieth century thousands of dances had been choreographed, not only in the United States, but around the world, especially in Britain, where country and western dancing has attracted a

Opposite: John Travolta's *Urban Cowboy* (1980) inspired something of a revival of interest in country and western music in the mainstream dance environment.

'... suddenly everyone threw away their disco glitter and donned cowboy boots and stetsons instead. Country and western dance clubs appeared to replace discos almost overnight.'

Above: Country and western really hit the big time in the 1990s with the growth in the popularity of line dancing.

particularly large following. There are numerous manuals and step guides published, both in book form and on the internet, and the teaching of country and western dance is big business. In Britain most country and western dancing takes the form of classes, since there are few clubs, but in the western United States, on the other hand, there are many honky-tonks – clubs and bars specializing in country and western dance and music.

Like the courtly dancers of much earlier eras, country and western dancers follow a formal etiquette, perhaps harking back to the roots of this dance form. For example, the dance floor is tacitly divided into 'lanes', around which dancers move, always in an anticlockwise direction. Faster dancers remain in the outer lanes, while those doing slower dances move closer to the middle, and the centre of the dance floor is given over to line dancers or to swing dancers. Collisions are frowned upon and always elicit sincere apologies. In addition, people who come to the dance or club as couples always dance at least the first and last dances together. Men are free to ask other women to dance, and must escort them back to their seats once the song is finished.

Line dancing

Line dancing developed its own identity relatively late in the day. Although its roots in contra dancing are obvious and a few line dances were always performed, it did not become common until the late 1970s. However, although it is a modern innovation, its step patterns remain true to its roots. Traditional forms, such as the schottische, the polka and the cha-cha-cha, are major influences, and like other forms of country and western dancing, line dances consist of a combination of set steps, which are then repeated after a quarter turn. There are usually four repetitions in total, one to each wall.

The profile of line dancing really soared in the 1990s, with the achey breaky, choreographed to the hit song, 'Achey Breaky Heart'. At this time there was a phenomenal rise in the popularity of country and western music. Album sales doubled during the 1990s, and it was estimated that around 40 per cent of the adult radio audience in the United States were listening to country stations. A wave of new country musicians, such as Garth Brooks, Reba McIntire and Randy Travis, won crossover popularity without sacrificing their stylistic integrity.

And as others forms of American regional music enter the mainstream, the public will continue to be exposed to new dances: for example, the growth in popularity of zydeco (Cajun) music from New Orleans has inspired a mini-craze in that complex dance style. Zydeco dancing is done to an eight-beat rhythm, and what makes it tricky is that while one foot moves to each beat, the other foot moves only to every other beat, a feat of coordination that takes novices some time to master.

Above: Line dancing, as its name implies, requires participants to perform a sequence of steps while in a line, facing in one direction.

'Zydeco dancing is done to an eight-beat rhythm, and what makes it tricky is that while one foot moves to each beat, the other foot moves only to every other beat ...'

Left: Olivia Newton-John and John Travolta in the high school dance competition sequence from the 1978 Hollywood version of the 1972 hit stage musical *Grease*.

A Chorus Line

As popular interest in dance grew throughout the 1970s, Broadway got into the act as well, presenting musicals and plays based around a dance theme. The 1950s-retro musical *Grease* (1972) had a successful run on Broadway and internationally, winning praise for its choreography, which presented a lively pastiche of 1950s rock and roll dance fashions, before spawning an even more successful Hollywood version (1978) starring John Travolta (yet again) and Olivia Newton-John. The film became the highest-grossing movie musical ever on its first release (its re-release 20 years later was also phenomenally successful).

A wave of new black musicals also hit Broadway, reasserting the link between African-American jazz dance traditions and the evolution of musical theatre and attracting a substantial African-American audience for the first time. Some of the shows, such as *Purlie* (1970), *Raisin* (1973), and *Ain't Supposed to Die a Natural Death* (1971), the last produced by Melvin van Peebles, were thematically hard-hitting, examining the social realities of being

'*A Chorus Line*, however, was a show purely about dance and dancers.'

Left: The Scarecrow, Lion and Tin Man from *The Wiz*, the all black version of *The Wizard of Oz*, which was first released in 1975.

black and American. Others looked firmly on the bright side. *The Wiz* (1975) was pure entertainment and attracted attention for its imaginative retelling of the classic *The Wizard of Oz*. George Faison's choreography created a visual landscape through dance – the initial tornado, for example, was created by whirling dancers dressed in black, while the Yellow Brick Road was symbolized by four dancers in yellow costumes, wearing yellow afro wigs and carrying poles. Still other shows were reassessments, by African-American producers and performers, of the history of black musical theatre. Revues such as *Bubbling Brown Sugar* (1976), *Ain't Misbehavin'* (1978) and *Eubie* (1979) were lively takes on rich heritage of black popular entertainers, such as Bert Williams (see pages 26–27) and Eubie Blake (see page 55).

The most exciting musical theatre event of the decade, however, was the Broadway show *A Chorus Line*, which opened off-Broadway in April 1975, transferring in July that year. Most musicals use dance as a way to enliven a show at the same time as communicating information about plot and character. *A Chorus Line*, however, was a show purely about dance and dancers.

The action of *A Chorus Line* takes place during an audition session for a nameless Broadway show. The director, Zach, who is heard but never seen, is looking for dancers to build up a chorus line of eight dancers, four men and four women, and has recalled 18 hopefuls for a longer interview. Because there is a chance that they may have a few lines, he wants to learn a little about them and asks them to tell him about their lives. Each narrative follows a subtle progression. One by one, the characters recount aspects of their life stories, through monologues and musical numbers, moving from childhood to adulthood. These solo or small-group pieces are intercut with montage musical sequences depicting the shared emotions of the aspiring chorus members. The show is essentially plotless, and there is no star - other than dance itself.

The show was developed through a series of workshops led by director and choreographer Michael Bennett (b.1943) , who conceived of *A Chorus Line* as a celebration of 'gypsies', the theatrical nickname for chorus dancers. A former dancer himself, Bennett was one of Broadway's leading choreographers of the

Above: The most successful dance musical of the 1970s, *A Chorus Line*, made the usually anonymous members of the chorus into the protagonists.

'... dancers move off and on the stage, in a dramatized version of a warm-up session that ends suddenly ...'

Above: *A Chorus Line* choreographer and director Michael Bennett with his Gold Record Award for the original cast album of the musical.

Right: Members of the *Chorus Line* make their debut as the show finally reaches the stage.

1970s, and his hits included Sondheim's *Company* (1970) and *Follies* (1971), a show about former show people. For *A Chorus Line* groups of dancers would meet to talk about their lives, and tape recordings of these sessions were used as the basis for the script, which was co-written by a playwright, James Kirkwood (1924-89), and Nicholas Dante, who, as a dancer, was involved in the workshops.

Although the stories that are told relate specifically to the experience and emotions of dance and theatre, they also have universal resonance, and the underlying message is that the audience and the performers are, at heart, the same. This encourages the audience to identify with the various characters as individuals. The final dance routine, 'One', when the dancers, dressed in identical costumes, perform as a perfectly polished chorus line, subsuming their individuality, comes as a shock, as the characterizations built up during the course of the show dissolve into the ensemble. Bennett said that he wanted to foster a feeling of dislocation in the audience: 'I want the audience to walk out of the theatre saying, "Those kids shouldn't be in a chorus!" And I want people in the audience to go to other shows and think about what's really gone into making that chorus.'

In addition to 'One', several other dance numbers stood out. The opening dance sequence, 'I Hope I Get It', lasted 10 minutes. To simple piano music, dancers move off and on the stage, in a dramatized version of a warm-up session that ends suddenly as the dancers seamlessly form a line, each holding his or her 'head shot' photograph. 'The Music and the Mirror' is Cassie's dance. Played in the original Broadway production by Donna McKechnie, Cassie is a former soloist (and former lover of Zach, the director), who, despite her measure of success, still needs this chorus job. This number was the longest solo dance ever created for a musical and depicted Cassie's emotional need for the dance and her desire, unrequited, to subsume her personal life into her dancing.

A Chorus Line was a wholehearted success, earning universally rave reviews and winning multiple awards. In addition to running on Broadway for 15 years, it spawned numerous touring productions around the world. In a sense, *A Chorus Line* harked back to the backstage musicals of the 1930s and 1940s, and it possesses its own versions of the hard-nosed choreographers and gritty hoofers who filled those shows. It reaffirmed the old belief that the story of a chorus dancer struggling to make a living against all the odds offers a useful metaphor for our own lives.

Street style

'Gradually – and disco is the first mainstream example of this – the DJs became more than simply providers of music, but creative artists in their own right.'

By the end of the 1970s the brutality and realism of punk and new wave seemed to signal the end of disco culture. Disco's influence on the subsequent history of social dancing, it was argued, would be as short lived and inconsequential as the renaissance in couple holds that it engendered. However, disco's influence was to be far more pervasive than anybody at the time thought, and by the time the twentieth century was drawing to a close dance music, and the culture in which it thrives, would become the dominant idiom of popular musical entertainment. The reason for this was not only the sense of performance and irony that disco brought to the dance scene, but because disco was the first dance culture that made creative use of one important social development – recorded music.

Street style

Disco DJs

Ever since the development of the 7-inch single in the 1950s and the arrival of the first jukeboxes in the coffee shops of teenage America, vinyl had provided a soundtrack for dancers to move to. The development of durable, portable records and small transistor radios meant that recorded music could replace live music in a dancer's affections, and they were available at any time and in any place. The subsequent rise of new record companies and the explosion of rock and roll music meant that records became the dominant means of providing new sounds to the market. As a result a new concept, the radio DJ, emerged.

In the early days, disc jockeys such as Alan Freed (see page 185) were the main conduit between the audience and the scene, but as recorded sound began to infiltrate the dance clubs in the 1960s the concept of the DJ extended to the dance floor. Someone was needed to access the records, spot the latest sounds and provide the musical background. Gradually – and disco is the first mainstream example of this – the DJs became more than simply providers of music, but creative artists in their own right.

Disco DJs recognized that they could mould an evening around their own tastes, and the best began to provide a

Left: One of the South Bronx pioneers of the hip-hop revolution, DJ Grandmaster Flash (right).

Right: In the foreground, Afrika Bambaataa, another of the New York DJs who changed the language of urban music and dance in the early 1980s.

thematic succession in the music they played. Pioneering work was done with linking one track smoothly with another. The ultimate intention, of course, was to keep the dancers on the floor for as long as possible. Record companies had already recognized this need and provided 12-inch versions of popular disco tracks; but the disco DJ also sought to 'interact' with the turntables in order to extend the audience's favourite tracks. This led to the development of twin turntables and the concept of repeating the same musical segment over and over again.

This one essential development – the recognition that the turntable was an instrument rather than simply a conduit for the music – was the single biggest development in popular music in the final decades of the twentieth century. It instantly multiplied the musical possibilities in dance music and provided the base on which late twentieth-century dance culture could develop.

The pioneers of this modern dance scene can again be traced to New York City, this time the South Bronx. In the early 1970s the South Bronx was already synonymous with social exclusion and degradation, but it possessed an underground dance scene of breathtaking vitality. Pioneer DJs, such as Kool Herc, Grandmaster Flash and Afrika Bambaataa, were pushing back the boundaries of what could be achieved with vinyl and turntables and, in the process, forging a street culture called hip-hop.

'Pioneer DJs, such as Grandmaster Flash ... were pushing back the boundaries of what could be achieved with vinyl and turntables and, in the process, forging a street culture called hip-hop.

Hip-hop and breakdancing

Hip-hop is a multi-faceted street culture – although its popularity at the end of the century was so far reaching that to call it 'street' is somewhat naive – which includes DJing, rap, graffiti and breakdancing, the last of which was the most notorious and visually exciting vernacular dance style to come out of the United States since the birth of the lindy hop.

Breakdancing is, in fact, a media invention. It is the name given to the early hip-hop dance styles that were being performed by the b-boys, or breakers, of hip-hop culture when it finally gained mass appeal in the early 1980s. An athletic combination of fast footwork, body spins and robotic freezing, breakdancing caught the media's attention at the end 1970s because of its 'power moves' – the head, back and hand spins – and this pushed it into the international spotlight.

The origins of b-boying can be traced to the late 1960s, when New York teenagers started doing a dance called the good foot, which was based on the way James Brown performed his 'Get on the Good Foot' on stage. Incorporating primitive drops and spins, the good foot also involved a step that consisted of raising one leg high at the knee, holding it there for a beat, and then dropping it and raising the other leg at the same time. As DJs in the clubs evolved ways of extending the back beats in records, the dancers found more ingenious ways of filling this 'break' beat – these

Above: Nights at the turntable took on a new meaning when the vinyl was in the hands of the likes of Kool Herc.

Right: Members of New York's Rock Steady Crew in a scene from *Beat Street*, the 1984 movie celebrating breakdancing.

included dropping to the floor and jumping up on the beat, and balancing on the hands to free the legs to shuffle and sweep. DJ Kool Herc named these dancers 'breakers'.

The athletic nature of breaking made it attractive to the young kids and street gangs of the South Bronx, where a strong tradition of dance battles existed. Breakdance battles became a way of settling scores on the street, and in this way crews developed who practised together, performed together and created new moves. The best known breakers of the mid-1970s were the Nigger Twins, Clark Kent and the Zulu Kings.

Breakers also began to incorporate the locking and popping dance moves, which were coming out of California. Locking owed its genesis to the popularity of science fiction shows on American television at the time – *Lost In Space*, for example – and it mimicked the move-and-freeze characteristics of the science fiction robots. A street dancer called Don Campbell developed this style, and, along with a TV choreographer, Toni Basil, he established a crew called the Lockers. They began to appear regularly on TV shows, including the influential *Soul Train* and *Saturday Night Live*, and their popularity led to the development of a Californian dance craze called the robot.

Popping is a development of locking, in which the movement is more fluid and gives the impression of an electric current passing through the dancer as he 'pops' each of his body joints in succession. Created by a group of brothers, including Pistol Pete of the movie *Breaking'*, it was called electric boogaloo, but it was as 'electric boogie' that popping entered the breakdancing repertory.

The first wave of breakdancing came to an end about 1977, when the 'freak' dance craze attracted the attention of the black community, but its popularity within the Puerto Rican community made sure that it continued to evolve. It was mainly the Puerto Rican teenagers, influenced by the Kung Fu films of the 1970s, who brought to the genre martial arts moves and the trademark power spins. Rock Steady Crew, in particular, which was formed in 1980, pushed back the limits of what could be done with breakdancing. They incorporated headspins, windmills, handglides and backspins alongside the old-style footwork.

By now the world was sitting up and taking notice. In 1981 Charles Ahearn's hip-hop film *Wild Style* brought the street scene of the Bronx to a wider public, but it was the movie *Flashdance* (1983) that really brought it into the mainstream. The most representative breaking film of this time was *Beat Street*, a dance battle between the two most important new-style breaking crews of the day, Rock Steady Crew and the New York City Breakers.

It was the media that gave b-boying the name breakdancing. It was an all-purpose title for a dance form that included footwork and spins and the body popping and locking that had originated

Below: Another action shot from *Beat Street* with the New York City Breakers showing the crowd a thing or two.

ROCK STEADY CREW: THE LEGENDARY 'SECOND GENERATION'

Crazy Legs: An 18-year veteran of the hip-hop scene, he featured in the films *Flashdance*, *Beat Street*, *Wild Style* and *Style Wars*. Signature moves include windmills and backspins.

Prince Ken Swift: Known as the inventor of many new moves including Kaboom, flowing downstream and airbabies, Prince Ken has won awards for his choreography.

Mr Wiggles: With experience of dancing on Broadway and on film, Mr Wiggles is one of the core members of GhettOriginal.

Orko: A native of Los Angeles, and a noted popper and breaker since the tender age of 12, Orko is renowned for his 1990 – 8 spins in a row.

Masami: Born in Japan, Masami is one of the pioneering b-girls who are exerting a strong influence on the breaking scene.

Above: Some of the more extreme moves involved in breakdancing were literally head spinning.

in Los Angeles. Almost as soon as the media took notice, however, breakdancing began to lose popularity. Unsuited to the new sounds in hip-hop and rap music, by the mid-1980s it was being replaced by what would become hip-hop dance. Breaking has proved a resilient dance form on the street, however, and in the 1990s it showed signs of a resurgence. Rock Steady Crew continues to perform throughout the world under the title of GhettOriginal, two major breaking festivals are held in the United States each year, and many new crews are making room for themselves within the modern hip-hop scene.

'Almost as soon as the media took notice, however, breakdancing began to lose popularity.'

Techno and house music

As hip-hop developed and rap became ever more personal and confrontational, so did hip-hop dancing. Old school hip-hop – breakdancing – was gradually replaced on the scene by the 'new school' style. The new trend was evident as early as the mid-1980s, and many of the new moves were showing up in the rap videos of the day. Moves such as the robocop, roger rabbit, wap and running man made increasing use of reggae, soul and martial arts moves, placing the importance firmly on footwork rather than acrobatics. The new genre was more inclusive and less competitive than its predecessor.

Broadly speaking, however, the rap scene was moving away from expressive dancing. As the genre moved more towards the political ideology of Public Enemy, the trend for 'gangsta rap' accelerated, with less importance being placed on dancers and dancing. New school hip-hop dancers found themselves moving over into the other emerging dance scenes of the time, particularly the electronic sounds of techno and house music.

The work of DJs Kool Herc and Grandmaster Flash and the other South Bronx pioneers quickly spread to other urban centres in the mid-1970s. In both Chicago and Detroit the twin turntable sound of New York was combined with the new electronic technology available in synthesizers and drum machines to produce whole new dance floor sounds. Electronic dance culture had arrived.

In Chicago this new sound became known as 'house music'. The father of house was DJ Frankie Knuckles, who moved to

Right: The acknowledged father of house music, Chicago-based DJ Frankie Knuckles, who pioneered the sounds at the city's Warehouse club.

'While you control your body in hip-hop in house dancing the music controls you.'

Right: Derrick May, one of the influential trio of Detroit DJs who took the basic elements of techno and forged them into a distinct style.

Chicago from New York. Knuckles and his contemporaries, such as Marshall Jefferson and Lil Louis, mixed disco and soul tracks with the more esoteric electronic sounds coming out of Europe – most notably Kraftwerk. The resulting sound was soulful and funky but with a heavy electronic rhythm. In 1977 Knuckles was mixing the new sound in a gay club called the Warehouse in Chicago; a decade later the English would seize Knuckles's sound and market it across Europe as house music.

The dancing that developed out of house music is a development of new style hip-hop. Like its predecessor disco, house music is an amalgamation of many different sounds. Exactly the same is true of house dancing. Hip-hop, salsa, milenge and the Brazilian martial art, capoeira, all get thrown into the mix. Once again the emphasis is on footwork, but the broader range of influences allows for a much freer style. One of the leading house dancers of the 1990s, Ejoe Willson (who cites the Nicholas Brothers and Fred Astaire among his influences), stressed the freestyle element of house dance when he said in an interview: 'I still like hip-hop dancing but I like house better because the beat is faster and it is more freestyle ... While you control your body in hip-hop, in house dancing the music controls you.'

Detroit, Michigan, is to techno, what Chicago is to house. It was the urban environment in which all the disparate elements of modern electronic music came together and coalesced into a functional whole. The music was deliberately technological and industrial, and it is no coincidence that it came of age in the industrial wasteland of 1970s Detroit. Techno's overriding aesthetic is the harmony between man and machine. There were few places on earth were this harmony had been so comprehensively eroded than Detroit.

The techno sound owed its origins to the likes of Kraftwerk, Afrika Bambaataa's 'Planet Rock', Parliament and the other early innovators of analogue music. It was the Detroit trio of 'Magic' Juan Atkins, Kevin 'Reese' Anderson and Derrick 'Mayday' May, however, who took on this sound and harnessed it into a distinct genre.

Rave and club culture

In Britain the Detroit dance sound was turned into a fully fledged cultural movement. Unlike the United States, Britain is small enough to have a more centralized culture, and for this reason new dance styles can be taken up and hyped by the media more quickly than elsewhere in the world. This is precisely what happened to house and techno in the late 1980s.

The north of England devoured house music as surely as it had fed on the Motown sound of the 1960s. In the same way that northern soul had been seized upon and turned into a way of life, so the new electronic dance music was taken up and turned into an ideological movement. The British did more than simply recreate a new club sound: they created a culture, and at its heart was a new dance phenomenon – the rave.

The rave phenomenon owes its spirit, at least in part, to the psychedelic counterculture of the 1960s. Like the great rock festivals and underground clubs of that era, the rave is a

drug-derived subculture that seeks to unite a community with dance and music and that, at least in some cases, stands outside of the law. By the end of the 1990s the term itself had fallen out of fashion – a victim of media hype – but dance party culture remains the dominant trend in worldwide social dance.

The first raves were spontaneous underground dance parties, held, mostly, in warehouses around the periphery of Britain's industrial towns and cities or at secret open-air venues. Clandestine and loosely organized, these parties were attracting crowds of over 5000 dancers by the summer of 1988. The term 'techno' was still in its infancy, and the music played at the parties was a mixture of European psychedelic rock – the Stone Roses and the Happy Mondays – and Chicago-based acid house. Acid house was an LSD-inspired Chicago variant on house music, which made use of the Roland 303 synthesizer to create a watery, trance-like sound. It was ideally suited to the recreational use of

Above and left: The rave scene which came out of disco club culture in the late 80s was characterized by drug-influenced music and psychedelic ambiance not unlike that of the hippie subculture of the late 1960s.

the drug ecstasy, which became widely available in Europe at the end of the 1980s. If the scene had overtones of the late 1960s, it was intentional. The similarities were found not only in the music. On the dance floor too – if that term can be applied to an open field – a freestyle, personal response to the music was all the dancing the sound required.

The rave is more than a simple dance party: it seeks to lift the audience into an altered physical and mental state. The mixture of sensual location, powerful sound systems, theatrical lighting (including strobes and lasers) and the passing of long periods of time (parties usually last through the night) lead the dancers into something approaching a trance-like state. In fact trance is the title of one form of techno music, and the term has a long history of association with the techno movement – not least because of the sensation of repetition in the industrial sounds that lie at the core of techno's evolution.

At the heart of the rave is the DJ. The DJ may have replaced the live musician as the provider of dance music, but he retains something of the aura of a live performer. Not only has the DJ power to use his turntables to create the perfect combination of sounds, but he controls the all-important 'vibe' of the event. The vibe is a term used by dancers to comment on the quality and spirit of an event, and, as in the great rock festivals of the 1960s, it illustrates the culture's aim to unite everyone in 'one nation under a groove'.

As the 1990s progressed rave parties spread across the world. The dance music available had grown at a dizzying speed, and by the end of the decade the term 'techno' barely covered the myriad of dance sounds that flowed through the speakers. House, techno, ambient, hardcore, breakbeat, trance, tribal, progressive, drum and bass and jungle are just some of the styles that fill the clubs as the music sub-divides and propagates.

The expansion and spread of rap, house, techno and the new dance culture in the last quarter of the twentieth century greatly increased the already cavernous divide between social and theatrical dancing. In effect, musical theatre and popular dance began to go their separate ways as soon as Bill Hayley rocked around the clock, but, by the beginning of the 1980s this separation had become a divorce. Instead, television replaced the theatre as the medium best suited to 'breaking' new styles, and street dancing and musical television began to feed on each other in a way not seen since the Broadway theatre devoured the Harlem jazz dances of the 1920s.

Below: Although the rave scene had its origins in Britain's industrial cities, the focus soon moved to Spain's Balearic islands, and Ibiza in particular.

'The British did more than simply recreate a new club sound: they created a culture, and at its heart was a new dance phenomenon – the rave.'

CLUB CULTURE STYLE GUIDE

Ambient: Soft, dreamy sound, characterized by sleepy keyboards and loose bass. Pioneered by Brian Eno and his *Music For Airports* (1978).

Drum and Bass: Highly evolved mix of break beats, jazz, funk and industrial sounds.

Garage: The offspring of DJ Larry Levan's modernizing of the 1970s disco sound, taking its name from the Paradise Garage club in New York City where Levans appeared.

Hip-hop: South Bronx pioneer of the break beat sound. Hip-hop culture led to the development of rap, the ubiquitous sound of modern pop.

House: Electronic music mixing heavy bass rhythms with soulful vocals. Developed in the late 1970s by DJ Frankie Knuckles at the legendary Warehouse in Chicago. The arrival of the Roland 303 synthesizer led to the derivative Acid House movement.

Jungle: Jamaican-British hybrid combining elements of Hip-Hop and Techno.

Techno: Development of the European analogue music of Kraftwerk and the like moulded into a dance sound in the Detroit of the late 1970s and early 1980s, Techno became a catchall term for most electronic dance music.

The music video

The most important development in this new trend was the arrival of the music video and, more specifically, the music video television channel. The Beatles had pioneered the concept of a short film as a means of record promotion back in the 1960s, most notably for their double-A side, 'Strawberry Fields' and 'Penny Lane'. By the beginning of the 1980s this idea of a free promotional film as a means of advertising was fairly well established in Britain, although rare in the United States. However, the market potential in the genre had not been recognized. In 1981 an American cable company, Warner Amex Satellite Entertainment Company (WASEC), responded to the results of extensive market research and began a 24-hour cable TV network that offered nothing but rolling musical video clips. It went on the air for the first time with a song and video called 'Video Killed the Radio Star'. It was meant to be prophetic, and it was: MTV (music television) transformed every aspect of the entertainment industry and revolutionized the way the rock acts were presented.

The arrival of the music video heralded a revolution in the way musical performance was translated on to film. Like Busby Berkeley's expressionistic, montage-based routines of the 1930s (see pages 123–126), the pop video was all about visuals and need not be hindered by responsibilities of narrative. As in the early 1930s, the pioneers of video production failed to recognize the possibilities for creativity within film technique.

The first videos were simply live band performances transferred to screen, which was enjoyable for those fans eager to glimpse their heroes but visually boring for everyone else. Guitar-based bands hiding behind their instruments did not make for good television, and, moreover, television did little for their reputations. Visual presentation, therefore, became increasingly important to the music, and dance has always been a central component of pop music presentation. It comes as no surprise to find that two of the megastars of pop music in the 1980s and 1990s were danced-based acts. Madonna and Michael Jackson both understood the power of the new medium and harnessed it to their advantage.

Moonwalking

By the time Michael Jackson came to revolutionize the music video, he already had a lifetime of professional experience behind him. Born in 1958, Jackson was only 10 years old when he and his brothers signed to Berry Gordy's Motown label in 1968 as the Jackson 5. Even before this, the Jacksons had been working at the Apollo Theater in Harlem, supporting classic soul acts such as the Temptations, Gladys Knight and the Pips and James Brown.

Left: British boy band Take That, whose musical output – as with that of many of their musical contemporaries – was promoted by singing and dancing videos that captured their stage act.

Below: Michael Jackson was responsible for one of the most famous pop videos to plug his album 'Thriller', in which he danced his way through 14 minutes of what in effect was like a mini feature film.

'It comes as no surprise to find that two of the megastars of pop music in the 1980s and 1990s were danced-based acts. Madonna and Michael Jackson understood the power of the medium ...'

James Brown, in particular, had a lasting effect on the youngster, who devoured every spin and split that the great man had to offer. Indeed, the incongruous combination of 'soulful' moves and an innocent boy was an important part of the young Michael Jackson's appeal.

By the 1980s the Jacksons had long since left Motown, and Michael had established his solo career. In 1983 he was asked to perform alongside his brothers for a TV show to celebrate 25 years of Motown. He agreed, on the explicit understanding that he could also perform a song from his solo album, 'Thriller'. His subsequent performance of 'Billie Jean' on *Motown 25* caused an absolute sensation. In front of one of the largest TV audiences ever for a variety show, Jackson unveiled a dance routine in which he appeared to move across the stage without lifting his feet from the floor. Later known as the moonwalk, it became his trademark.

Above: Michael Jackson (second right) had always been a song and dance performer in the old showbiz sense, from his child prodigy years when he fronted the Jackson 5.

Michael Jackson did not, in fact, originate the moonwalk – he adapted it from moves he had seen on the breakdancing scene around this time – but he polished it and made it his own. It incorporates the robotic popping that originated in Los Angeles in the 1970s and that was assumed into breaking, but it also bears a strong resemblance to a minstrel dance called the Virginia essence from a century before. Whatever the genesis of the moves, Jackson was showing how the new street dances could be taken up, mixed with an existing aesthetic and turned into something fresh. In effect, he was doing what Fred Astaire had done 50 years before - trawling the world of popular dance to find anything that could be used to create an effect. Jackson recalls that in the aftermath of his performance on *Motown 25* he was contacted by Astaire and invited to his house. It is said that he spent an afternoon teaching Astaire and the great choreographer Hermes Pan the fundamentals of the moonwalk.

Michael Jackson's moonwalk was incorporated into three videos that accompanied singles. These films pushed back the boundaries of the form, and showed the role that dance could play within it. *Billie Jean* (1983), *Beat It* (1983) and *Thriller* (1987) were, to all intents and purposes, fully fledged musical films, made with a budget and production values to match. *Billie Jean*, the first to be released, made use of Jackson's trademark moves, including the moonwalk, spins and freezes. Ironically, the

Left: After pioneering his moonwalk, 'Jacko' as the press came to refer to him, became something of a parody of his former self.

'In concept, choreography, rehearsal and cost, Thriller bears comparison with the great Hollywood musicals of the past.'

director, Steve Baron, had to be persuaded that dance had a place in the video, but Jackson insisted, and the video's phenomenal success proved him right.

Beat It made the most direct reference to the culture from which Jackson's dancing sprang. Using real-life gang members from Los Angeles, the video loosely tells the story of an imminent gang battle brought to a peaceful conclusion through the unifying power of dance. Directed by Bob Giraldi and choreographed by the Broadway and salsa star Michael Peters, *Beat It* can be compared with the choreographed street fights of *West Side Story* in the 1950s (see page 176).

Thriller, the final release in the trilogy, was by far the most ambitious. Running for a full 14 minutes, *Thriller* had all the components of a movie packed into its structure – scripted scenes, an intricate storyline and, at its centre, a fully realized cinematic dance routine. It was directed by John Landis, an accomplished film-maker in his own right, who had made *An American Werewolf in London* a few years before and now brought many traditional film-making techniques to *Thriller*. In concept, choreography, rehearsal and cost, *Thriller* bears comparison with the great Hollywood musicals of the past. The companion video, *The Making of Thriller* (which was made in part to finance the original

Above: Like that of Madonna, Michael Jackson's stage show was heavily reliant on a strong dynamic dance element to accompany songs that otherwise were often less than memorable.

film), sold well over a million copies alone, while *Thriller* itself was voted in 1989 'the greatest video in the history of the world'. Even allowing for the hyperbole of the entertainment industry, this was no mean feat, and it is an accolade few would quibble with.

Michael Jackson's subsequent career has failed to reach the heights of his *Thriller* period. He has continued to innovate choreographically, but his creativity has become bogged down in multinational responsibilities – in 1991 he signed a multi-million pound deal with Sony – and personal controversy. The 'Black and White' video from his 1991 album *Dangerous* is a case in point – provocative choreography, including the repeated grabbing of his crotch and a move that seemed to mime the unzipping of a trouser fly, caused moral outrage. Of course, sexual suggestion has always been an important component of popular dance, but the counterpointing of Jackson's innocent persona and the explicit nature of his dancing began to cause deep public concern. The process was exacerbated by allegations of sexual impropriety in 1993.

Madonna

Unlike Michael Jackson, Madonna built a career on the explicit connection between sex and popular dance. Like Jackson, she recognized the potential in the music video to create and manipulate a screen persona, and throughout the 1980s and 1990s she used the medium to reinvent herself repeatedly.

'Throughout her career Madonna has created choreography that mixes club and street style with more disciplined styles of contemporary dance.'

Opposite, left and above:
From her earliest 'Like A Virgin' days (opposite), Madonna, through a chameleon-like series of image changes that were often unrecognizable as the same person, always relied on dance and dramatic theatrics to sell her disco-driven music.

Ever since the young Madonna Louise Veronica Ciccone (b.1958) first stepped into a dance class, she knew that dance and music offered the best outlet for her ambition. She studied ballet briefly at the University of Michigan and originally went to New York City to find work in the New York modern dance scene (she danced briefly for the Paul Taylor Company). Instinctively rebellious, Madonna soon realized that the rarefied air of contemporary dance was not for her, and gravitated towards the New York club scene. It was DJ Mark Kamis who broke Madonna's first single 'Everybody' by playing it in his shows.

Throughout her career Madonna has created choreography that mixes club and street style with more disciplined styles of contemporary dance. Her early singles, such as 'Holiday' and 'Lucky Star', were, in production terms, naive. They offered little more than a young woman full of attitude and with an exceptional love for exhibitionism. However, by the end of the decade and the release of her *Like a Virgin* video (1986), she had transformed herself into a unique performer who could create provocative and irresistible choreography. Her 1990 single, 'Vogue', demonstrated how she could latch on to a movement in the club scene – in this case the trend for flamboyant pose battles known as vogueing - and repackage it in a marketable and unique way.

Madonna's original success came out of the New York club scene, and she continued to put dancing at the heart of her act. Her live shows, such as her 1990 Blonde Ambition Tour, presented audiences with a succession of polished and ambitious routines choreographed for each number. While her contemporaries were filling stadiums with the paraphernalia of rock music – guitars, speakers, drumkits – Madonna's band was pushed out of sight and she packed the stage with dancers. With their intricate choreography and stage direction, these shows fell somewhere between a rock concert and musical theatre.

If Michael Jackson showed how underground street styles could be successfully incorporated into mainstream pop, Madonna illustrated how vigorous choreography could help sell a song. Together they heralded an era in which dance routines became an essential part of pop acts. Alongside the ubiquitous boybands and teen groups that flooded the market in the 1990s, female performers, such as Paula Abdul, Gloria Estefan and Janet Jackson, built careers on the ground broken by Madonna.

'With their intricate choreography and stage direction, Madonna's shows fell somewhere between a rock concert and musical theatre.'

Left: Paula Abdul was one of the many female vocalists in the 90s whose stage act with its dance routines owed much to Madonna.

This new environment demanded a new generation of street-wise choreographers – dancers and performers who understood the language of the new styles. For this reason a rash of young dancers, such as Leslie Segar, Marjory Smarf and Fatima Robinson, worked their way into the business from a background not in the traditional training grounds of the musical theatre or classical dance but the clubs. Robinson is a good example. A native of California, she began her career by winning dance contests at her local clubs and appearing in rap videos without any official dance training. By 1992 she was choreographing Michael Jackson's *Remember the Time* video for which she was nominated for an MTV choreography award. Since then, she choreographed for a whole host of artists, including Will Smith, the Backstreet Boys and Whitney Houston, and is a repeated winner of the Music Video Producer's Association award for best choreography. Together with her contemporaries she continues the tradition of using social dances of the day to set the entertainment agenda for her generation.

Above: Where once they held guitars, even if they could not play them very well, pop groups in the 90s like the Backstreet Boys had highly rehearsed dance routines augmenting their music on stage.

Left: Michael's sister Janet was another solo performer whose performances involved big set numbers with backing dancers.

Glossary

Acrobatic tap The name given to a style of tap dancing in which gymnastic and athletic effects – most commonly leg-splits or body flips – were woven into tap routines for excitement.

Animal dances A range of popular rag-time dances in which the walk and characteristics of animals are imitated. The best known is the turkey trot.

Ballin' the jack An African-American jazz dance made famous by its appearance in the Harlem musical, *Runnin' Wild* (1923). It was characterized by no foot movement, while the body undulates and the hips swing.

Big apple A novelty dance of the 1930s and 1940s, which originated in North Carolina, USA, but was made popular by Arthur Murray and his dancing schools. Dancers stand in a circle and respond to a series of instructions shouted out by an elected leader.

Black bottom Developed in New York City in the mid-1920s, a dance of African-American origin, incorporating shuffling, stomping and swaying knees.

Boogie-woogie An African-American dance in which the knees are held together while the hips sway from side to side and the dancer moves forwards.

Bossa nova A dance of the late 1950s, evolved from the fusion of Brazilian samba and North American bebop jazz. Danced in syncopated 2/4 time, it has samba-derived body movements.

Boston A slower and less physical version of the old style rotary waltz, which was popular in the opening years of the twentieth century. Originating in North America, its style is more relaxed and less formal than its predecessor, with the focus on lateral rather than rotational movement.

Breakdance A street dance style that emerged from the hip-hop culture of the South Bronx, New York City, in the 1970s. It is an athletic mix of fast footwork, body spins and 'robotic' freezing. It is also known as b-boying and breaking.

Buck and wing A predecessor of rhythm tap, it is characterized by wing steps on the balls of the feet.

Bump A couple dance, popular in the disco craze of the 1970s, which involves bumping against the partner on the beat, starting with the hips and moving to other parts of the body.

Cakewalk An African-American dance, characterized by elaborate steps and attitudes. A prize in the form of a cake was traditionally given to the best performer. It later became a staple of minstrel and vaudeville shows.

Capoeira A traditional Brazilian dance form and martial art, which became popular in the 1990s as an integral part of new-style hip-hop and house dancing.

Cha-cha-cha A derivative of the mambo, popular in the 1950s, it is based on a pattern of three steps followed by a shuffle.

Charleston A popular dance craze of the mid-1920s, combining heel kicks with a bobbing motion of the body caused by bending and straightening the knees. It is danced in syncopated 4/4 time.

Class act The name given to tap acts that combined smoothness and sophistication in appearance with precise and intricate tap routines, often executed at the same time.

Conga A Cuban-derived dance style, which was popular in Europe and America in the 1930s and 1940s, in which the participants form a line.

Country and western A style, indigenous to the United States, which includes couple dances and group dances, such as square and line dances.

Eccentric A speciality dance act that made use of unusual, eccentric, or individual steps for a particular effect. It often incorporated tap, legomania and comic styles.

Flash tap Tap acts that wove 'flash' steps, characterized by acrobatic or athletic moves, into their routines.

Foxtrot A ballroom dance consisting of a series of slow steps followed by a series of quick steps. The name derives from the style's creator, Harry Fox.

Freak An individual dance style, which was popular in the late 1970s disco scene. It is a slow, grinding version of the twist and was associated with the Chic song of the same name.

Habanera A Cuban folk dance, popular in the nineteenth century, which evolved from the European *contredanse*.

Hokey-cokey A novelty dance, popular in the 1930s and 1940s, in which dancers are joined in a circle and execute a series of shouted manoeuvres. It is known in the United States as the hokey-pokey.

Hustle A quintessential partner dance of the 1970s disco scene, it was influenced by Latin dances and the lindy hop. The basic step structure can be elaborated by improvised spins, lifts and breakaways.

Irish jig A traditional Irish solo dance style, characterized by percussive foot movements, and an upright and controlled upper body carriage. It was made internationally popular in the 1990s by the success of *Riverdance*.

Jitterbug A refined form of the lindy hop, this was popular in Europe during and immediately after the Second World War

Jive The internationally recognized competitive form of swing dancing today and the most ubiquitous form of swing dance at the birth of rock and roll.

Lambeth walk A novelty dance, popular in the late 1930s, which derived from the British musical *Me and My Girl* (1937). A pastiche of 'cheeky-chappie' cockney behaviour.

Legomania The name given to the trend in vaudeville or cabaret acts for excessive use of comic or athletic leg movements.

Lindy hop The original and most athletic form of swing dancing. It is believed to have been named after Charles Lindbergh's flight across the Atlantic in 1927, and it was made famous by the dancers of the Savoy Ballroom in Harlem, New York, in the 1930s.

Line dancing A generic term for unified dance moves performed by groups of dancers standing in a line or in lines. It is popular in the rock and roll, disco and country and western dance genres.

Locking A 'robotic' dance style developed in Los Angeles in the 1960s and 1970s. It is characterized by repeated move-and-freeze steps, giving the dancer a mechanical appearance.

Mambo A Cuban dance style, usually attributed to Perez Prado, that is musically identified by its mixture of Cuban rhythms with swing jazz.

Maxixe The ballroom forerunner of the samba, this Brazilian dance was popular during the tango craze just before and after the First World War. It is danced in 2/4 time.

Merengue The national dance of the Dominican Republic, this was popular in the United States in the 1950s and 1970s. It is best known for its sideways 'limp' step.

Milonga An Argentine dance that was popular in Buenos Aires immediately before the arrival of the tango. It combined elements of the polka and the Cuban habanera.

Mooche An African-American dance style involving the sensuous rotating of the hips. Made famous by Bert Williams and popular in the ragtime dance craze, it was also known as the 'Georgia grind'.

Moonwalk A breakdancing-derived dance style made famous by Michael Jackson. The dancer proceeds backwards and forwards across the floor, manipulating the feet to give an appearance that he is not moving.

One-step A simple ragtime dance, requiring only a single step to the beat.

Polka A popular couple dance of the nineteenth century, which originated in Bohemia. It was a lively dance in 2/4 time, combining close couple turns with high-stepping footwork.

Popping A dance originated in LA in the 1970s. It was a development of locking and is characterized by the appearance of an electric current passing through the dancer as he 'pops' his body joints in succession. It is also known as electric boogaloo and electric boogie.

Precision dancing The name given to dance routines performed by teams of dancers executing uniform movements.

Rhythm tap A style of tap dancing that evolved in the 1920s. It uses intricate footwork and frequent use of the heel for rhythmic effect. Also known as jazz tap and heel and toe.

Rumba A generic term for Cuban dance styles including the son, danzón and guaracha. Traditionally danced in 4/4 time, with rapid sideways steps and a single slow forward step, it is accompanied by swinging hips.

Salsa A generic term for Cuban-derived Latin dances and music, incorporating the mambo, cha-cha-cha, rumba and others

Samba A Brazilian dance that achieved international prominence in the 1940s. It is danced in syncopated 4/4 time with forward and backward steps and swinging, rocking movements.

Shake A solo, derivative dance of the twist era, characterized by vigorous shaking of the body.

Shimmy An African-American dance made famous by Gilda Gray and Mae West. Characterized by a vigorous shaking of the shoulders and the upper body.

Soft shoe A precursor to modern tap, it is danced in a slow 4/4 time in soft shoes on a sandy surface.

Stroll A line dance made popular in the 1950s by its regular performance on the US television programme *American Bandstand*. It was inspired by the single 'C.C. Rider' by Chuck Willis.

Suzy-q An African-American jazz dance, characterized by hands being held in front of the knees, the body moving to the side and the arms swinging in the counter direction. Popular in the 1920s and 1930s, it was revived in the 1960s.

Swing A generic term for American dances emanating from the North American swing jazz movement and incorporating huge regional variety. It includes the lindy hop, jitterbug and jive among others.

Tango A ballroom dance originating in Buenos Aires, Argentina, at the beginning of the twentieth century. It is a couple dance characterized by rapid long steps, and sudden turns of the head and feet.

Twist A dance, popular in the early 1960s, in which the dancer stands with one foot forward, swivelling the foot while simultaneously swinging the hips and rocking the arms from side to side. It was made famous by the Chubby Checker song (1960) of the same name.

Two-step A marching dance popular at beginning of the twentieth century, due in the main to John Sousa. It still exists in some country and western styles.

Waltz A dance, in triple time, in which couples rotate around each other as they circle the dance floor.

Index of people

Index

Acknowledgements

AKG, London: 9 Top, 10–11, 12, 13, 14, 17, 25 Bottom, 28–29 Centre, 36–37, 50 Top, 57 right, 59, 67 Bottom, 68 left, 68 right, 69, 74 Bottom, 75, 80, 107 left, 122, 123 Bottom, 128 left, 152–153 Background, 155, 170, 177 right, 179 Top /**Nelly Rau-Haring** 7

American Tap Dance Orchestra: 114

Brown Brothers: 21, 26 Top, 34 Bottom, 47, 60 left

Corbis UK Ltd: 6 top, 16, 24, 61 right, 70 background, 110–111 background, 186, 216 /**Tony Arruza** 89 right /**Archivio Iconografico** 15 main picture /**Bettmann** 6 bottom, 23 top & bottom, 26 bottom, 30 left, 31,32, 39 right, 41 left, 41 top right 44, 50 bottom, 51, 52, 55 bottom, 62 bottom, 65, 66, 70 bottom, 77 left, 81 left, 81 right, 82–83 centre, 84, 86, 88 bottom, 96, 99 right, 112,132–133 centre,135 left, 136, 140, 141 left, 148–149 centre, 149 right, 150–151, 161 top, 167, 172 top, 173 right, 176, 180–181 background, 182–183 centre, 185, 187 right, 191 Bottom, 193 top, 206–207 background, 208, 209, 211, /**Colita** 90 /**Henry Diltz** 111 right /**Philip Gould** 217 /**Hulton-Deutsch Collection** 49 left, 63, 67 top, 83, 142, 143, 181 right /**Stephanie Maze** 73, 93 /**Ethan Miller** 196 /**Minnesota Historical Society** 134 /**Museum of the City of New York** 22 /**Genevieve Naylor** 74–75 background /**SIN** 227, 234–235 background, 236 bottom /**Bradley Smith** 42 /**Ted Streshinsky** 195 top /**Underwood & Underwood** 61 left, 64–65

Culver Pictures Inc.: 43, 49 right, 62 top, 102, 103, 124, 158

E.T. Archive: 18, 45 top

Hulton Getty Picture Collection: 1, 11, 15 bottom, 25 left, 25 right, 30–31 centre, 33 left, 33 right, 34–35 centre, 39 left, 45 bottom, 60 right, 87, 88–89 centre, 95 right, 144, 145 left, 145 right, 146, 148 left, 151 top, 156–157, 160–161 centre, 164–165, 195 bottom, 214 right,194 left

Image Bank/Archive Photos: 156 left, 207 top /**Fred Fehl**175 bottom /**Jason Trigg** 116 /**Scott R.Sutton** 117 top /**Tim Boxer**/224/29 top, 35 right, 114–115

Kobal Collection: 37, 78, 94–95 background, 100, 104 left, 106, 107 right, 108, 121, 125, 132 bottom, 165, 174–175 background, 178, 210, 212, 213 /**Castle Rock** 215 /**Michael Ginzberg** 231 top /**Paramount** 219

Mander & Mitchenson:19

Peter Newark's American Pictures:20–21, 27, 29 bottom

National Film Archive: 4–5

Private Collection: 40, 53, 54, 57 left, 79 right & left, 92 left, 98, 101, 137, 174 left, 182 bottom, 183 top, 189, 190, 191 top Left, 193 bottom left, 198 right, 237

Redferns: 9 bottom, 199, 238 top /**Richie Aaron** 241 /**Glenn A. Baker Archives** 192, 206 /**Michael Ochs Archive** 198–199 bottom right /**Fin Costello** 204 /**Brigitte Engl** 117, 118, bottom, 221 /**Jat Guenter** 242 /**Mick Huston** 236 top /**Salifu Idriss** 234 /**JM International** 245 top /**Max Jones Files** 139, 141 right /**Bob King** 205, 245 bottom /**Marc Marnie** 72 /**Michael Ochs Archive** 56, 85/138 bottom, 138 top, 184 top, 184 bottom, 187 left /**Jan Olofsson** 191 right /**RB** 198 bottom /**David Redfern** 147, 188, 194 right, 239 /**Ebet Roberts** 228, 243 right /**Nicky J.Sims** 119, 220/Robert Smith 183 bottom /**Jon Super** 226–227 background /**Toby Wales** 91

Retna: /**Andy Catlin** 229 /**Adrian Green** 235 /**Ernie Paniccioli** 230 /**Neal Preston** 244

The Ronald Grant Archive: 2 left, 2–3 background, 8 top, 38, 41 bottom right, 46, 48, 55 top, 58, 71, 76, 77 background, 97, 99 left, 104 right, 105, 109, 113, 120–121 background, 123 top, 126, 127, 128–129 centre, 129 right, 130, 131, 133 right, 134 right, 153 right, 154, 158 bottom, 159 top, 160 left, 161 bottom, 162, 163 top, 163 bottom, 164 left, 166, 168, 169 left, 169 right, 171, 172 bottom, 172–173 centre, centre Left, 177 top, 179 bottom, 197 top, 200 background, 201 right, 203 top, 214 left, 222 top, 222 bottom, 222–223 Centre, 223, 224–225, 231 bottom, 232, 238 bottom, 240, 243 left, 202–203 background